Stress Management
A
Comprehensive Guide
To Wellness

Stress
Management
A
Comprehensive Guide
To Wellness

By:

Edward A. Charlesworth, Ph.D.
Sid W. Richardson Institute For Preventive Medicine
The Methodist Hospital
Baylor College of Medicine

and

Ronald G. Nathan, Ph.D.
Departments of Psychiatry and Family Medicine
Louisiana State University Medical School in Shreveport

biobehavioral
press

Published by:

Biobehavioral Publishers and Distributors, Inc.
P.O. Box 1102
Houston, Texas 77001

10 9 8 7 6 5 4 3 2

PRINTED IN THE UNITED STATES OF AMERICA

Library of Congress Cataloging in Publication Data:

Charlesworth, Edward A., 1949 —
    Stress management.

    Bibliography: p.
    1. Stress (Psychology) 2. Stress (Physiological).
I. Nathan, Ronald G. II. Title.
BF575.S75C44 1982   158'.1   82-1143
ISBN 0-938176-03-X   AACR2
ISBN 0-938176-02-1 (pbk.)

To
Robin, Myra
And
Our Parents

Special recognition is given to these scientists and writers — original contributors to the foundations of stress management training.

Robert E. Alberti
Herbert Benson
Barbara B. Brown
Kenneth H. Cooper
Albert Ellis
Michael L. Emmons
Meyer Friedman
Thomas H. Holmes
Edmund Jacobson
Alan Lakein
Arnold Lazarus
Wolfgang Luthe
Neal E. Miller
Richard H. Rahe
Ray H. Rosenman
Johannes H. Schultz
Hans Selye
Joseph Wolpe

This book is part of what may become the most important health care revolution of this century. People want to do more with their lives than merely cope with the overwhelming cost of ever-mounting stress. They are seeking new and effective ways of taking control of their lives, preventing disease, and enhancing their health.

Those who are successful seem comfortable in almost any situation. Their lives are full and yet unhurried. They look relaxed and confident, even when they are making critical decisions or meeting important people. Physically fit and seldom tired, they project a sense of quiet strength. These stress management pioneers are also preventing the very diseases which now pose some of the greatest challenges to modern medicine.

More and more twentieth century illnesses have been shown to be related to the smoking, drinking, eating and hurrying behaviors of patients. It is estimated that as many as 75% of all presenting medical complaints are stress-related. The list of these disorders is long and growing: Ulcers and stomach disorders, migraine and tension headaches, high blood pressure, rapid irregular heart beats, insomnia, back pain, muscle aches, and skin diseases, as well as many psychiatric disorders. Fifty percent of the people living in the United States report suffering from at least one psychosomatic symptom on a regular basis. These disorders and symptoms are reaching near epidemic proportions.

One of the great paradoxes of modern medicine is that improved health technology and living conditions have been accompanied by an increasing demand for medical services. In fact, health care costs in the United States increased from 190 billion dollars in 1979 to 229 billion in 1980. These figures are expected to nearly double by 1985. Unfortunately, you cannot buy good health!

One way to contain skyrocketing costs and treat stress-related diseases is to find ways to help people adopt health-promoting behaviors, rather than find new ways of operating, medicating, or radiating away the effects of unhealthy life-styles. Behavioral medicine is the revolutionary new, multidisciplinary field devoted to understanding and changing these and other health-related behaviors.

This is an exciting time to practice medical psychology, one of the major branches of behavioral medicine. As teachers in medical schools, we have found a refreshing openness to the behavioral sciences among both students and faculty. Industry has also become aware of the costs of stress and the potential savings when employees learn stress management skills. These savings include reduced personnel turnover, alcoholism, absenteeism, lateness, premature employee death or disability, and other symptoms of burn-out. In fact, the Mental Health Association of America has recently received a grant from a number of large industries to create a clearinghouse for information about stress and employee assistance programs.

Both of us have been involved in stress management training for many years. Edward A. Charlesworth, Ph.D. began developing an educational tape series in 1972 and in 1980 we completed an extensive manual to share with clinicians several effective techniques for treating stress-related disorders. Working with hundreds of patients, executives, employees, police officers, teachers, students, secretaries, nurses, doctors, and people from all walks of life, we have learned a great deal about stress management. But perhaps the most exciting thing we have learned is that stress management can not only be successful, but it can also be fun. In fact, wellness behaviors are known to be positively addicting.

Many stress management programs emphasize how to treat a disease, prevent illness, or lengthen ones life. We prefer to emphasize the pleasures of good health, as well as the consequences of high-risk living. Donald R. Dell, a leader in the Wellness movement makes a frank, comic appeal to vanity. "I like to tell people that wellness is fun, romantic, hip, sexy and free. People who practice it are stronger, better-looking, have higher morale, superior bowel movements and more antibodies against disease. They also become widely popular, tax-exempt and get elected to office." While we cannot guarantee these sorts of changes, we hope to go well beyond just stress management for your physical health.

Our goal is to help you achieve maximum well-being and to enjoy a richer and more rewarding life-style. Many of our patients come to us for psychosomatic problems and leave not only symptom-free, but with a far greater sense of self-confidence, self-esteem, and involvement in life. They are no longer the victims of stress, but the victors over stress.

This book provides ways to assess your stress so that you can begin to understand and change your stress response. Stress and tension can be used in creative ways to make use of energy which would otherwise be lost through distress and disease. For example, when we are tense and anxious, we may find it difficult to enjoy the world around us and we may develop physical disorders. It is important to learn new ways of coping, but it is also important to enjoy a renewed sense of self-sufficiency, and begin living life more fully.

We will present those techniques which can be learned through self-guided exercises in a short period of time. To this end, we have provided you with self-assessment forms, charts, case examples, and questions for review.

Part of this book will help you to establish goals and rehearse their attainment. We will teach you how to be more relaxed in even the most stressful situations. However, we want you to go beyond just lowering your level of tension. You will learn how to overcome fears or phobias and reach out for experiences you might otherwise avoid. We also want you to find new and rewarding goals, such as those of Dag Hammarskjold, a past president of the United Nations, who wrote, "If only I may grow firmer, simpler, quieter, and warmer."

In one of the chapters, you will learn the hazards to your heart of time-urgent living. There is more to life than increasing its speed or slowing it down. The process of discovering this can become a source of great pleasure. For example, when we discuss time management with an executive, he may think of greater productivity and efficiency on the job. But our goal is a much larger one. We hope that he will not only be able to increase his work productivity, but also have more quality time with his family and children. Again, the goal is to enhance not only your health, but also your life.

Two of the chapters in this book involve exercise and nutrition. The basic fitness behaviors and sources of nutrition for health are fairly well-established in scientific circles. We have outlined these findings, but we have also shared how to begin making these a permanent and pleasant part of your life-style. We are hoping that rather than will power, you will learn enjoyable ways of more fully developing and maintaining your body.

Another part of this book will help you to learn about assertiveness training. Too often we clamp a lid on our true feelings until we are ready to explode. Assertiveness training provides new skills for expressing yourself to others honestly and without fear.

For many, "Life is like playing a violin solo in public and learning the instrument as one goes on." While this is true for most of us and is part of the adventure of life, this book will provide some effective ways of approaching the instrument and finding more of the joy in playing it well. Men and women are the most adaptive creatures on the face of the earth. We can live in any environment, even in space or under the sea. To survive happily and successfully, the next generation will have to find enjoyment in adapting to a rapidly changing world.

Some writers have proposed that happiness involves having more pleasant thoughts and images than unpleasant ones. If this is true, then happiness is available to each and every one of us at almost any time. While we cannot and would not want to promise you unending bliss, this book will help you learn new, healthier ways of perceiving and dealing with events. As Shakespeare wrote, "Things are neither good nor bad, but thinking makes them so." For example, a crisis or mistake may be stressful, but both can be thought of as opportunities to learn and grow from the experience of life. Thus, by taking on the challenge of stress in our lives and approaching life in new ways, we can learn about ourselves, accept our strengths and weaknesses, and grow from both our successes and our failures.

The responsibility for much of your health and happiness rests squarely on your shoulders. We hope that you will use this book to feel new things, think new things, and do new things which will not only alleviate distress and disease, but also bring you pleasure and wellness.

Houston, Texas   E. A. Charlesworth
Shreveport, Louisiana   R. G. Nathan
January, 1982

Acknowledgments

Many people have contributed to this book and helped to bring it to press. We wish to thank Nema Frye, M.S., R.D. who shared her expertise and collaborated with the authors in writing the chapters about exercise and nutrition. Special and deep appreciation is extended to William Braud, Ph.D. and Eugene Doughtie, Ph.D. for their early inspiration, research and academic guidance in exploring the physiological and psychological aspects of stress management.

Both Paul Baer, Ph.D. and Ben Williams, Ph.D. gave countless hours of time in developing early research and clinical materials that allowed us to explore the effectiveness of our techniques. The basic outline of this book reflects their contributions which deserve full acknowledgement and are sincerely appreciated. Beverly Graves, R.N. and Carol Loggins, R.N. were also highly instrumental in helping to test our materials in a corporate setting.

We are truly in debt to Shirley Hickox for her painstaking editing and proofreading of several drafts and the galleys of our manuscript. If this book is readable much of the credit belongs to Shirley who generously volunteered hundreds of hours to help our readers. Various drafts were also read and critiqued by Robin Charlesworth, M.A., Sue Crow, R.N., William Day, M.D., Sharon P. Davidson, M.S.W., Fred Kotzin, Ph.D., Mary Lou McNeil, M.D., Bill Myerson, Ph.D., and Art Peiffer, Ph.D. Thank you for your valuable comments.

Danell Gable and Sherry Hardin of Silent Secretary deserve special recognition for composing and typing this guide. We are also greatful for the creativity and flexibility with which Bob and Peggy Cooper of Graphics South designed and typeset the cover, illustrations and charts for this guide. We would also like to thank Ruby Harris for her dedication and hard work in typing and retyping early drafts of the manuscript.

A few words of acknowledgement are hardly sufficient to indicate the importance of the many hundreds of participants in our stress management groups. These are the true authors of this book. They have been some of our best teachers. Only through their work have we been able to sift through the effective and ineffective techniques and suggestions that we have presented over the last decade. A sincere "Thank You" to each and every one of you.

Finally, a very special thanks to our families for their consistent support, encouragement and love. To our parents who worked so hard to give us a head start on the road of life. To our wives who have endured many long weekends of "work without play," and insulated each of us from other demands when we needed a rest. They have sacrificed much and we are grateful. We also wish to thank Jennifer, Travis and Webster for the long, thoughtful walks they eagerly accompanied us on.

Feedback And Suggestions

We have prepared what we hope will be a helpful guide to stress management training. We would like to know what parts of this book were most helpful to you. In this way, we can be sure to include them in future editions of this guide. If there were parts that were confusing, we would like to know what we might try to rewrite. Please list your suggestions by page and line. In addition, if you have learned something from your outside reading or from your training that might benefit others, we would like the opportunity to share it with future readers.

Please address all correspondence to:

Drs. Charlesworth and Nathan
c/o Biobehavioral Press
P. O. Box 1102
Houston, Texas   77001

We look forward to hearing from you.

Table of Contents

SECTION III: OVERCOMING YOUR SPECIAL STRESSORS

SECTION IV: ATTACKING YOUR STRESSFUL BEHAVIORS, THOUGHTS AND ATTITUDES

SECTION VI: PLANNING THE DAYS OF YOUR LIFE

SECTION VII: **ENHANCING HEALTH AND PREVENTING DISEASE: WHEN YOUR BODY WEARS OUT, WHERE ARE YOU GOING TO LIVE?**

SECTION VIII: PUTTING IT ALL TOGETHER

Section I

Learning About Stress
And Your Life

Chapter 1

How Do You Respond To Stress?

Stress And Our Ancestors

The 20th century has been called the "Age of Anxiety." The history books that our grandchildren read will speak of the alarming increases of health problems related to tension and anxiety in what may be called the "Century of Stress." However, you may well ask, "Has man always been nervous and anxious?" The plays of Shakespeare included many examples of the stress response. One of the most respected medical textbooks of the 1600's gave excellent descriptions of anxiety states. In fact, our nervous responses can be traced to the prehistoric caveman.

Imagine a caveman sitting near a small fire in the comfort of his cave. Suddenly, in the light of his fire, he sees the shadow of a saber-toothed tiger. His body reacts instantly. To survive, the caveman had to respond by either fighting or running. A complex part of our brains and bodies called the Autonomic Nervous System prepared the caveman for "fight-or-flight." This nervous system was once thought to be automatic and beyond our control. Here is a partial list of the responses set up by the Autonomic Nervous System and how you may know them from your own experience.

1. Digestion slows so blood may be directed to the muscles and the brain. It is more important to be alert and strong in the face of danger than to digest food. Have you ever felt this as "butter-flies" in your stomach?

2. Breathing gets faster to supply more oxygen for the needed muscles. Can you remember trying to catch your breath after being frightened?

3. The heart speeds up and blood pressure soars. This forces blood to parts of the body that need it. When was the last time you felt your heart pounding?

4. Perspiration increases to cool the body. This allows the body to burn more energy. Do you use extra deodorant when you know you are going to be under stress?

5. Muscles tense in preparation for important action. Have you ever had a stiff back or neck after a stressful day?

6. Chemicals are released so that the blood clots more rapidly. If injured, this can reduce blood loss. Have you noticed how quickly some wounds stop bleeding?

7. Sugars and fats pour into the blood to provide fuel for quick energy. Have you ever been surprised by your strength and endurance during an emergency?

The caveman lived in the jungle or the wilderness and faced many environmental stressors. Often these were immediate, life-threatening events involving dangerous animals or human enemies. For the caveman, this "fight-or-flight" response was very valuable for survival.

Stress And Modern Man

Modern man continues to have the same automatic stress responses that the caveman used for dangerous jungle situations, only now man is seldom faced with a need for "fight-or-flight." If a cat is threatened, it will arch its back. A deer will run into the bush. When civilized man is threatened, he braces himself, but he often struggles just to contain his nervous reactions. This is because the threat is not usually one of immediate, physical harm. Bosses, budgets, audiences, and examinations are not life threatening, but sometimes we feel like they are.

Smaller stressors and briefer stress responses can add up to hundreds a day. These can be parts of our lives that we hardly notice and almost take for granted. If you work in an office, stress may accumulate with every ring of the telephone and every meeting you squeeze into your already busy day. If you are a homemaker, all the endless necessities can mount up just as quickly and take just as much of a toll as those faced in the office.

Man's ability to think of the past and imagine the future is still another way in which stress responses can be triggered at any time and in any place. In addition, distance is no longer a buffer. By simply turning on a television we are made instantly aware of wars, famine, disasters, political unrest, economic chaos, and frightening possibilities for the future.

The rate of change in our lives is accelerating. We only have to read Alvin Toffler's Future Shock to realize that the unexpected has become a part of our everyday lives. These are not the types of situations that we can try to physically overcome. Tigers are seen primarily in zoos, but it is as if we see their stripes and saber teeth in all sorts of things in our everyday world.

Not only do we seem to trigger our stress response more often, but most situations do not provide an outlet for the extra chemical energy produced by our bodies. The "fight-or-flight" response is not useful for most of modern life where we have few physical battles to fight and almost nowhere to run. In the past, the demands for fulfilling basic needs for food, shelter, and safety made good use of our heightened arousal. Today, few of these outlets are available.

Physical Stress Versus Emotional Stress

When we think about what has happened or what might happen, we cannot run from our anxieties or fight our fears. This is emotional stress. The body has only limited ways of using the output of its various stress reactions.

Physical stress is different from emotional stress. Even exercise triggers a stress response. In fact, until recently, scientists relied on the research in exercise physiology as a basis for understanding the effects of both psychological and physical stress upon the body. Although the effects of physical and emotional stress are similar, we now know that there are differences between the two.

There are many hormones which are elevated during the stress response. Three of these are norepinephrine, epinephrine and cortisol. Norepinephrine and epinephrine are more commonly known as adrenalin. In response to a physical stressor, such as extremes in environmental temperature, or the stress induced by exercise, there is primarily an increase in norepinephrine. In addition, there is also a small increase in epinephrine. In response to a psychological stressor, there is also an increase in cortisol. To understand the effects of stress, we need to study the effects of each hormone that is secreted in response to a stressor.

In general, norepinephrine has the greatest effect in increasing heart rate and blood pressure. Epinephrine has the greatest effect in releasing stored sugar. All of these actions tend to aid in preparation for vigorous physical activity.

Cortisol also acts to aid in preparation for vigorous physical activity. But, unfortunately, one of its functions is to breakdown lean tissue for conversion to sugar as an additional source of energy. Cortisol also blocks the removal of certain acids in the blood stream. When cortisol is elevated in the blood for prolonged periods of time, it causes ulcerations in the lining of the stomach because of increased acid formation.

Some of the results of increased cortisol secretion are higher levels of fatty acids in the blood, breakdown of lean tissue, and increased gastric acidity. With the potential for ulcerations in the stomach lining and the breakdown of healthy, lean body tissue, it is clear why emotional stress responses with excesses of cortisol have led scientists to claim that man, the once victorious predator, is now preying upon himself.

Other Effects Of Emotional Stress

Even if we could exercise or somehow "burn off" all the chemicals produced by emotional stress, upsetting psychological distress can interfere with productivity, learning, and interpersonal relationships. If our stress reactions increase, we become less and less able to handle even minor stress. Usually, our ability to interact with and understand other people is also disrupted. We can exhaust our adaptive energy reserves and become more susceptible to diseases. It is clear that, for life in the 20th century, our "fight-or-flight" and emotional stress mechanisms are often both unnecessary and harmful.

Balancing Emergency And Maintenance Systems

The Autonomic Nervous System has two divisions. One division is called the Sympathetic Nervous System. The word sympathetic has two parts. "Sym" means before and "pathetic" means to arouse the feelings. Thus, sympathetic means before feelings are aroused. Let's return to the caveman sitting in

front of his fire. The caveman's response to the tiger included
increased heart rate and breathing. These responses were
automatic and occurred before the tiger aroused the caveman's
feelings of fear.

The Parasympathetic Nervous System is also part of
the Autonomic Nervous System. This division influences the body
in ways that are almost the exact opposite of how the
Sympathetic Nervous System influences the body. In fact, "para"
implies a modification. The Parasympathetic Nervous System may
be thought of as modifying the Sympathetic Nervous System
response. For example, the Parasympathetic Nervous System
decreases heart rate, slows breathing, retards perspiration, and
accelerates stomach and gastrointestinal activity for the proper
digestion of food.

If the sympathetic division can be thought of as an
emergency system, then the parasympathetic division can be
thought of as a maintenance system. This maintenance system is
responsible for the conservation and replenishment of energy.
Scientists have evidence to suggest that our Parasympathetic
Nervous System can be activated through the sort of relaxation
procedures used in stress management training programs. Maybe,
we can all learn to replace "fight-or-flight" responses with
what have been called "stay-and-play" responses.

Hans Selye And The General Adaptation Syndrome

Dr. Hans Selye is often referred to as the "father of
stress research." His early pioneering work demonstrated that
every demand on the body evokes not only physiological responses
specific to the demand, but also the nonspecific and uniform
stress responses we have already discussed. Selye classified
reactions to stress as the General Adaptation Syndrome. The
General Adaptation Syndrome has three stages: (1) alarm
reaction, (2) resistance, and (3) exhaustion.

The Alarm Reaction

During the alarm reaction, the stressor activates the body
to prepare for "fight-or-flight." Both electrical and hormonal
signals are involved in mobilizing the energy needed for an
emergency. Heart rate, breathing and perspiration increases.
The pupils of the eyes dilate. Adrenalin and cortisol are
released. Stored energy floods the blood stream. According to
Selye, if the stress is strong enough, death may result during
the alarm reaction.

The Stage Of Resistance

During the resistance stage of adaptation to stress, the signs of the alarm reaction are diminished or non-existent. Resistances to noxious stimuli and illnesses, such as infectious diseases, increase above their normal level.

The Stage Of Exhaustion

If the stressful stimuli or responses are not diminished, then the stage of resistance is followed by a stage of exhaustion. During this stage, the exposure to a stressor has nearly depleted the organism's adaptive energy. The signs of the initial alarm reaction reappear, but they do not abate. Resistance is decreased and illness or death may follow.

The General Adaptation Syndrome has great importance as an early theory of stress and disease. It stimulated much research contributing to our understanding of stress and resistance as factors in every illness. Stress may interfere with our ability to resist most disease, but we now also know that the ability to manage stress adaptively can be learned. When this skill is used, then stress is enjoyed as a challenge, rather than dreaded as a threat.

Stress And Disease

If your doctor has recommended that you relax or take it easy, you may be suffering from a stress-related disorder. It is estimated that up to 75% of all visits to physicians are made by people with a stress-related problem. Stress is a major factor that may be involved in hypertension and coronary heart disease, migraine and tension headaches, ulcers, and asthmatic conditions. Stress may lead to harmful habits such as smoking and overeating. These have been shown to cause or intensify still other diseases. Stress is also suspected to aggravate chronic backache, arthritis, allergies, hyperthyroidism, vertigo, and multiple sclerosis.

Dermatologists find that stress is a factor in many skin disorders such as hives, eczema, and dermatitis. It has also been strongly associated with many gastrointestinal disorders including irritable colon and gastritis. Some of the excess hormones that the adrenal glands release during repeated stress responses can also interfere with your body's stress immunity to infection. This may make you more susceptible to bacteria and viruses, such as the flu virus.

Stress And Mental Health

Stress not only affects our bodies, but it also affects the way we think and feel. Have you ever come home after an unusually stressful day at the office, feeling irritable and thinking about things at work? At times, our family already knows without asking how things went at work.

Sometimes, we pass our irritability along to others. For example, the stock market drops and the boss blows up at his secretary for not doing enough work. She goes home and screams at her children for being too loud. Her children scold the dog for being bad, when he just wanted to play. Do you have any idea what happened to the cat when the dog finally caught it? Stress can disrupt our lives as it ripples from person-to-person and even person-to-pet. This is just one of the many ways daily stress affects our mental health and our relationships with others.

The effects of long-term stress can be devastating. Most of us can bounce back from a bad day at the office or at home, but this may not be possible if stress continues day after day. Under long-term stress, our personalities may seem to change. We may suffer from depression and feel hopeless and helpless. Occasionally, we may feel tense and explosive. Sometimes, we may find ourselves compulsively repeating meaningless tasks in an attempt to control our lives. At times, we may also act impulsively without thinking about the consequences. At other times, we may have exaggerated fears of such things as leaving our house, traveling by airplane, or riding in an elevator.

The changes we experience after long-term stress may have many causes. These causes may be very complex or as simple as learning an unhealthy response. Whether the cause is simple or complex, the problem physical or mental, stress can intensify our difficulties.

The Current Score In The Stress Arena

Although we have begun to conquer the "Age of Stress," we still have an enormous task ahead. Stress is clearly ahead at this time. Here are some of the current scores in the arena of stress. These could be called the three D's: Disorders, Drugs, and Dollars.

Disorders

30 million Americans have some form of major heart or blood-vessel disease.
1 million Americans have a heart attack every year.
25 million Americans have high blood pressure.
8 million Americans have ulcers.
12 million Americans are alcoholics

Drugs

5 billion doses of tranquilizers are prescribed each year.
3 billion doses of amphetamines are prescribed each year.
5 billion doses of barbiturates are prescribed each year.

Dollars

$19.4 billion is lost by American industry because of premature employee death.
$15.6 billion is lost by American industry because of alcoholism.
$700 million is spent each year to recruit replacements for executives with heart disease.

These numbers are somewhat impersonal. They do not reflect the pain and suffering of the victims of stress and their loved ones.

Healthy Stress

All stress is not harmful. As a source of motivation, stress can spur us on to creative work and it can enrich our pleasurable activities. Hans Selye makes this clear in his book entitled Stress Without Distress. There is an important difference between life's stimulating thrills and its overwhelming anxieties. This is why it is best to manage the stress responses, rather than to try to remove them. Before going further, let's look closely at some of the things that trigger stress responses.

Chapter 2

The Challenge Of Stress
And The Benefits Of Wellness

Have you ever wondered how some people seem to be comfortable with almost any situation? They seem calm and collected even when they make the most important decisions. They project a sense of quiet confidence and seem to have overcome the fears most of us associate with modern life.

Many of the people we just described have felt the same anxiety that others feel, but they have cultivated ways of relaxing in the most difficult of situations. Instead of focusing on the fears or anxieties of life, these people view life as an opportunity for more than just coping. They see life as a challenge, but still something to be enjoyed.

These are the winners in the game of life. There are signs that more and more people are enhancing their enjoyment for life, and not just coping with the status quo. Men and women are the most adaptive creatures on the face of the earth. We can live in almost any environment, even in space and under the sea.

The people who are most likely to survive and succeed in this and future generations will be those who can find enjoyment in adapting to a rapidly changing world. Before we talk about the skills of the winners in life, let's talk about some of the approaches which have failed to work.

Bottled Tranquilizers

To help overcome excessive and chronic stress responses and to relieve feelings of being "uptight," many people turn to a variety of tranquilizing medications, narcotic drugs, and alcohol. These external agents have helped many through periods of trauma, but they do not modify the "fight-or-flight" response mechanism.

Over time, many users actually increase their stress by fighting the sedative side-effects of the drugs to maintain alertness. Instead of increasing their internal control over stress, many become more and more dependent on a drug to offset the effects of stress.

These drugs and chemicals cannot think for us. They cannot decide what stress is good and what stress is bad. A tranquilizer cannot decide if a stress response comes from healthy excitement or debilitating anxiety.

Discovering Alternatives To Drugs

Because of the short-comings of drug therapy, much scientific research has gone into finding alternative means of stress management. From this work, a number of effective procedures have emerged. Some of these teach you ways to relax and gain control over stress, tension, and anxiety. Other techniques teach you how to change stressful attitudes, beliefs, and actions. There are also procedures that help you release the emotional and physical effects of stress.

As a nation, we have begun to face the challenge of the "Age of Anxiety," and the "Century of Stress." Total consumption of fats and cholesterol is on the decline. Cigarette use has decreased over 25% since 1964. An estimated 400% more people with high blood pressure have successfully lowered their blood pressure since 1970. More and more people are exercising and practicing relaxation and stress-management skills. Large companies are building "wellness" centers for stress release, physical fitness and relaxation.

Wellness: Enhancing Your Health

These changes are signs of progress, but we are just beginning to understand the psychology of stress. There are truly vast frontiers to explore in regard to the physical and psychological health-enhancing properties of stress management and relaxation training. Thus, techniques like the ones you are about to learn have the potential to go beyond the treatment or the prevention of disease and into the frontiers of health enhancement. If this is true, a stress management program could not only help prevent some diseases, but also make you healthier and more productive. This is what we mean by "wellness."

The beauty of non-pharmacological approaches to the management of stress and the enhancement of health is that such techniques are non-addictive. In addition, these can readily be called up as situations demand. They can also be set aside until they are needed. For many people, this program will help replace tranquilizing pills with calming skills.

Enjoying Life

Thousands of people have learned ways of relaxing in potentially difficult situations. These people can view stressful situations as opportunities to learn and use new life-enhancing skills. Stress management training will show you ways of learning these sorts of skills. With practice, you will be able to enjoy life rather than feeling "uptight," overwhelmed, and unable to cope.

Most people report not only healthy physical changes, but also a new appreciation for the richness of life. After all, when one is anxious, it is difficult to "take time to smell the roses."

One successful stress management student compared her new skills to the wax on a well-kept car. When it rains on a waxed car, the water beads up and runs off. She said stressors in her life still rained on her, but now she could relax and watch their effects roll off of her.

Stress Management Can Be Fun

Learning to enjoy the challenge of stress will take practice. It can also be fun, as you see yourself more and more able to cope and enjoy life. With daily use, you will fully benefit from this program of stress management. The skills are much like other physical skills in that they take some time to learn. Home practice will be helpful when learning these exercises, but soon you will be able to relax and take action calmly without written or spoken instructions.

Stress management is very much like learning to ride a bicycle. At first, you need training wheels or someone to guide you. Later, after practice, you are able to take the training wheels off and ride the bicycle alone. It is also similar to learning to drive a standard shift car. At first, the car probably jolted forward. Then you talked yourself through the procedure: "Slowly push the gas pedal down. Now, gently let the clutch up..." If you are currently driving a standard shift car, it is probably an automatic habit to depress the gas or clutch pedal and move the gear shift. The same is true when you master stress management skills.

The first part of this program would be of some help if it taught you to relax when following instructions at home in a reclining chair. However its greatest value is allowing you to be relaxed in the face of real-life stressors. Take the example of riding a bicycle one step further. In learning to ride a bicycle, the goal is to use it not only in your driveway or on the sidewalk, but also on streets and busy bike-paths. Likewise, the goal of stress management training is to use it whenever you need it.

Stress management training is not a cure-all. Instead, it is a change in life style and a way of viewing the world. You acquire the habit of relaxation and trade the stress and strain of daily living for a relaxed and enjoyable way of seeing and doing things. You might be able to reduce your stress by dropping out of society, but you would be throwing out the good with the bad. Stress management is another alternative. You can learn to manage your stress and enhance your wellness by changing your responses to modern society.

Chapter 3

Discovering Where
Stress Comes From

"Stress" has become a household word, but what is it? How does it affect you? How can you recognize stress in your life?

Stress has many meanings, but most people think of stress as the demands of life. Technically, these demands are called "stressors," and the actual "wear and tear" on our bodies is the stress.

The demands, or challenges of life, can come from people and events around us, as well as from our inner thoughts and struggles. When these demands increase, people often feel like they are "under more stress."

One of our goals is to present better ways, not only of learning to live with stressful situations, but also to help you find more enjoyment in meeting and mastering the challenges of our changing world. You should not have to give up the challenges of life that you enjoy and want to keep. You might be bored if you were forced to spend your days sitting in an easy chair. When you live successfully in a stressful world, you will neither be over-stressed nor under-stressed.

Most people are not aware of their minute-to-minute stress responses. For better or worse, we learn to ignore, overcome, or just accept them as part of living. What are these important stress responses?

Short-Term Stress Responses

At times, we are all too aware of how stress effects us. Have you ever felt that your stomach was jittery or "full of butterflies"? Maybe you had a lump in your throat, or maybe your chest felt tight. Perhaps your pulse raced and your heart pounded. You may have felt pain in your neck and shoulders from tension. Maybe you felt sweaty or "all wound up." Thoughts may have raced through your mind, but when someone asked a question, your mind went blank. You may have "flown off the handle" at the drop of a pin. Can you remember getting upset and having any of these responses? Most of us have experienced some of these feelings at one time or another.

Long-Term Responses To Stress

The short-term stress responses are physical or behavioral warning signs. If the stress becomes chronic and incessant, then the short-term warnings become more serious stress responses. Some people work longer and harder, but actually become less productive. For many, the words, "I don't have time," become a way of life. Dangerous stress disorders can follow changes in the way we feel and in the way we act. For example, some people become withdrawn or depressed.

Smoking and drinking may become problems. One's sexual life may suffer. Pain associated with headaches, arthritis, and other chronic diseases may increase. Some people eat more and gain weight, while others eat less and lose weight. Sleeplessness and sleepiness may become problems. Daydreaming and difficulties with concentration are common. Feelings of suspiciousness, worthlessness, inadequacy, or rejection may become prominent.

Too many of us have some of these experiences too much of the time. We may find ourselves anticipating the worst and being nervous before anything has happened. We may not recognize how our personality has changed. Even if the change is pointed out to us, we may not believe we have changed.

The following explanations and diagram will help you to understand what your stressors are, and how you respond to them. Notice that no matter where stress comes from, if the short-term effects occur intensely and frequently, the long-term costs are the same -- the quality of your life suffers. On the other hand, if you increase and refine your coping skills, your life and health actually improve.

Stressors: Where Does Stress Come From?

We broadly define stressors as the external demands of life or the internal attitudes and thoughts that require us to adapt.   Stressors can include traffic jams, pollution in the city, that fifth cup of coffee, the pushy salesman who will not take no for an answer, or the angry boss.   Stressors can also include the work that never seems to get done, the children who never seem to listen, or the way some people put themselves down for their shortcomings.   Notice that some of these stressors come from things around us and others from our inner struggles.   Some stressors come from both sources.

Many elements contribute to a stressor being stressful. There are certainly individual differences among us.   Hans Selye says it this way, "You can't make a racehorse out of a turtle." How much control we have over the stressor will determine our own response.   Whether we feel we have a choice in our exposure to a stressor, will also determine our response.   For example, if you "have to" work late because your boss "made you" you will respond differently than if you "choose to" work late, because you wanted "to finish" the project and take the weekend off. The compatibility between a person's individual background, aspirations, and interests and their work will also determine how stressful the work seems.

Thinking of stressors in different categories will help you become more aware of the varieties of stress in your life and which stressors are stressful for you.   As you read the brief descriptions that follow, think about an average day and consider how each stressor may be reducing your enjoyment of life.

THE TWO STRESS CYCLES:

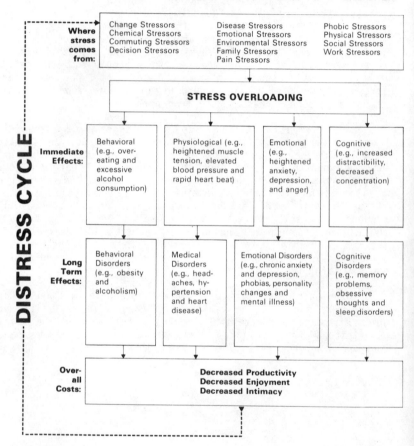

DISTRESS CYCLE

Where stress comes from:

Change Stressors
Chemical Stressors
Commuting Stressors
Decision Stressors

Disease Stressors
Emotional Stressors
Environmental Stressors
Family Stressors
Pain Stressors

Phobic Stressors
Physical Stressors
Social Stressors
Work Stressors

STRESS OVERLOADING

Immediate Effects:

Behavioral (e.g., over-eating and excessive alcohol consumption)

Physiological (e.g., heightened muscle tension, elevated blood pressure and rapid heart beat)

Emotional (e.g., heightened anxiety, depression, and anger)

Cognitive (e.g., increased distractibility, decreased concentration)

Long Term Effects:

Behavioral Disorders (e.g., obesity and alcoholism)

Medical Disorders (e.g., head-aches, hypertension and heart disease)

Emotional Disorders (e.g., chronic anxiety and depression, phobias, personality changes and mental illness)

Cognitive Disorders (e.g., memory problems, obsessive thoughts and sleep disorders)

Over-all Costs:

Decreased Productivity
Decreased Enjoyment
Decreased Intimacy

DISTRESS AND WELLNESS

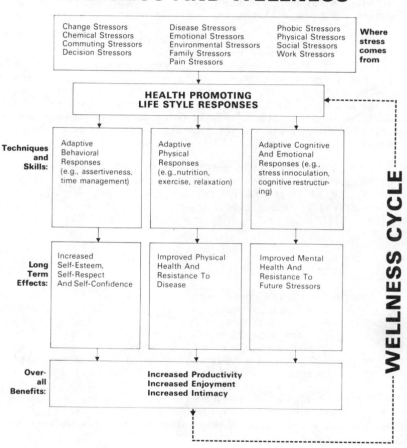

	Change Stressors Chemical Stressors Commuting Stressors Decision Stressors	Disease Stressors Emotional Stressors Environmental Stressors Family Stressors Pain Stressors	Phobic Stressors Physical Stressors Social Stressors Work Stressors	**Where stress comes from**

HEALTH PROMOTING LIFE STYLE RESPONSES

Techniques and Skills:

Adaptive Behavioral Responses (e.g., assertiveness, time management)

Adaptive Physical Responses (e.g., nutrition, exercise, relaxation)

Adaptive Cognitive And Emotional Responses (e.g., stress innoculation, cognitive restructuring)

Long Term Effects:

Increased Self-Esteem, Self-Respect And Self-Confidence

Improved Physical Health And Resistance To Disease

Improved Mental Health And Resistance To Future Stressors

Over-all Benefits:

Increased Productivity
Increased Enjoyment
Increased Intimacy

WELLNESS CYCLE

Emotional Stressors

Emotional stressors include the fears and anxieties with which we struggle: "Will inflation ever slow down?" "What if we run out of gasoline?" "What if I lose my job?" Additional emotional stressors include worrying about unpaid bills, fretting about the children, or taking an exam.

The things we may silently tell ourselves about our actions and the actions of others are also emotional stressors. Telling ourself how "awful" we are going to do in some activity is an emotional stressor which may lead to poor performance. On the other hand, consistently denying that we need to be prepared and "do our homework" may also be an emotional stressor and can lead to failure. Both "awfulizing" about tomorrow and procrastinating about today's activities can trigger stress responses.

Each individual has a unique set of emotional stressors. Some of them may even seem contradictory. One person may not be concerned if bills are paid late, but may be very concerned if his girlfriend is not on time. Another person may be very upset paying a bill late, but hardly concerned if his girlfriend is not on time.

Family Stressors

Interactions with family members can be stressful. The family structure has been changing drastically. The institution of marriage was once a strong, supportive factor that could help family members cope with other stressors. Now, nearly half of all marriages end in divorce and an estimated 40 percent of children born in the last decade will spend at least part of their youth in homes with only one parent.

The percentage of people aged 20 to 34 years who have never married has increased by nearly 20 percent in the last 16 years. Since 1960, the number of unmarried couples living together has more than doubled.

Families go through various stages of stress even if divorce is not a factor. The birth of a child places new demands for adaptation on a family. Children striving for independence during their teenage years can lead to struggles between parent and child. In addition, families must adapt as the teenagers become adults and move away. Finally, families must cope with aging parents and grandparents.

Social Stressors

Social stressors involve our interactions with other people. Asking an attractive person for a date, giving a speech, and expressing our anger are common social stressors. Attending a round of company parties may be stressful for the person who likes quiet evenings at home. On the other hand, the outgoing person may find staying at home every night stressful.

Social stress is also related to feeling that we have a place in the social order. Often when communities toiled together, strength was drawn from awareness and interactions with other members of the same community and social class. Now, many people are uprooted and chronically strive to regain a feeling of community.

Social stressors vary widely from person-to-person. What brings relief from stress for one person, may contribute to the stress of another person.

Change Stressors

It has been said that there are discoverable limits to the amount of change that humans can absorb. Since 1900, the rate of change has been accelerating at a previously unimagined speed. We may be subjecting masses of people to changes that they will not be able to tolerate.

We experience change stressors when we alter anything important in our lives. When we leave a job, a house, or a relationship, part of our adjustment to our loss or to our new situation involves stress. Change is involved in technological advances, as well as the shifting framework of traditions and customs.

If we do not make enough changes in our lives, we can feel stagnant and bored. This can also be a source of change stress. Even the alleviation of pain or disease can be a change that demands readjustment.

Stress management training is a change stressor, because training requires giving up old habits and thoughts. Stressful ways of living are harmful, but they are also comfortable and hard to exchange for healthier ways of managing stress.

Chemical Stressors

Chemical stressors may include any drug a person abuses, such as alcohol. Chemical stressors also include the pesticides or sweeteners in foods we may eat. Caffeine is a common chemical stressor. Nicotine in tobacco is another. Most drugs, both those that are sold by prescription and those that are sold over-the-counter are chemical stressors.

We choose to ingest most chemical stressors. We may ingest excessively large quantities of alcohol or smoke. Some chemical stressors are less under our control. For example, we may live in a city where we breathe chemicals from the air or drink chemicals in the water. Likewise, many foods have chemical additives.

Work Stressors

Work stressors are those tensions and pressures we usually experience between 9 and 5 o'clock at our place of work. If you are a homemaker, your hours may be longer. Asking the boss for a raise, trying to meet impossible deadlines, explaining an embarrassing mistake, disciplining the children, or cleaning the floor a second time to remove fresh mud tracks are all work stressors.

Work stressors, like social stressors, differ from individual-to-individual. One person may work well with the pressure of deadlines and may find "slow" periods boring and stressful. Another person may get "uptight" and stressed when given a deadline.

Some occupations generally involve more work stressors than other occupations. Did you know that secretaries suffer more from stress than executives do, as measured by the incidence of such stress-related problems as heart and artery disease, high blood pressure, ulcers, and nervous disorders? The National Institute of Occupational Safety and Health compiled a list of the 12 occupations most susceptible and least susceptible to stress-related diseases. The following two lists are given in order of susceptibility and may offer some surprises.

Most Stressful Occupations	Least Stressful Occupations
Laborer	Seamstress (hand-stitcher)
Secretary	Checker
Inspector	Stockhandler
Clinical lab technician	Craftsman
Office manager	Maid
Foreman	Farm laborer
Manager or administrator	Heavy-equipment operator
Waitress or waiter	Freight handler
Machine operator	Child-care worker
Farm owner	Packer, wrapper
Miner or machine operator	College or university
Painter (not artist)	professor
	Personnel or labor relations

The above list of stressful occupations does not reflect one of the common components of work stress. We believe the changing nature of our working world is a major contributor to stress. In 1900, J. P. Morgan commented that he didn't know everyone on his staff by their first name. Since that time, businesses have mushroomed, and we are frequently faced with hierarchies of managers. Most of us have little personal contact with our "real"boss; and it can be frustrating to meet or even communicate our needs. The "home office" or the "corporation" often acquired identies of their own; but how do you discuss your needs with the "home office" or the "corporation"?

Other changes have occurred in the working world. Fifty percent of the labor force is white-collar. Fewer jobs are linked to end products such as merchandise, food or the consumer. It has become more and more difficult to see the importance of our individual contributions.

The sexual composition of the work force is also changing. Nearly 50 percent of women over 16 years of age are now in the labor market. This includes half of all the mothers with school-age children. Economist predict that over the next ten years, the number of working women will increase and six women will enter the work force for every five men.

It has become more and more difficult to make decisions both on and off the job. Rational decisions depend on our ability to predict the consequences of our actions. Now our ability to make the best predictions is often compromised by more alternatives and less decision time. A good example of vocational decision stress is reflected in the alternatives facing us in terms of job selection. There was a time when a man became an apprentice to his father and a woman became a mother. Now the number of choices we have are overwhelming. A brief look at the thousands of jobs in the Dictionary of Occupational Titles is all we need to confirm the potential confusion.

Decision stress on the job is also increasing. We often hear in the workshops we conduct that certain jobs carry too much responsibility with too little authority. People experience role ambiguity and conflicting job demands. Predictability and control in our rapidly changing world are increasingly unattainable. There are more possibilities to consider, but humans have only a limited capacity to receive, process, and remember information. Push beyond certain limits and your stress response may sound an alarm.

Commuting Stressors

Many people commute long distances to work. Some people drive "rush-hour traffic daily. Others spend hours on a bus or train. Depending on your distance from work, the amount of traffic you encounter, and your mode of travel, this may or may not be a major stressor.

Phobic Stressors

Many people have exaggerated fears of certain animals, places, objects, or situations which the individuals know pose no immediate danger. These intense and recurrent fears are called phobias. The range of phobias is unlimited and there are Greek names for almost anything a person can fear.

Some of the common ones and the objects of the unreasonable fear include claustrophobia (small enclosed spaces), acrophobia (heights), aquaphobia (water), and, in children, school phobia. "Social phobias" can be specific fears of activities such as speaking in front of large groups or meeting new people.

Some of the more unusual and esoteric phobias include ergasiophobia (work), gymnophobia (nudity), cibophobia (food), phobophobia (phobias), and, yes, even onomatophobia (names or terms).

One of the authors was bitten by a dog at the age of six. For eighteen years, he was afraid of dogs--not just the dog that bit him, but most dogs, chained or unchained! This is an example of a conditioned fear. Many people have learned their phobia through this type of conditioning. Many of these people do not remember the connection or link that was learned. The author realized that his fears were exaggerated, and how they started, but by carefully avoiding dogs, he had never learned to overcome his phobic anxiety.

The author fell in love with a woman whom he wanted to marry. However, there was a problem. She not only loved him, but also Irish Setters. She wanted to raise one of these beautiful dogs when they could afford a home with a yard. This did not stop the author from marrying the woman he loved, because buying their own home seemed very far off in the future. However, time passed quickly, and a few months before the day of reckoning, the doctor looked in the mirror and recalled the words, "heal thyself." Using the techniques to be presented, the author was able to overcome his phobia and enjoy the companionship of "man's best friend." A stressor had become a source of pleasure and recreation.

Physical Stressors

Physical stressors are those demands that change the state of our bodies. Physical stressors can involve the strain we feel when we physically overextend ourselves, fail to get enough sleep, lack an adequately nutritious diet, or suffer an injury. Pregnancies and menstrual discomforts are examples of physical stressors which are specific to women.

Physical stressors often involve increased physical demands. Working 80 hours each week without getting adequate rest can certainly place a physical demand on the body. An abrupt change from high, sustained activity to the boredom of low activity can also be a stressor. For example, some heart attacks may occur immediately after a busy period of time and when a person finally has a chance for rest.

Disease Stressors

Disease stressors are those stressors we experience as a result of long- or short-term disorders. Many disease stressors are short-term and place us under immediate, but time-limited stress.

We will concentrate here on chronic diseases, particularly those which may have been inherited and may last a lifetime. For example, some people are born with a predisposition to develop headaches, arthritis, asthma, allergies, ulcers, high blood pressure, diabetes, dermatitis, hyperthyroidism, multiple sclerosis or hyperkinesis.

These may or may not be caused by stress. Nonetheless, they may be aggravated by stress. With stress, the disease may increase in intensity. The attacks of the disease may last longer, and the frequency of the episodes may increase.

There is a theory that each person genetically has one or more weak systems within his or her body. For example, a young man may find that one or both of his parents had hypertension. He should monitor his blood pressure more frequently than a person without a family history of hypertension. It may be that he will have a predisposition toward manifesting stress through increases in his blood pressure. Knowing what your weak system is, whether it is based on a genetic predisposition or other information, will enable you to use your body as a barometer of stress.

Pain Stressors

Pain stressors are the aches and pains of new and old injuries, accidents, or diseases. Those pains that cause people stress over a long period of time are particularly important. For example, old traumas to the joints can leave a person with a painful osteoarthritis. This condition, like a chronic disease, can flare up in times of stress.

A person may lose the use of his legs from an automobile accident and be plagued by chronic pain. In periods of stress, the pain may become more severe, last longer and occur more frequently.

Part of the stress of any chronic pain may result in a decrease of both physical and social activities. Thus, the stress of chronic pain may lead to still more stress through isolation and inactivity. Ultimately, it may lead to depression.

Environmental Stressors

Environmental stressors include those aspects of our surroundings that are often unavoidable, such as noisy typewriters, muggy rooms, cramped offices, choking exhaust fumes, the glare of the sun, and the burning heat of summer or the chilling cold of winter.

The extreme conditions to which we are exposed can be either too much or too little. Loud noise is stressful, but studies in special, sound-insulated rooms called "anechoic chambers" have demonstrated that "total" silence is also highly stressful. In such sensory deprivation, people may experience boredom, perceptual distortions, and even hallucinations.

Stressors That Are Better Reduced Than Managed

This book will help you to learn exciting and effective ways to live more successfully with many of the stressors we have just defined. However, some stressors are better approached in direct ways to help reduce or eliminate the stressor, rather than learning ways to cope more effectively with it. For example, drinking too much coffee may make you jittery or irritable. It is more efficient to reduce this chemical stressor by substituting water or caffeine-free drinks, than to use the techniques in this book to attempt to be less irritable or shaky.

For many people, such changes are easier said than done. In these cases, a number of the techniques in this book may be useful in helping to reduce the "urge" for coffee and helping to adjust to life with less caffeine. This is also true for other chemical stressors such as alcohol or nicotine. The use of these chemicals is often related to difficulties in coping with other stressors that we will explore in this book.

Likewise, the majority of environmental stressors can be managed most efficiently with environmental changes. For example, if you work in an excessively noisy environment, some of the techniques you can learn from this book would help to reduce the muscle tension you might experience in response to the noise. However, a more direct approach might be to use earplugs. Other techniques, in this book, might help you if you were afraid to ask your boss for a change in the level of noise. Thus, some of the relaxation or assertiveness techniques in this book could help you indirectly to make an environmental change; but making the change would be your real goal.

To help you make such environmental changes, think of yourself as an environmental engineer or architect. Some of your ideas and blueprints may come from the chapter on time management. For example, to avoid expressway traffic jams, a growing number of executives are changing the times that they arrive and leave their offices. Others "van-pool" and enjoy reading a newspaper or talking with friends on the way to work. Still others listen to pre-recorded "books on tape." Thus, they change the drudgery of commuting to the enjoyment of recreational "reading." Take a good look at your work and play. Be creative -- the rewards are many.

Chapter 4

Beginning To Manage Your Stress

You now know something about the stressors in your life, the stress responses of your body, and the long-term effects of chronic stress. Knowing this, you may want to eliminate stress from your life. This seems like a worthwhile goal, but it brings to mind two thought-provoking cartoons.

The first shows a man in flowing robes who is sitting cross-legged on an isolated mountain top. Three physicians are standing in front of the man. They are dressed in white coats with stethoscopes in their hands. One doctor says to the others, "Well, at least we know it's not stress-related!"

The second cartoon pictures a glassy-eyed begger in a gutter calling out to a well-dressed man carrying a black bag. "Don't you remember me, doc? I'm the man you told to slow down and let my business take care of itself!"

Let us assure you that we are not going to teach you how to escape to mountain tops or eliminate all stressors in your life. We are also not suggesting a stress-reduction program. Rather, we are offering you a stress management program. Stress can be stimulating and can make your life exciting. Our goal is to help you learn how to live with your stressors, without letting them interfere with the quality of your life. We want you to reduce the wear and tear on your body, but we also want you to enjoy life.

Stress Hygiene And You

What you will learn is not a cure-all. It will not be a pill that you can take and then feel forever young. Hopefully, what you learn about the management of stress will be what soap-and-water is to dirt. Most people wash themselves to feel clean and refreshed. If you let dirt and grime build up, you begin to feel uncomfortable and you may actually develop infections. Sometimes you may need to wash more than at other times.

At times we make washing our bodies a chore. Another way to wash is to recline in the tub for a slow, warm bath. The same is true of the stress management skills you will learn here. You will want to use regularly what you learn. But, there will also be times of stress when you will need to use the procedures more frequently, slowly and deliberately.

No one forces you to bathe daily or to wash your hands throughout the day. The same is true with stress management skills. When you give yourself permission to improve the quality of your life and to decrease the wear and tear on your body, then you may choose to practice the suggestions in this book. Only you can decide when you are ready to take better care of your needs. We hope you will choose to try these techniques and find ways to make your life a more relaxing and more rewarding experience.

It may help you to list your personal reasons for beginning stress management training:

Example: _I always feel tense about making_
mistakes. This seems to lead to headaches.

1. _____

_____

2. _____

_____

3. _____

_____

4. _____

_____

At times during this program, as in any new undertaking, you may get discouraged or feel that it is not worth the effort. Have you ever started to learn a new sport and wondered how anyone could ever enjoy it? At such times, it may be helpful to review your list of reasons for learning how to manage stress better.

If you do not have a list of reasons that are convincing to you, then you may want to study the last chapter of this book. This may help you to become aware of what is keeping you from getting started. Then come back and write a new list of reasons for learning how to manage stress.

Barriers To Beginning

We hope that each of you will continue using this book and will become successful stress managers. However, we also realize that some people may decide that they "Don't have the time," "Don't have the interest" or "Don't need to relax." The problems people mention most often are difficulties finding a quiet place and enough time to practice stress management training. The following example illustrates some of these common difficulties.

Ms. Aptaker is a highly-successful, executive secretary and a single parent. She was referred to us for a mild ulcer and frequent tension headaches. She complained of neither having the time nor a quiet place to practice relaxation.

After examining these problems more closely, Ms. Aptaker discovered that she could use her coffee and lunch breaks at work to practice relaxing in a room that was not in use. She also discovered that her eight-year-old son, Sean, was curious about her new activity and wanted to try it.

Ms. Aptaker and Sean began practicing relaxation together in the afternoon when he came in from playing in the park and before she prepared supper.

After scheduling these practice times and finding quiet places, Ms. Aptaker went on to say "One of the reasons I complained so much about neither having the time nor the place to practice was that I felt guilty about doing this for me. I felt like I always had to be productive at work or showing attention to Sean at home. Now I'm doing something that's good for me. My work is better, and Sean and I are closer."

There are many reasons why people find problems difficult to overcome. The obstacles may be very real, but can be exaggerated by our guilt over a feared loss of productivity should we take the time to relax. It may be reassuring to know that most of our patients find their productivity actually increasing with stress management training.

As you begin to examine any personal barriers to beginning stress management, keep in mind what motivates you. There are only two major motivators in life. One is fear, and the other is desire. Fear constricts us and impairs our ability to reach our goals. Desire, on the other hand, pulls us like a magnet to our goals. Focus on your desire to be a successful stress manager, but be aware of what your fears or obstacles may be. Obstacles can be the fertilizer for creativity, once you recognize and begin to overcome them.

Most people find it helpful to list personal obstacles and problems that may interfere with their learning and practicing stress management skills. Knowing what your own obstacles are will help you plan ways of overcoming them. List below you personal obstacles to beginning stress management training and the potential solutions for these problems.

Example. Problem: _I have a tendency to give up too soon when I try something new._

        Solution: _I'll practice with someone else and remember that some habits take time to change._

1. Problem: _____

    Solution: _____

2. Problem: _____

    Solution: _____

Discuss your personal reasons for beginning stress management training and the potential obstacles that you may face with close friends or relatives. Do not make your decision to begin stress management lightly.

The stress in most of our 20th century lives will not decrease. Just as animals evolve and adapt to new environments, the survivors of our generation will be the individuals who learn to adjust to and enjoy the "future shocks" of our changing world. We cannot change all the future stressors that we will probably face, but we can change our responses to them.

An additional suggestion that we would like to make, is to find a partner to train with. This is particularly important if you are not working with a professional. Finally, once you have decided to start, it may be helpful to discuss your plans for practice with a family member or close friend. Such people can offer valuable suggestions and encouragement. In addition, a public commitment to practice is often more difficult to break and a better source of motivation than a private one.

How This Book Is Organized

Each chapter in this book introduces a technique that research or clinical work has shown to be an effective way to manage stress. We have selected those stress management skills which people have been able to learn in relatively short periods of time. In fact, the things you will learn were chosen by the hundreds of people whom we have helped to become successful stress managers. Some skills are more difficult to learn than others and are best learned after some easier ones have been mastered. We have arranged the chapters to help you build on skills that are found in the earlier chapters of this book.

How To Use This Book

Most of the individuals and groups that we counsel and train are taught one technique each session. We explain the method and give participants instructions so they can practice the skill during the session. Most of the relaxation procedures, such as those in Section Two, have some immediate positive effects. After the session, the participants are encouraged to practice the new technique every day during the next week. This is usually enough practice to learn the skill and begin receiving some of its benefits by applying it in stressful situations.

To get the most from this book, we recommend progressing through it like a workbook and practicing one procedure at a time. Many hospitals and clinics now teach stress management individually or in groups. You may be using this book as part of such a program. If a psychologist or other qualified professional is guiding your training, follow his or her recommendations. The whole stress management program from start to finish takes several weeks to several months of practice. Very few people can learn to use and enjoy stress management skills effectively in less time.

On the other hand, as psychologists, we know that people vary widely in the way they learn and change. Perhaps you have already learned ways to relax your body quickly and deeply through earlier training or experimentation. If so, you may want to skim the chapters in Section Two and start learning some of the skills in the remaining chapters.

Some people will want to practice a few skills while reading through this book and come back to master the skills they found most useful. If you decide not to follow our recommendations to practice one skill at a time, try to look back over things you have learned successfully in the past and use the same type of approach in learning to manage stress.

Some people may prefer reading this material as a book, rather than using it as a workbook. If you are the sort of person who enjoys reading a book from cover-to-cover, we invite you to do so. In some ways, this would be like reading a good cookbook. Perhaps you would try out some of the recipes for stress management or save one for a special occasion. Maybe you would put some of the recipes in a convenient place, and at a later time plan your strategy for coping effectively with a stressful situation.

Professional Help

More and more psychotherapists are learning how to conduct stress management training and adding it to the services they provide. Psychotherapists can be psychologists, psychiatrists, social workers, nurses, or counselors. These professionals can also help you assess the appropriateness of stress management training for your problems.

Some of the long-term psychological effects of chronic stress, such as depression and personality changes, may require other forms of treatment. Intense and recurrent fears of things that are not dangerous are called phobias. Many phobias, such as fears of airplane travel or public speaking respond well to the stress management training described in this book. Others, may require treatments that only a psychotherapist can provide. A professional can help you decide on the best treatment for you.

If you have a stress-related disorder, but always seem to find reasons why you can not slow down and practice stress management, then read the time management chapter and the last chapter in this book. If you still are having difficulty, then a psychotherapist may help you to understand your difficulties and decide if you want to change your lifestyle. If you want or need additional guidance, the last chapter will help you choose one of these professionals.

Biofeedback Training

Some mental health professionals offer biofeedback training as part of stress management training. Biofeedback machines measure and display some of the physical changes brought about when we use certain stress management skills. Just as a bathroom scale is useful if you are dieting, a biofeedback machine can be useful in learning stress management. If you are interested, you may want to refer to some of the suggested readings at the end of this chapter.

If you are considering the purchase of biofeedback equipment, you may wish to contact the publisher for additional information (Biobehavioral Press, P.O. Box 1102, Houston, TX 77001.)

Warnings And Precautions

If there is any possibility that the problems you are experiencing may relate to a physical illness, read no further - see your physician. Diet, hormonal imbalances, and other physical problems can wear the masks of stress or anxiety symptoms. If you have not had a recent physical examination, this is recommended.

If you are currently under a physician's care for diabetes, hypertension, a thyroid disorder, or a serious depression, consult with your physician before starting this stress management training program. The dosages of the medications your physician prescribes for these conditions may need to be monitored as your skills in stress management increase. Finally, if you have heart disease or severe headaches, your stress management training should be conducted under professional supervision.

Relaxation Training

Section Two emphasizes relaxation training. Relaxation is a very important part of stress management. The ability to relax quickly in any situation, will serve two purposes. First, as soon as you begin using it, it will help you decrease daily wear and tear on your body. Next, it will give you the self-control to decide how you want to handle stressful situations so as to decrease anxiety, anger or "fight or flight" responses and enjoy the experience. Being able to stay calm, relaxed and in control is an important part of being able to change stressful situations in positive ways. Without this ability, you can be at the mercy of your stressors and you may react to them, rather than acting on them.

You may wish to use relaxation tapes to help learn stress management skills. There are several cassette tape relaxation programs available commercially. At the end of each chapter on relaxation we recommend compatible prerecorded instructions. Some of these have instrumental and environmental backgrounds to enhance the relaxation training. Also, many psychologists and other health care professionals have recorded relaxation exercises for use by their clients.

You may want to use the detailed relaxation instructions in this book to record your own relaxation tapes. Appendix I lists different musical and environmental selections that are compatible with relaxation practice. If you record your own relaxation, you may want to use some of these selections. Many of the selections have a calming effect on mood, as well as heart rate and respiration. Select the musical or environmental backgrounds that you find especially relaxing.

Recommended Books and Recordings

At the end of many chapters we have listed both prerecorded relaxation tapes and other recommended listening materials. The recorded materials can help you to practice new techniques or learn related information.

We have also included recommended books at the end of most chapters. These readings can also help to expand and deepen your knowledge of the topics covered in this book.

If you have difficulties locating any of these educational materials, they may be obtained through Biobehavioral Press, P. O. Box 1102, Houston, Texas 77001.

REVIEW QUESTIONS

Directions: Circle the letter in front of the best response to
each question.   The correct answers are provided on the page
following the last question.

1. Having an argument at home is a

    a. chemical stressor.
    b. environmental stressor.
    c. family stressor.
    d. work stressor.

2. The "fight-or-flight" response refers to

    a. an automatic increase in heart rate.
    b. certain chemicals released for energy.
    c. sympathetic nervous system responses.
    d. All of the above.

3. Modern man is faced with threats that are primarily

    a. immediate and physical.
    b. psychological and philosophical.
    c. material and physical.
    d. chronic and physical.

4. The "fight or flight" response was generally adaptive for
    _____ man, but it is often unnecessary and harmful
    for _____ man.

    a. modern; prehistoric.
    b. prehistoric; modern.
    c. modern and prehistoric; modern and prehistoric.
    d. None of the above.

5. Our outdated "fight or flight" reactions can lead to stress
    disorders such as

    a. high blood pressure.
    b. tension and migraine headaches.
    c. ulcers.
    d. All of the above and more.

6. Stress takes many forms. It is clear that

   a. all stress should be avoided.
   b. some stress is healthy.
   c. all people have the same stressors.
   d. most stress is physical.

7. To help overcome excessive stress-reactions, people often turn to

   a. tranquilizing medications.
   b. narcotic drugs.
   c. alcohol.
   d. Any of the above.

8. Tranquilizing drugs

   a. help people through brief periods of situational stress if used as prescribed by a physician.
   b. permanently modify the "fight-or-flight" response mechanism.
   c. help us decide which stress increases productivity or excitement and which drains us of adaptive energy.
   d. are all non-additive and safe for prolonged use.

9. Alternatives to tranquilizing drugs

   a. have not been discovered, nor are they likely to be discovered.
   b. have not been shown to be effective with people experiencing stress.
   c. teach a person to exercise voluntary control over stress and anxiety.
   d. All of the above.

10. Stress management training is designed to

    a. teach you to relax only when listening to instructions.
    b. teach you to relax only at home in a particular room.
    c. teach you a habit, so you can trade, at will, the tension and strain of daily living for a relaxed way of seeing and doing things.
    d. Only (a) and (b).

ANSWERS TO REVIEW QUESTIONS

1. c	6. b
2. d	7. d
3. b	8. a
4. b	9. c
5. d	10. c

SUGGESTED BOOKS AND RECORDINGS

BOOKS

Executive Health by P. Goldberg. New York: McGraw-Hill, 1979.

Executive Stress by H. Levinson. New York: Mentor, 1975.

Mind As Healer, Mind As Slayer by K. Pelletier. New York: Dell, 1977.

Stress Without Distress by H. Selye. New York: Lippincott, 1980.

RECORDINGS

Stress Management Training Program: Hospital Edition -- Introduction by E. Charlesworth & A. Peiffer. Houston: Stress Management Research, 1977.

Quieting Response Training -- Introduction by C. Stroebel. New York: B.M.A., 1978.

Section II

Relaxing Ways
For A Stressful World

Chapter 5

Progressive Relaxation:
How Can I Relax By
Tightening My Muscles?

How often, when we are stressed and worried, do we hear someone say "Just relax"? Perhaps a friend suggests this when you are feeling "uptight" about job frustrations or about other demands. Maybe your dentist says "Just relax" when the drill begins to hum. When patients complain of nervousness, headaches, backaches, or just plain exhaustion, physicians often tell them to relax. Many people tell us to relax, but never really tell us how.

For most people, relaxation is the best skill to learn at the beginning of stress management training. Progressive Relaxation is a technique for muscle relaxation which was developed in the 1920's by Dr. Edmund Jacobson. As a medical student, Dr. Jacobson realized that, even when he was relaxed, his muscles were still somewhat tense. He became aware that this muscle tension might reflect the increasing pace of life.

In the 1920's, Dr. Jacobson was beginning his career as a physician. Even then, almost every individual was facing ever growing demands that were almost unknown to earlier generations. The average businessman was striving for greater and greater achievements in hopes of security. Businessmen often fought off fatigue until they were nearly exhausted. Social events were becoming more complex and recreational activities often failed to provide the needed relaxation and diversion.

Then, as now, there was more and more competition and preoccupation with the appearances of being in control. The great stock market crash created anxieties similar to our current inflation and unemployment. A success image was created. Through advertising, people were trained to want more and more gadgets from the market place. To be successful, one had to strive unendingly to fulfill heightened expectations. The barrage of new needs has continued, as we are now expected to buy only designer clothes or the newest electronic instruments.

Dr. Jacobson realized that he, as well as his patients, needed something more than just encouragement to relax. Through his long and distinguished career, he developed a systematic program for training people to relax their muscles completely.

Dr. Jacobson studied the effectiveness of his techniques by measuring the amount of electrical activity produced in the muscle fibers. The results suggested that many people report feeling totally relaxed when asked to simply "sit and relax." However, Dr. Jacobson discovered that he was not alone. In fact, most of the people had what he called "residual tension," of which they are unaware. His later studies demonstrated that people can produce greater relaxation by practicing Progressive Relaxation than by simply trying to "sit and relax."

Over the years, Dr. Jacobson and other scientists have carefully studied and refined Progressive Relaxation. It now offers a proven, systematic way to control muscle tension. In addition to helping people learn how to relax, the techniques have been used for many disorders, including anxiety, insomnia, headaches, backaches and hypertension. Physiological research has demonstrated that the procedures produce a profound relaxation. When measured with sensitive, electromyographic instruments, major muscle groups can be trained to what is called a zero (0) firing threshold. This is total muscle relaxation.

The physical relaxation produced is pleasant and tends to leave the individual with a sense of refreshment. Dr. Jacobson believed that tense muscles had a lot to do with tense minds and that mental relaxation would follow physical relaxation.

Many people use Progressive Relaxation techniques as a form of recreation. More and more of the techniques are being incorporated into physical fitness programs and exercise classes. Some people find that after vigorous exercise it is helpful to bring their bodies back into a resting state by using these relaxation procedures.

Why Learn Relaxation?

Many people question the need to learn how to relax. For some individuals, muscle tension is a sign of strength. For others, tension equals fitness rather than flabbiness. However, in the rush of everyday living, men and women have, in part, forgotten how to live without unnecessary discomfort. Muscle tension is not always a sign of strength, but can be a sign that energy is being wasted.

To have various muscles, constantly tense, as we wrinkle our forehead, squint our eyes, tap our fingers, and shift our positions is not a sign of strength. When we nervously make a path to the coffee machine or automatically light up a cigarette, we are often looking for ways to release pent up tensions.

Learning and practicing relaxation, can be a sign of strength in how to be selectively tense when a particular task must be performed. You also learn how to avoid wasting energies needlessly by conserving them for important accomplishments.

A football player may get up slowly and walk back to the huddle, as if he were dead tired. Yet, a minute later, the same football player is carrying would-be tacklers with him down the field. He does not run to the huddle and jump up and down waiting for the next play to be called. He saves his energies for those things he truly wants to do.

It is important to know that people who learn to relax do not lose motivation. An executive who complained of neck and shoulder pain, came to us, but insisted that he was not tense and did not need to become more relaxed. He was a successful man in a large oil company and feared that, if he learned how to relax, he would become less productive.

It was only after several weeks of encouragement and practice that this high-level executive realized that he had been chronically carrying tension in his shoulder and neck muscles throughout the day and during the commute home. He was surprised that, without a decrease in his job performance, he was able to learn to relax these muscles. Consequently, he felt more energetic and productive. This energy was directed into more productive work and recreational activities.

It is important to remember that, when we talk of teaching you to relax, we do not mean we will teach you how to become lazy, bored or tired. In fact, a medical student, in one of our classes, reported that his father learned Progressive Relaxation as a bomber pilot during World War II. By using Progressive Relaxation, the pilots could remain alert and avoid fatigue.

Where To Find Muscle Tension

To progressively relax muscles, you begin by tensing and relaxing the major muscle groups of the body. In this way, you become aware of exactly where your muscles are located. Tensing and relaxing muscles, helps you to increase your awareness of your body's muscular response to stress. As one becomes more aware of the location and feeling of muscle tension, then the absence of tension becomes clear. In essence, you begin to recognize muscle tension and the difference between being tense and being relaxed.

The muscle groups around the head, face, neck and shoulders are particularly important areas of stress. A great deal of tension may accumulate in these muscles. However, every person is different. Other muscle groups should also be explored, including the arms, hands, chest, back, stomach, hips, legs, and feet.

It is often important to know which muscles seem to stay tense. Take a moment to look in the mirror and think about being angry or anxious. Are your legs in a defensive stance? Is your jaw tight? Do your eyes seem intense? During the next few days, observe how you sit and stand in different places and at different times. Try to find out which of your muscles seem to stay tense.

Testing Your Muscle Relaxation

It is important to know that, after tensing, a muscle will automatically relax more deeply when released. The feeling of relaxation is increased further by experiencing the difference between muscle tension and muscle relaxation.

Relaxation simply means doing nothing with your muscles. In fact, one way to test a person's depth of relaxation is to have someone lift or bend a relaxed arm at the elbow. If the arm is resisting or assisting the movement, it is not relaxed. The arm should be as easy to move as any other object of the same weight.

Why Start With Progressive Relaxation?

Progressive Relaxation is an excellent place to begin stress management training. It increases general bodily awareness and the recognition of specific muscles where tension is troublesome.

As you may recall, the oil-company executive we just wrote about discovered that he had been living with excessive tension in his shoulders and neck. His reaction to this discovery was one of surprise. He had insisted that he did not need relaxation, but Progressive Relaxation increased his awareness of the difference between tension and relaxation.   The realization that his shoulders stayed needlessly tight did not come to him immediately, but Progressive Relaxation helped him to recognize that muscle tension was mounting, before he experienced pain.

Most people feel surprisingly comfortable after their very first session of Progressive Relaxation. Progressive Relaxation techniques may seem simple. The exercises themselves are neither spectacular nor difficult. Do not be fooled! The important parts of this part of the stress management program are the systematic exercise sequences, awareness of residual tensions, and the regular practice needed to make this new muscle relaxation a routine way of life.

Differential Relaxation

Another use of Progressive Relaxation is differential relaxation. Differential relaxation involves relaxing the parts of the body not needed for a certain task, while tensing the necessary muscles that are in use. For example, when driving a car, it is not necessary to tense every muscle in your body. Often people find their jaws or shoulders are tense while driving.

After practicing with Progressive Relaxation, your ability to relax the muscles that are not needed to perform a task becomes easier. At the same time, one learns how to keep only a moderate amount of tension in the needed muscles. This is very helpful in many situations such as typing a report, preparing a meal, standing in line, and discussing business on the phone.

Building Relaxation Into Everyday Living

It is useful to leave reminders in the office and at home to help you remember to observe your tension and to relax differentially. Small pieces of colored tape may be attached to your watch, the telephone or rear view mirror. These will help remind you to scan your body for any signs of tension every time you look to see what time it is, receive a telephone call or prepare to change lanes.

Looking at your watch or a clock is often associated with nervousness and excessive tension. Converting "What time is it?" tension habits to the habit of responding with creative relaxation helps to build a sense of control over your body's tensions.

It may also be useful to put a sign on the bathroom mirror, desk or dashboard of the car. Something like "Am I relaxed?" or simply "Relax" will work. Even the letter "R" can represent a cue to relax. A vacation snapshot around the office can also provide a pleasant reminder of relaxation. In fact, a concerned wife of one of the authors of this book gave both writers needlepointed paper weights. Each paper weight displays the word "Relax!"

Ms. Thomas' Headaches

Remember to continue practicing relaxation until it is as automatic as breathing. One of our patients whom we will call Ms. Thomas, suffered from daily tension headaches at work in the afternoons. Occasionally, the pain was so intense that it forced her to leave work early. This only added to the stress she had to face the next day. As a secretary, she already had enough work stressors. Before she was referred by her physician for stress management training, she was unaware of the muscle tension in her neck and shoulders that preceded the onset of her headaches.

When Ms. Thomas began learning Progressive Relaxation, she discovered that her tension had been increasing over the course of each day. She placed reminders to relax in the typing paper drawer and on the corner of her desk. In addition, she brought a travel alarm clock into work and set it under a pillow to ring quietly each hour. This helped her to remember to check her tension level and practice Progressive Relaxation. She also began to use her morning and afternoon coffee breaks as additional opportunities for practice.

Over the course of several weeks, Ms. Thomas' headaches decreased in frequency and intensity. As with many of our patients, who discover the joy of managing stress, she had more energy for her personal life.

About a month later, she felt cured of her headaches and began skipping her relaxation at work. Her headaches returned. However, as one would expect, she experienced relief when she once again began to practice regularly.

Creative Cueing

Be creative with relaxation cues and use "spare time" to practice Progressive Relaxation. There are many times during the day when most of us have a few seconds to practice.

Practice while waiting for an elevator, sitting in an office, holding on the telephone or stopping at a red light. These situations should become cues to scan the body for tension. If unnecessary tension is found, then use the time to "Relax and let go."

You may find an occasional need to tense and release certain muscles that are difficult to keep relaxed. Briefly tensing all of the muscles at once and then letting all of them go is helpful. Additional tensing and releasing may be especially helpful when first beginning stress management training.

Keeping daily records will help you become aware of which muscles are most troublesome. For these muscles, you may want to tense and release them several times throughout the day. After practicing Progressive Relaxation several times, relaxing even the most difficult muscles should become easy by merely taking a deep breath, and silently saying "Relax and let go" as the breath slips out. This should become automatic.

When you push an elevator button and wait for the elevator to arrive, scan your body for tension, take a deep breath, and say "Relax and let go." Do the same when the phone rings, or when any other frequent event occurs. In this way, you can teach yourself to relax your body automatically and quickly.

BEGINNING PROGRESSIVE RELAXATION PRACTICE

Scheduling Formal Relaxation Practice

We recommend practicing Progressive Relaxation twice each day for 20 to 30 minutes at the same time. Practice may be scheduled in the morning and afternoons. Try to wait at least an hour after eating to practice relaxation or you may tend to fall asleep. During the work week, use the morning coffee break or lunch hour, and then practice in the afternoon before or after going home. Some individuals prefer to practice after returning home from work and then later in the evening.

Relaxation practice is especially important at work if the job is even mildly stressful. Practicing at least twice a day at work may be necessary if you do not have a quiet place at home. If work is noisy, arrange quiet times at home.

If your home and work settings are not appropriate, find a quiet park, recreational center, or local library. However, be aware that the harder it is to get to your place of practice, the more difficult it is to maintain regular practice.

Scheduling Brief Relaxation Practice

Many people feel good in the morning, but become more and more tense as the day wears on. They may finish work only to find themselves unable to enjoy their leisure time because of headaches, heartburn, fatigue, or other discomfort. The minor, but constant problems encountered during the day generate tension and anxiety. This stress may grow as they wonder if there will be more problems and how long they can cope. The stress spirals upward.

Brief relaxation practice throughout the day can help break the dangerous stress spiral. These brief practice periods may last less than five minutes; but they can bring great benefit by helping you keep tension below critical levels. If you are unable to schedule formal relaxation practice into your working day, at least take brief breaks to relax.

Alternate Schedules For Learning Relaxation

We have found that, for a person to thoroughly learn stress management, they need to practice relaxation daily. We recommend that a person practice twice daily and work with one technique until they have mastered it. This usually takes at least a week. We also recognize that some people will be able to schedule only one formal relaxation session per day. If this is the only way you can schedule your day, then be sure to take brief breaks throughout the rest of your day.

An alternative approach to learning stress management involves an initial overview. Some people may prefer to go through each relaxation exercise one time before returning for extensive practice of each technique. In fact, when we are training groups of people, we sometimes introduce all the different types of relaxation first, and then begin individual practice of each technique.

If you are a person that likes to read a book rapidly from cover-to-cover, then by all means do so. You may want to read each chapter, practice each new relaxation exercise once, and then continue reading. When you have finished the book, you can come back to this chapter and begin really exercising so that Progressive Relaxation becomes a part of your life.

Remember your first experience with the alphabet. You may have repeated each letter after someone, one letter after another, but you really learned it by practicing over and over saying "A, B, C,..." until you could also say "...X, Y, Z." This may sound dull, but it does not have to be. Remember the colorful pictures in your alphabet book? Some people use colorful anatomy books or images to better understand which muscles they are learning to relax. Others find friends to practice with. Learning the alphabet was the first step to reading your favorite books; and Progressive Relaxation is just the beginning of finding satisfaction through stress management.

Hospital And Other Programs

If you are learning stress management training through a hospital, clinic, or health resort program, you may practice as often as their program recommends to insure that you gain maximum benefits in the shortest possible time. After you have completed their formal program, you may want to go back to each of the recommended steps of stress management training. In this way, you can increase your ability to apply all of the skills to your daily life.

Keeping Good Progress Records

Before and after your first Progressive Relaxation session, complete one of the rating scales for the exercises you practiced. Progressive Relaxation rating forms are included in this chapter. They are titled "Subjective Ratings of Muscle Relaxation." Write in the numbers that describe your feelings of muscle tension. Add them up to find out how relaxed you were before and after relaxation.

After your practice session, record your overall pre- and post-practice rating on the Home Practice Chart on the last four pages of this book. Record the technique you used, how long you practiced, and how relaxed you became.

In future Progressive Relaxation practice sessions, rate your relaxation before and after your practice. Continue to record these levels on the Home Practice Chart. You may wish to make duplicates of the "Subjective Ratings of Muscle Relaxation" form to continue rating your practice.

Preparing For Progressive Relaxation Practice

For the most successful beginning, it is best to find a place where all outside noise is reduced to the lowest possible level. Practice the exercises in a quiet room and keep the lights dim. The room temperature should be comfortable. If needed, have a blanket available to cover yourself. The exercises may be practiced while reclining on a sofa, lying on a bed, or sitting in a comfortable chair. We recommend using a lounge chair that reclines.

Lying on one side or with the chest down may strain parts of your body. This is not to say that it is impossible to benefit from relaxation in this, or other positions, but it is easier to learn the exercises the first time while reclining on your back. Later, it will be beneficial to practice while sitting up and standing.

Clothing should always be comfortable and loose when practicing relaxation. Belts can be loosened in preparation for the exercises. It is often best to remove ties, jewelry, shoes and eye glasses or contact lenses.

Problem Solving: Cramps And Falling Asleep

If the room is very cold and your muscles are tired, do not tense the muscles too tightly or they may tend to develop mild cramps. If a cramp occurs, knead the muscle and stretch it out. The most frequent cramp occurs in the calf muscle. If this occurs, pulling the toes toward your face and kneading the calf muscle will usually relieve the cramp. Using a room with a comfortable temperature and being sure that your muscles are not tired, should eliminate cramping.

Never over-strain a muscle when you tense it. If you have had any physical problems that may may me affected by tensing various muscle groups, then seek your physician's advice before practicing.

Some individuals have difficulty staying awake and will need to practice in a sitting position. It may be necessary to rest your elbow on the arm of the chair or surface of the bed while holding your hand up. In this position, if you start to fall asleep the hand should drop to the side and wake you up.

Remember, the major advantage in learning relaxation comes from being able to relax when you are awake. If you wish to use the exercises to help you fall asleep at night, then practice when you go to bed. Studies with insomniacs have shown that their sleep onset time can be decreased an average of about 20 minutes. If you use the exercise to go to sleep, be sure to continue your daily, relaxation practice. There is no substitute for regular,daytime practice.

One of our patients, who suffered with insomnia, described his use of Progressive Relaxation in the following way. He was tensing and releasing each muscle group and adding the words "legs relax and sleep, feet relax and sleep, toes relax and sleep..." At this point in his practice, his wife came into the bedroom dressed in a sexy nightgown. The patient smiled and said, "O.K., everybody up!" The joy of stress management is knowing you can raise or lower your stress response, depending on whether you are facing distress or healthy stress. Drugs and external chemicals can't make this important distinction for you.

HOW TO DO PROGRESSIVE RELAXATION

Using Relaxation Tapes

If you are using recorded relaxation exercises, schedule times now and begin listening to the tape of Progressive Relaxation. Review the suggested relaxation tapes at the end of this chapter to help select an appropriate practice tape. Use the "Subjective Ratings of Muscle Relaxation" in this chapter to record your relaxation levels for each muscle group before and after your relaxation practice sessions. Also, remember to list for each practice session your overall relaxation levels on the Home Relaxation Chart on the last four pages of this book.

Guiding Yourself

If you will be guiding yourself through the relaxation exercises, then review the directions below. You may find it helpful to read the directions several times. You may also want to ask someone to read the relaxation instructions slowly to you. If possible, you may want to record these instructions onto a tape and then use the tape to practice.

Helpful Hints To Tape And Self-Instruction Users

Begin learning relaxation by lying on a bed or reclining in a comfortable lounge chair. Although you may begin practice by lying down, in time you will want to be able to do these exercises while sitting, and even while walking. Practice in a quiet environment and loosen any tight clothing. Be certain that the temperature is pleasant and not distracting. Remember, if you find you have a tendency to fall asleep, rest your elbow on the arm of the chair or next to you on the bed, and balance your hand in the air directly over your elbow. If you start to fall asleep, your arm will drop, and this should arouse you.

The following written exercises recommend a particular sequence of relaxing your body. This begins with your head and ends with your feet. We have found that most people prefer to relax their facial and head areas first. After relaxing the rest of the body, it may be annoying to tense and relax facial muscles. However, some individuals prefer to start with their hands or feet and finish with their head. If you find this to be your preference, then modify the sequence or return to the head area after completing the progression through the rest of the body.

Some people find certain muscles more difficult to relax than others. For example, the neck or shoulders frequently require extra practice to relax. Return to difficult muscle groups and repeat the tension-relaxation contrast for these muscles after progressing through all the other exercises.

When you have read this chapter and practiced the exercises at least once, then answer the review questions and check your answers. If you miss some questions or fail to understand some of the ideas, you might consider reviewing parts of this chapter.

We recommend that you read the next chapter while you practice Progressive Relaxation. In it, you will learn how to become deeply relaxed by scanning your body for tension and breathing deeply for relaxation. The time it takes for you to become deeply relaxed will grow briefer, as you refine your relaxation skills. Eventually, relaxation will become as automatic as breathing.

OUTLINE FOR PROGRESSIVE RELAXATION

I. Basic Technique

    A. Separately tense your individual muscle groups.
    B. Hold the tension about 5 seconds.
    C. Release the tension slowly and, at the same time, silently say, "Relax and let go."
    D. Take a deep breath.
    E. As you breathe slowly out, silently say "Relax and let go."

II. Muscle Groups and Exercises

    A. Head
       1. Wrinkle your forehead.
       2. Squint your eyes tightly.
       3. Open your mouth widely.
       4. Push your tongue against the roof of your mouth.
       5. Clench your jaw tightly.

    B. Neck
       1. Push your head back into the pillow.
       2. Bring your head forward to touch your chest.
       3. Roll your head to your right shoulder.
       4. Roll your head to your left shoulder.

    C. Shoulders
       1. Shrug your shoulders up as if to touch your ears.
       2. Shrug your right shoulder up as if to touch your ear.
       3. Shrug your left shoulder up as if to touch your ear.

    D. Arms and hands
       1. Hold your arms out and make a fist with each hand.
       2. One side at a time: Push your hands down into the surface where you are practicing.
       3. One side at a time: Make a fist, bend your arm at the elbow, tighten up your arm while holding the fist.

    E. Chest and lungs
       1. Take a deep breath.
       2. Tighten your chest muscles.

    F. Arch your back

G. Stomach
    1. Tighten your stomach area.
    2. Push your stomach area out.
    3. Pull your stomach area in.

H. Hips, legs and feet
    1. Tighten your hips.
    2. Push the heels of your feet into the surface where
        you are practicing.
    3. Tighten your leg muscles below the knee.
    4. Curl your toes under as if to touch the bottom of
        your feet.
    5. Bring your toes up as if to touch your knees.

WORD-BY-WORD PROGRESSIVE RELAXATION

Preparation

Spend a little time getting as comfortable as you can. While you are finding a good position, you will also want to loosen any tight clothing. Loosen your belt or tie if they are not already loose. If your shoes feel tight, you may wish to take them off. Your legs and arms should be slightly apart.

Slowly open your mouth and move your jaw gently from side to side....Now let your mouth close, keeping your teeth slightly apart. As you do, take a deep breath.... and slowly let the air slip out.

While you tighten one part of your body, try and leave every other part limp and loose. Keep the tensed part of your body tight for a few seconds and then relax and let it go. Then take a deep breath, hold it, and as you breathe out, silently say, "Relax and let go." In time, this will be a technique you can use to produce rapid relaxation. Now begin your relaxation practice.

Total Body
Tension

First, tense every muscle in your body.
Tense the muscles of your jaws, eyes, arms,
hands, chest, back, stomach, legs and feet.
Feel the tension all over your body....Hold
the tension breifly and then silently say,
"Relax and let go" as you breathe out....
Let your whole body relax....Feel a wave of
calm come over you as you stop tensing.
Feel the relief.

Gently close your eyes and take another
deep breath....Study the tension as you hold
your breath....Slowly breathe out and
silently say, "Relax and let go." Feel the
deepening relaxation. Just allow yourself to
drift more and more with this relaxation...
As you continue, you will exercise different
parts of your body. Become aware of your
body, and its tension and relaxation. This
will help you to become deeply relaxed on
command.

<u>Head And Face</u>   *Keeping the rest of your body relaxed,
wrinkle up your forehead. Do you feel the
tension? Your forehead is very tight.
Briefly pause and be aware of it....Now,
relax and let go. Feel the tension slipping
out. Smooth out your forehead and take a
deep breath. Hold it. (Briefly pause.) As
you breathe out silently say, "Relax and let
go."*

*Squint your eyes tightly as if you are in a
dust storm. Keep the rest of your body
relaxed. Briefly pause and feel the tension
around your eyes....Now, relax and let go.
Take a deep breath and hold it.
(Briefly pause.) Silently say, "Relax and
let go" as you breathe out.*

*Open your mouth as wide as you can. Feel
the tension in your jaw and chin. Briefly
hold the tension....Now let your mouth gently
close. As you do, silently say, "Relax and
let go." Take a deep breath. Hold it.
(Briefly pause.) As you breathe out say,
"Relax and let go."*

*Close your mouth. Push your tongue against
the roof of your mouth. Study the tension
in your mouth and chin. Briefly hold the
tension....Relax and let go. Take a deep
breath. Hold it. (Briefly pause.) Now
silently say, "Relax and let go" as you
breathe out. When you breathe out, let
your tongue rest comfortably in your mouth,
and let your lips be slightly apart.*

*Keep the rest of your body relaxed, but
clench your jaw tightly. Feel the tension
in your jaw muscles. Briefly hold the
tension....Now relax and let go, and take a
deep breath. Hold it. (Briefly pause.)
Silently say, "Relax and let go" as you
breathe out.*

*Think about the top of your head, your fore-
head, eyes, jaws and cheeks. Make sure these
muscles are relaxed....Have you let go of
all the tension? Continue to let the tension
slip away and feel the relaxation replace
the tension. Feel your face becoming very
smooth and soft as all the tension slips
away....Your eyes are relaxed....Your tongue
is relaxed....Your jaws are loose and
limp.... All of your neck muscles are also
very, very relaxed.*

*All of the muscles of your face and head are
relaxing more and more....Your head feels
like it could roll from side to side, and
your face feels soft and smooth. Allow your
face to continue becoming more and more relaxed as you now move to other areas of your
body.*

Shoulders   *Now shrug your shoulders up and try to touch your ears with your shoulders. Feel the tension in the shoulders and neck. Hold the tension....Now, relax and let go. As you do, feel your shoulders joining the relaxed parts of your body. Take a deep breath. Hold it. (Briefly pause.) Silently say, "Relax and let go" as you slowly breathe out.*

Notice the difference, how the tension is giving way to relaxation. Shrug your right shoulder up and try to touch your right ear. Feel the tension in your right shoulder and along the right side of your neck. Hold the tension....Now, relax and let go. Take a deep breath. Hold it. (Briefly pause.) Silently say, "Relax and let go" as you slowly breathe out.

Next, shrug your left shoulder up and try to touch your left ear. Feel the tension in your left shoulder and along the left side of your neck. Hold the tension....Now, relax and let go. Take a deep breath. Hold it. (Briefly pause.) Silently say, "Relax and let go" as you slowly breathe out. Feel the relaxation seeping into the shoulders. As you continue, you will become as loose, limp and relaxed as an old rag doll.

Arms And Hands

Stretch your arms out and make a fist with your hands. Feel the tension in your hands and forearms. Hold the tension....Now, relax and let go. Take a deep breath. Hold it. (Briefly pause.) Silently say, "Relax and let go" as you slowly breathe out.

Push your right hand down into the surface it is resting on. Feel the tension in your arm and shoulder. Hold the tension....Now, relax and let go. Take a deep breath. Hold it. (Briefly pause.) Silently say, "Relax and let go" as you slowly breathe out.

Next, push your left hand down into whatever it is resting on. Feel the tension in your arm and shoulder. Hold the tension....Now, relax and let go. Take a deep breath. Hold it. (Briefly pause.) Silently say, "Relax and let go" as you slowly breathe out.

Bend your arms toward your shoulders and double them up like you might to show off your muscles. Feel the tension. Hold the tension....Now, relax and let go. Take a deep breath. Hold it. (Briefly pause.) Silently say, "Relax and let go" as you slowly breathe out.

Chest And Lungs   *Move on to the relaxation of your chest. Begin by taking a deep breath that totally fills your lungs. As you hold your breath, notice the tension. Be aware of the tension around your ribs....Silently say, "Relax and let go" as you slowly breathe out. Feel the deepening relaxation as you continue breathing easily, freely and gently. (Briefly pause.)*

Take in another deep breath. Hold it and again feel the contrast between tension and relaxation. As you do, tighten your chest muscles. Hold the tension....Silently say, "Relax and let go" as you slowly breathe out. Feel the relief as you breathe out and continue to breathe gently, naturally, and rhythmically. Breathe as smoothly as you can. You will become more and more relaxed with every breath.

Back

Keeping your face, neck, arms, and chest
as relaxed as possible, arch your back up
(or forward if you are sitting). Arch it
as if you had a pillow under the middle and
lower part of your back. Observe the ten-
sion along both sides of your back. Briefly
hold that position....Now, relax and let go.
Take a deep breath. Hold it. (Briefly
pause.) Silently say, "Relax and let go" as
you breathe out. Let that relaxation spread
deep into your shoulders and down into your
back muscles.

Feel the slow relaxation developing and
spreading all over. Feel it going deeper
and deeper. Just allow your entire
body to relax. Face and head relaxed....
Neck relaxed....Shoulders relaxed....Arms
relaxed....Chest relaxed....Back relaxed....
All these areas are relaxing more and more,
becoming more deeply relaxed than you thought
possible.

<u>Stomach</u>

Now begin the relaxation of the stomach area. Tighten up this area. Briefly hold the tension....Relax and let go. Feel the relaxation pour into your stomach area. All the tension is being replaced with relaxation and you feel the general well-being that comes with relaxation. Take a deep breath. Hold it. (Briefly pause.) Silently say, "Relax and let go" as you slowly breathe out.

Now, experience a different type of tension in the stomach area. Push your stomach out as far as you can. Briefly hold the tension....Now, relax and let go. Take a deep breath. Hold it. (Briefly pause.) Silently say, "Relax and let go" as you slowly breathe out.

Now, pull your stomach in. Try to pull your stomach in and touch your backbone. Hold it....Now, relax and let go. Take a deep breath. Hold it. (Briefly pause.) Silently say, "Relax and let go" as you breath out.

You are becoming more and more relaxed. Each time you breathe out, feel the gentle relaxation in your lungs and in your body. As you continue to do these exercises, your chest and stomach area will relax more and more. Check the muscles of your face, neck, shoulders, arms, chest and stomach. Make sure they are still relaxed. If they are not, then tense and release them again. Whatever part is still less than fully relaxed is starting to relax more and more. Soon you will be able to tell when you have tension in any part of your body. You will learn that you can always relax and let go of the tension you may find in any part of your body.

Hips, Legs
And Feet

Now, begin the relaxation of your hips and legs. Tighten your hips and legs by pressing down the heels of your feet into the surface they are resting on. Tighten these muscles. Keep the rest of your body as relaxed as you can and press your heels down.. Now, hold the tension....Relax and let go. Feel your legs float up. Take a deep breath. Hold it. (Briefly pause.) Silently say, "Relax and let go" as you breathe out. Feel the relaxation pouring in. Notice the difference between tension and relaxation. Let the relaxation become deeper and deeper. Enjoy the relaxation.

Next, tighten your lower leg muscles. Feel the tension. Briefly hold the tension.... Now, relax and let go. Take a deep breath. Hold it. (Briefly pause.) Silently say, "Relax and let go" as you breathe out.

Now, curl your toes downward. Curl them down and try to touch the bottom of your feet with your toes. Hold them and feel the tension... Relax and let go. Wiggle your toes gently as you let go of the tension. Let the tension be replaced with relaxation. Take a deep breath. Hold it. (Briefly pause.) Silently say, "Relax and let go" as you slowly breathe out.

Now, bend your toes back the other way. Bend your toes right up toward your knees. Feel the tension. Try to touch your knees with your toes. Feel the tension. Hold the tension....Relax and let go. Feel all the tension slip right out. Take a deep breath. Hold it. (Briefly pause.) Silently say, "Relax and let go" as you slowly breathe out. Feel the tension leaving your body and the relaxation seeping in.

Body Review   You have progressed through all the major muscles of your body. Now let them become more and more relaxed. Continue to feel yourself becoming more and more relaxed each time you breathe out. Each time you breathe out, think about a muscle and silently say, "Relax and let go"....Face relax....Shoulders relax....Arms relax....Hands relax....Chest relax....Back relax....Stomach relax....Hips relax....Legs relax....Feet relax....Your whole body is becoming more and more relaxed with each breath.

Spend a few more minutes relaxing, if you would like. If, during your day, you find yourself getting upset about something, remember the relaxation you have just experienced. Before you get upset, take a deep breath, hold it and as you breathe out, silently say, "Relax and let go." With practice, you will be able to use this to relax whenever you begin to feel the stress of everyday living.

PROGRESSIVE RELAXATION SUMMARY

We recommend that you practice your Progressive Relaxation every day, twice a day if possible. Be sure to mark your practice on the Home Practice Chart on the last four pages of this book. We usually recommend that a person continue to practice with Progressive Relaxation exercises twice daily for at least a week.

If you are under the guidance of a psychologist or other professional, follow his or her instructions. If you are overviewing the book first, then practice Progressive Relaxation once and continue reading the book. Use the rating forms on the following pages to rate your pre- and post-session relaxation. After all sessions, you will want to put your overall pre- and post-session estimates on your Home Relaxation Chart.

After a few sessions, you will be able to relax unneeded muscles differentially while you perform tasks with needed muscles. For example, you do not need a tight jaw or clenched fist while writing a memo at your desk. Be sure to use Progressive Relaxation whenever you see the cues that you have set up in your home or office to help you relax.

If you drive to work, you may want to use stopping at a red light as a cue to mentally scan your body. Whatever your cues, ask yourself different questions like, "Is my forehead wrinkled?" "Are my jaw muscles tight?" "Is my stomach knotted up?" Then let your breathing become smooth and rhythmic. Allow the relaxation to replace any tension, and a wave of calm comes over your body. Try to be creative and find more places where you can practice your new skills.

SUBJECTIVE RATINGS
OF MUSCLE RELAXATION

Directions: Before and after your relaxation sessions, rate your subjective relaxation from 0 (very relaxed) to 10 (very tense) for each muscle group. Carefully record these ratings in the spaces provided. Then add these ratings to get your total scores for before and after the session.

Be sure to transfer your total score for before and after the sessions from the bottom squares to the Home Practice Chart. Circle the muscle groups that you find particularly difficult to relax. These may need extra practice.

DATES OF PRACTICE

	BEFORE AFTER	BEFORE AFTER	BEFORE AFTER

FOREHEAD AND EYES
Very relaxed 0 1 2 3 4 5 6 7 8 9 10 Very tense

JAW AND MOUTH
Very relaxed 0 1 2 3 4 5 6 7 8 9 10 Very tense

NECK
Very relaxed 0 1 2 3 4 5 6 7 8 9 10 Very tense

SHOULDERS
Very relaxed 0 1 2 3 4 5 6 7 8 9 10 Very tense

ARMS AND HANDS
Very relaxed 0 1 2 3 4 5 6 7 8 9 10 Very tense

CHEST
Very relaxed 0 1 2 3 4 5 6 7 8 9 10 Very tense

BACK
Very relaxed 0 1 2 3 4 5 6 7 8 9 10 Very tense

STOMACH
Very relaxed 0 1 2 3 4 5 6 7 8 9 10 Very tense

HIPS
Very relaxed 0 1 2 3 4 5 6 7 8 9 10 Very tense

LEGS AND FEET
Very relaxed 0 1 2 3 4 5 6 7 8 9 10 Very tense

TOTALS

©1982 Edward A. Charlesworth, Ph.D. and Ronald G. Nathan, Ph.D.

DATES OF PRACTICE	BEFORE	AFTER	BEFORE	AFTER	BEFORE	AFTER	BEFORE	AFTER	BEFORE	AFTER	BEFORE	AFTER	BEFORE	AFTER	BEFORE	AFTER	BEFORE	AFTER	BEFORE	AFTER	BEFORE	AFTER
HEAD																						
JAW																						
NECK																						
SHOULDERS																						
ARMS																						
CHEST																						
BACK																						
STOMACH																						
HIPS																						
LEGS																						
TOTALS																						

REVIEW QUESTIONS

Directions: Circle the letter in front of the best response to each question. The correct answers are provided on the page following the last question.

1. Progressive Relaxation involves tensing and relaxing muscles. This helps us

   a. learn where our muscles are.
   b. learn what muscle tension feels like.
   c. relax, because if a muscle is tensed, it will relax more deeply when released.
   d. All of the above

2. Progressive Relaxation was developed by _____.

   a. Hans Selye, M. D.
   b. Edmund Jacobson, M. D.
   c. Sigmund Freud, M. D.
   d. Alfred Adler, M. D.

3. The Progressive Relaxation exercises may best be described by which of the following?

   a. tension-relaxation cycle
   b. muscle-tension cycle
   c. gradual relaxation cycle
   d. self-hypnosis training

4. To insure a successful beginning for Progressive Relaxation training, all outside noises should be _____ to the _____ possible level.

   a. reduced; highest
   b. increased; highest
   c. reduced; lowest
   d. increased; lowest

5. _____ practice is needed to help make this new muscular relaxation a routine way of life.

   a. Monthly
   b. Weekly
   c. Regular, daily
   d. Occasional

6. If our arm is relaxed, then it can be _____ by another person with little effort.

   a. bent or lifted
   b. tickled
   c. rubbed
   d. stuck with a needle (as in acupuncture)

7. "Differential Relaxation" means that you

   a. relax all muscles when you are driving a car at night.
   b. check all your muscles to be sure they are working, not just those that need to be tense.
   c. relax some muscles while tensing others, such as when driving a car.
   d. keep your forehead and stomach tense even while watching television.

8. The stress management program was designed to

   a. teach you to relax only when listening to instructions by another person.
   b. teach you to relax only at home, in one room, and only at certain times.
   c. teach you a habit, so you can trade, at will, the tension and strain of daily living for a relaxed way of seeing and doing things.
   d. Only (a) and (b).

9. The recommended and alternate schedules for successfully learning Progressive Relaxation include

   a. practicing two times every day for twenty to thirty minutes until you can relax easily.
   b. reading through this book; and, when you have completed it, returning to the exercises to begin daily practice.
   c. practicing for brief periods throughout the day.
   d. All the above.

10. Part of the Progressive Relaxation training of tensing and relaxing the muscles systematically, is

    a. slow breathing followed by quick breathing.
    b. quick breathing all the time.
    c. holding one's breath and letting it go slowly.
    d. uneven breathing all the time.

ANSWERS TO REVIEW QUESTIONS

1.	d	6.	a
2.	b	7.	c
3.	a	8.	c
4.	c	9.	d
5.	c	10.	c

SUGGESTED BOOKS AND RECORDINGS

BOOKS

Progressive Relaxation by E. Jacobson. Chicago: University of Chicago, 1974.

You Must Relax by E. Jacobson. New York: McGraw-Hill, 1978.

RECORDINGS

Relaxation And Stress Management Program -- Progressive Relaxation by E. Charlesworth. Houston: Stress Management Research, 1981.

Relaxation Training Program -- Tense -- Slo -- Relax by T. Budzynski. New York: B.M.A., 1974.

Quieting Response Training -- Relaxing Skeletal Muscles by C. Stroebel. New York: B.M.A., 1978.

Chapter 6

Scanning For Tension
And Breathing For Relaxation

The last chapter showed you how to recognize and reduce muscle tension. The instructions for Progressive Relaxation also taught you how to scan your body for muscle tension, but only in very general terms. Scanning is a very helpful technique. It is worthy of thorough study and daily use. You may want to continue practicing Progressive Relaxation twice each day as you learn more about scanning.

What Is Scanning?

Scanning means to examine or pass over quickly. Most people think of scanning as rapidly looking something over with their eyes. Body scanning uses your inner awareness, rather than your eyes, to examine your body. This kind of scanning involves directing your attention quickly and easily to various parts of your body.

Body scanning is very much like looking in a mirror; but the mirror is the awareness in your mind. You can use this inner awareness to check whether you have collected any unhealthy muscle tension.

Scanning is a skill that you may want to use every day for the rest of your life. Yes, every day for the rest of your life! Fortunately, with time and practice, scanning can easily become a habit as automatic as looking in the mirror. Many of our most successful patients have found scanning a favorite technique. It is quick and can be done anywhere. You need not sit or recline. You can even learn to scan as you are walking through the office or your home.

Your Body's "Mirror"

We look in the mirror to see if our hair is just right, our make-up needs refreshing, or our tie needs straightening. If everything on the outside looks okay in the mirror, we are usually satisfied; but a mirror cannot tell us if everything on the inside is also okay.

A mirror is a common convenience for checking our appearance. It is also a helpful cue that reminds us to straighten our tie or fix our hair. Unfortunately, there are few such reminders around for scanning our muscles, so we have to be creative and come up with some of our own. We suggested several ideas in Chapter 5. Remember the pieces of colored tape that could be placed on your watch and signs that could be arranged in different places?

A number of situations allow us enough time to scan and look at our body's tension. These can also act as cues. They include slowing through a school zone, stopping at a red light, waiting for an elevator, being put "on hold" when on the telephone, and standing in line. As you can tell, most of these situations involve waiting of some kind. Most of us have many short periods daily of such "free time." The cues associated with these situations (for example, the elevator or the red light) can be important for helping us remember to look into our body's "mirror."

An ulcer patient, who was a sergeant in the service, found scanning to be an answer to the Army's "Hurry up and wait." We may chuckle at the Army, but think of all the time you have while you wait for people who are late and meetings that do not start on time. Think of the hours you spend each month in your car waiting for your children or in the waiting rooms of doctors or lawyers you see. Previously trying situations can become opportunities to enjoy some calm relaxation.

Cues For Using Your Body's "Mirror"

In the spaces below, write down the cues you have already begun to use and some cues you will want to try out during the next few days.

Cues I use now: Cues I plan to try using:
Example: *Relaxation sign*   Example: *Wearing a special*
on my desk   *piece of jewelry or clothing*

1. _____   1. _____

2. _____   2. _____

3. _____   3. _____

4. _____   4. _____

5. _____   5. _____

Think about the things you do and see every day that could
be effective cues for scanning. Maybe the mirror we have been
using to describe scanning can also be a cue to look inside.
You may wish to put a "scan" sign on a few of your mirrors.

If you teach school, the buzzer or bell can become a cue.
If you answer the telephone, let it become a cue. With enough
practice, you will be able to check your tension and relax
during the first two or three rings before you answer the
phone. When you hang up you can scan your body again.

Any change in what you are doing can be used as a cue to
change your level of tension. Secretaries can scan for muscle
tension while the copying machine scans the originals to make
copies. Sales clerks can use the cash register as a cue to
relax any unnecessary tension. Television viewers can use
commercials. Many physicians, whom we have trained, use the
beepers they wear as cues to scan. Bathroom breaks and meals
can also be times to make certain we are not uptight.

Scanning And Everyday Living

The more cues you can find and use, the more unhealthy
tension you will scan away. The object is to use scanning to
remain relaxed throughout the day. Try to become aware of small
amounts of tension before they build up. Rather than one thing
leading to another, many things can lead to scanning for tension
and breathing for relaxation.

How To Do Scanning Relaxation

When we look in a mirror, we check our appearance, but we
probably look at a number of aspects of our reflection. We may
pay attention to clothes, hair and several other parts of our

bodies. This is also true of scanning. As you will see in the exercise that follows, when you scan, you will imagine various parts of your body and check to see if they are tense. Some people imagine a picture of their body, others imagine the muscles as they would be drawn in an anatomy book, and, still others imagine parts of a stick figure. One individual found it easier to imagine an x-ray machine scanning her muscles.

Most people simply scan their bodies by becoming aware and directing attention to each part of their body where tension might be. At first, it may seem like a long journey through all the muscle groups. With practice, the scan can be made very rapidly. Eventually, when you take one breath, you may be able to scan all the muscles from head to toe, and "Relax and let go" as you breath out.

Just as most people take special care to look at certain parts of their appearances when they look in a mirror, a good scanner will learn to do the same in his body's "mirror." Most people have areas that are tense more often than other areas. Many people carry tension in their shoulders, others put it into their wrinkled brow. Still others, clench their teeth. Most people begin to identify these areas. As time goes on, they know where they will find tension before they even start to scan their body.

An Executive Scan

For example, a hard-driving executive, who attended one of our groups on stress management, found that he always clenched his jaw when driving. He reported that this was almost a habit. He did it whether he was in a hurry getting to work or he was driving leisurely while on a vacation. In fact, long trips left him exhausted.

After learning how to scan, he began using red lights and stop signs to and from work as short scanning breaks. When driving long distances on the freeway, he used the reactions of other drivers. He also had a sign on his speedometer to remind him to scan his body whenever he looked to see how fast he was going. During the first week, he found that his jaw muscles were less tense and that he could relax quickly.

The executive also began to listen to "books on tape" in the car. These are recorded novels available from Books on Tape, P.O. Box 7900, Newport Beach, CA 92660. With continued scanning practice and "reading" while he drove, the executive reported that he enjoyed driving more and looked forward to it as a time to relax.

At a follow-up session, six months after completing our group training; he continued to report ease in driving, as a result of frequent body scanning. He was surprised how little effort it took to remain relaxed and to enjoy driving.

Experiment and see what works best for you in a variety of settings. When you first start your scanning practice, try not to overlook any opportunities to practice on any area of tension in your body. After frequent practice, looking into your body's mirror, can become as effortless as glancing in a mirror to check your appearance. Knowing how relaxed you are, can be as comforting and pleasing as knowing your nose is powdered or your tie is straight.

Using Relaxation Tapes

Once Progressive Relaxation is learned, scanning is one of the easiest techniques to master without a tape. For this reason, many of the pre-recorded tape series do not include a specific scanning tape. However, you may wish to use an excellent tape by C. H. Hartmann entitled "Mixed Scanning Relaxation Program." The first side presents Progressive Relaxation and stretching exercises, followed by a basic scanning technique.

The Hartman tape, and other taped scanning programs with which we are familiar, do not include the emphasis we place on breathing. We have found that by pairing breathing with scanning, relaxation can become as automatic as breathing. Since we breathe all the time, breathing itself can become an unbeatable cue for relaxation.

Guiding Yourself

If you will be guiding yourself through the exercises, review the directions below. At first, it may be very helpful to have someone read the instructions slowly to you. If possible, you may want to record these instructions onto a tape and then use the tape for practice.

Helpful Hints To Tape And Self-Instruction Users

Begin slowly at first. Many people see scanning as an easy technique and gloss over it. This is one of the reasons we decided to spend a full chapter on scanning to help you to understand it.

Another common problem is making the change from Progressive Relaxation to Scanning Relaxation. In Progressive Relaxation you are physically active. Scanning involves steady breathing, but uses more of the power of your mind. At first, it may be helpful to touch the parts of your body you are scanning or to look at them as you imagine and explore them in your mind's "eye."

You may want to continue your Progressive Relaxation training. Progressive Relaxation can help you get tuned into where your muscles are and what they feel like. Start practicing with the Word-By-Word Detailed Scanning Relaxation. Find a quiet place, take your time and enjoy the sensations. You may wish to use Scanning Relaxation after practicing Progressive Relaxation to check if all of your muscles responded to the tension-relaxation exercises.

For a couple of days, you may want to use Scanning Relaxation with the longer detailed instructions. Then you may begin alternating between the brief and long forms of instructions. If things are going well, start using the brief Scanning Relaxation everywhere you can, whenever you have a free moment.

We have provided the "Scanning Chart" for those of you who are "going all out" to learn stress management and for those of you who are under the care of a professional. Charting has been shown to be of great value for promoting behavior change. Use the "Scanning Chart" to mark down the cues you have chosen and how often you used them each day. Try to increase the number of cues and the frequency of your scans.

OUTLINE FOR SCANNING RELAXATION

I.   Basic Technique
     A. Breathe in while scanning one area of your body for tension.
     B. As you breathe out, relax that area.
     C. Progress through each area of your body.

II. Muscle Groups
     A. Face and neck.
     B. Shoulders and arms.
     C. Chest and lungs.
     D. Stomach area
     E. Hips, legs and feet.

III. When to use Scanning Relaxation
     A. Starting or completing a stressful task to help you to relax and prepare or relax and unwind.
     B. Standing in line, stopping at a red light, waiting for an elevator or during any "free time."

WORD-BY-WORD DETAILED SCANNING RELAXATION

Preparation

I want you to scan all the parts of your body as I call them out. This is called "Body Scanning." Think about a muscle area and, as you breathe out, feel the tension slipping away. Move progressively through your body. Remember, as you breathe in, scan the muscles for any tension, and, as you breathe out, feel the tension slip away. Let's begin.

Face And Neck

As you breathe in, scan your face and neck....As you breathe out, feel the tension slip away. Face and neck relax. Once again, as you breathe in, attend to your forehead, eyes, jaw and neck....As you breathe out, your relaxation is becoming deeper and deeper.

Shoulders And Arms

As you breathe in, scan your shoulders and arms....As you breathe out, feel the tension slip away. Arms and shoulders relax. Once again, as you breathe in, attend to your shoulders, arms and hands....As you breathe out, your relaxation is becoming deeper and deeper.

Chest And Lungs | As you breathe in, scan your chest and lungs....As you breathe out, feel the tension slip away. Chest and lungs relax. Once again, as you breathe in, attend to your chest and lungs....As you breathe out, your relaxation is becoming deeper and deeper.

Stomach Area | As you breathe in, scan your stomach area.... As you breathe out, feel the tension slip away. Stomach area relax. Once again, as you breathe in, attend to your stomach area....As you breathe out, your relaxation is becoming deeper and deeper.

Legs And Feet | As you breathe in, scan your legs and feet....As you breathe out, feel the tension slip away. Legs and feet relax. Once again, as you breathe in, scan your hips, legs and feet....As you breathe out, your relaxation is becoming deeper and deeper. Now allow your breathing to become smooth and rhythmic.

Return To Activity | Let your body continue to relax, as you return to your daily activities. Continue to feel calm and at ease....If at any time during your day, you begin to feel tense or uptight, scan your body to find the tension and then relax and let go with each breath.

BRIEF SCANNING RELAXATION

Practice using this brief scanning while you are waiting for an elevator, a red light, or a line. In the time it takes to breathe in and out three times, you can become aware of any tension and release it.

1. As you breathe in, scan your face, neck, shoulders, and arms.

2. As you breathe out, feel any tension slip away.

3. As you breathe in, scan your chest, lungs, and stomach.

4. As you breathe out, feel any tension slip away.

5. As you breathe in, scan your hips, legs and feet.

6. As you breathe out, feel any tension slip away.

Directions: Write in the cues you plan to use to help remind you to scan your body. Every day during the next week, estimate the number of times you used the cue to remind yourself to scan. Mark the total number of scans you made in response to each cue under the corresponding day of the week.

DAY OF WEEK

CUE USED	1	2	3	4	5	6	7
Example: *Jewelry*	2	3	4	3	5	2	6

REVIEW QUESTIONS

Directions: Circle the letter in front of the best response to each question.   The correct answers are provided on the page following the last question.

1. Body Scanning is

    a. a short form of Progressive Relaxation that can help you learn the longer technique.
    b. a long form of Progressive Relaxation that can help you learn the shorter technique.
    c. a technique for checking your appearance so you will not have to worry about it as much.
    d. a skill you can use to check and release unhealthy muscle tension.

2. Scanning is very much like looking in a mirror, but the mirror is

    a. a small one that you can carry with you.
    b. a long one in which you can see your whole body.
    c. the awareness of your body in your mind.
    d. a short one that only reflects your head and shoulders.

3. Scanning can be used

    a. everyday for the rest of your life.
    b. for only one week before learning a new skill.
    c. in one place and at only one hour each day.
    d. cautiously and only once a day.

4. Cues that can be used to remind us to scan our body's "mirror" include

    a. red lights.
    b. elevators.
    c. standing in lines.
    d. All the above and many more.

5. When people scan, they can

    a. imagine a picture of their body parts.
    b. imagine the muscles as they would appear in an anatomy book.
    c. simply direct their attention to the different muscles of their bodies.
    d. Any of the above.

6. Most people have areas of their bodies that are tense more often than others. As they become good at scanning they

   a. know where they will find tension before they even start to scan.
   b. give up, knowing that they were just born that way.
   c. try to keep those muscles tense, so as to have something to scan.
   d. find scanning more and more time consuming.

7. Scanning involves breathing in, scanning part of your body for tension, and breathing out as you relax that part of your body. You then scan the same part of your body or the next one. This description is

   a. missing some part of the technique.
   b. presented in the wrong order.
   c. the correct, basic technique.
   d. the wrong technique for scanning.

8. Muscle groups scanned should include at least: The face, neck, shoulders, arms, chest, lungs, stomach area, hips, legs and feet.

   a. True
   b. False, because you scan only the upper part of your body
   c. False, because you scan only the lower part of your body
   d. False, because you do not scan muscles

9. Progressive Relaxation and Scanning

   a. should not be practiced during the same week.
   b. are just different names for the same technique.
   c. can be used after one another to check muscle relaxation.
   d. can be helpful, even if they are used only a few times.

10. When you use scanning, you

   a. mentally scan your body for muscle tension.
   b. breathe and release the tension you find.
   c. find cues to remind you to do it as often as you can.
   d. All the above.

ANSWERS TO REVIEW QUESTIONS

1.	d	6.	a
2.	c	7.	c
3.	a	8.	a
4.	d	9.	c
5.	d	10.	d

Chapter 7

Reaching Deeper Levels Of Relaxation

Deep Muscle Relaxation is a form of Progressive Relaxation. It makes use of your new skills, but does not include the tensing part of the Progressive Relaxation exercises. Deep Muscle Relaxation involves suggestions of relaxation directed to each muscle group in turn. The step-by-step nature of these exercises is similar to Progressive Relaxation, but now you learn to rely more on mental awareness, deep breathing, and calming words or phrases.

Some individuals have learned Deep Muscle Relaxation without first practicing Progressive Relaxation. The main reason we recommend the tension-relaxation exercises first, is that Deep Muscle Relaxation uses only the power of your mind to relax your muscles. This can be more difficult than using a physical exercise to achieve relaxation.

A successful young lawyer, whom we will call John, joined a stop-smoking group conducted by one of the authors. He had tried Deep Muscle Relaxation before, but always felt "silly" trying to tell his body to relax. He had no real idea of what to expect or where to expect it. When the use of relaxation came up in the stop-smoking group, John was disappointed and he told the group about his previous experiences.

None of his earlier attempts at relaxation had involved the Progressive Relaxation technique discussed in Chapter 5. John had experienced only frustration in his attempts at Deep Muscle Relaxation, primarily because he started with an advanced relaxation procedure without first learning the basics. He was a little skeptical, but he gave Deep Muscle Relaxation another chance after he learned Progressive Relaxation. To his surprise, it became a favorite technique for coping with stress after he permanently gave up smoking.

What You Have Achieved

Progressive Relaxation instructions helped you to systematically tense and release each of the muscle groups in your body. When you focused on a specific area, such as your forearm, you tensed the muscle tightly and then released it slowly, as you said "Relax and let go." This achieved two goals.

First, by tensing the forearm muscle, you became aware of the location of the muscle and what it felt like when it was tense. Learning this, helped you to recognize when your muscles were tense, which muscles were tense, and how tense your muscles were. Some people teach themselves early in life to ignore tension and keep striving. If people do this, they have trouble knowing when they are tense and not tense. Progressive Relaxation helps reverse this early learning.

The second goal of tension-relaxation exercises was to gradually increase the depth of your relaxation until the word "relaxation" came to have a clear and very real meaning. Focusing on a muscle and suggesting relaxation, may be very frustrating and almost worthless until you know what relaxation feels like. By first tensing and then relaxing a muscle, momentum is built up so that the muscle relaxation becomes deeper with each release. It is as if tension is gradually being used up. Consequently, through the release of tension, a very deep level of relaxation is reached and a clear memory trace is laid down in your mind.

With practice, you eventually reach the point where you can use this memory to simply focus on a muscle, think about the feelings of releasing tension, and produce deep relaxation. This is why Deep Muscle Relaxation is also called Recall Relaxation.

Looking Forward

You can look forward, later in your training, to relaxing by simply taking a deep breath, and silently saying "Relax and let go" as you slowly breathe out. At that time, tensing a muscle may only be necessary for muscles that are particularly difficult to relax or, for the few situations in which tension becomes extreme. Of course, all of this comes with a great deal of practice. Hopefully, after having practiced Progressive Relaxation every day, you will now be able to bring back some of these feelings of relaxation without first having to tense your muscles.

You may feel that you have not practiced enough Progressive Relaxation to learn where your tension builds up and what relaxation feels like. If this is the case, you may want to finish reading this chapter, but practice more Progressive Relaxation before trying Deep Muscle Relaxation. Remember how John, the lawyer, found Deep Muscle Relaxation frustrating before he had learned Progressive Relaxation.

Resist the temptation to "rush" through this book. You may want to preview future chapters, but learn to practice relaxation the way you learned to read. You had to know the alphabet before you could learn to read words, sentences and paragraphs. You learned to count before you learned to add, subtract, multiply or divide. You learned to crawl before you walked, walked before you ran, and ran before you learned to play sports. The basics of relaxation must also be practiced and learned before advancing to other techniques.

Cultivating Deep Muscle Relaxation

For a moment, turn your attention from this book to your body. Are you comfortable? Is your body supported and resting? Are your back muscles tight? Are your jaw muscles tight? Is there any muscle tension in your stomach area? What about your arms and hands? How are you holding this book?

You just observed how your body was supported, the amount of tension in your body, and how you were holding this book. Did you move around to become more comfortable, slacken your jaw muscles or loosen your grip? If you did, you were using mental awareness similar to what we will teach you to use for Deep Muscle Relaxation.

Have you ever noticed your jaw becoming clenched while driving in heavy traffic? Do you grip the steering wheel too tightly? Imagine you are in a heated discussion at work, or you are telling children to stop doing something. Do your legs and stomach become tense as you assume a defensive posture?

In all these situations and even while reading this book, it may not be possible or practical to tense and relax your muscles. Of course, you would not want to tense and relax your muscles if it would interfere with an activity, or if it would be embarrassing. You can, however, learn to use Deep Muscle Relaxation for the muscles you are not using without interfering with your activity or calling attention to yourself.

Beyond Releasing Muscle Tension

Becoming aware of tension and releasing it is helpful, but Deep Muscle Relaxation does even more than this. Deep breathing exercises are practiced to be sure your breathing is calm and regular. In addition, Deep Muscle Relaxation helps you to learn cues which quickly produce the relaxation on command. After you are able to recall the feelings of relaxation and deepen them, key words and phrases are added to help you remember and to reinstate these feelings whenever and wherever you want.

Some people pick up a tennis racket and seem to be a "natural." Others need extra practice and discipline. The same is true with relaxation. Some individuals will be able to progress through the exercises rather quickly. Others will feel a need to continue tensing and releasing certain muscles that are troublesome. Your only competition is tension. Take your time and be patient. Remember, trying too hard and rushing can make you tense. Go at your own pace.

HOW TO DO DEEP MUSCLE RELAXATION

Scheduling And Recording Relaxation Practice

Deep Muscle Relaxation should be practiced during the same times you previously practiced Progressive Relaxation. Again, we recommend you practice twice daily. For example, during the work week, you may wish to use the morning coffee break or lunch hour and then practice in the afternoon after arriving home.

Any time you find muscles that have not become completely relaxed after finishing Deep Muscle Relaxation, tense them and release them by using Progressive Relaxation. Occasionally, we even recommend that a person work on Progressive Relaxation during one practice session and Deep Muscle during the other. This is helpful if a person feels moderately confident about his or her results with Progressive Relaxation, but has some difficulty relaxing certain muscle groups.

Before and after the relaxation sessions, complete the rating scale for Deep Muscle Relaxation. The Deep Muscle Relaxation rating form is identical to the forms used for Progressive Relaxation. Write in the numbers that describe your feelings of muscle tension and then add them up to find out how relaxed you were before and after relaxation. Then record your practice ratings on the Home Practice Chart on the last four pages of this book. Remember to record the technique used, how long you practiced, and an estimate of how relaxed you became each session.

Preparing For Deep Muscle Relaxation

Once again, as with Progressive Relaxation, plan on practicing Deep Muscle Relaxation in a place that is private, quiet, comfortable and free from distractions. Be sure family, friends, and co-workers will not interrupt you.

At this stage of your training, it will be best to practice while sitting rather than lying. Most people practice their relaxation while in a large, comfortable, over-stuffed chair. Ideally, this chair should have a high back to support your neck and head. If you practice at work, you may need to move your desk chair next to a wall to gain this support.

If you do not have a good chair to practice in at home, you can practice on a bed. It may be best to pile pillows at the head of the bed and sit up with your feet out and your back, neck, and head supported by the pillows. Experiment if you like. Remember, the goal during practice is not to fall asleep. You are certainly relaxed when you do, but unless it is bedtime and you are using the relaxation to promote sleep, then your goal is to become very relaxed while being awake and alert.

Common Problems And Their Solutions

One of our relaxation patients had a painful and chronic degenerative nerve disease. Mary had always been an active, hardworking and conscientious individual. She kept busy throughout her life and rarely had a spare minute. She liked life this way and the only thing that was more active than her body was her mind. Mary always thought of new things to do, and always seemed to get a lot of them done. Her friends described her as "vivacious" and "full of life." With the onset of her disease, she found that she had less and less physical energy. Her mind was still active, but it was now out of step with her physical capabilities.

Mary was able to gain moderate success in relieving some of her pain, sleeping better and relaxing better during activities. However, she found Deep Muscle Relaxation very difficult. Her concentration on the relaxation exercises was constantly interrupted by intruding thoughts of wanting to do something active. With Progressive Relaxation, tensing and releasing the muscles tended to be active enough to occupy her mind. Deep Muscle Relaxation did not offer the same advantage, but the following suggestions helped her to benefit fully from Deep Muscle Relaxation.

Prescriptions For Intruding Thoughts

If you experience problems with intruding thoughts, you may want to try some of the following techniques. First, be gentle with yourself and do not get angry when you realize you have lost your concentration. Allow your thoughts to leave your mind as quickly as they came and bring your attention back to the exercises or muscle group you were practicing.

For more persistent thoughts, you may want to command yourself very firmly to "Stop!" the distracting thoughts and return to the relaxation. At first it may be nesessary to say "Stop!" out loud. With practice you can say it in a whisper and, finally, you can say it silently to yourself. A similar approach is to repeat the silent "Stop!" or "No!" several times and then return to the relaxation exercises. These techniques are called "thought stopping." The techniques can be used in many situations where you want to control unwanted thoughts.

It is also helpful to make the relaxation very brief. For example, set an alarm (you can use a kitchen timer) for five minutes to see if you can concentrate that long. If not, then set it for fewer minutes. When you succeed, gradually increase the time until you can do all of the exercises.

Another technique involves attempting to relax just a few groups of muscles without losing your concentration. Decide you will first go through just the face and neck. Congratulate yourself on your success and then move to your arms and hands. In this fashion, go through the other muscles briefly. Try the chest and stomach, the hips and thighs, and then the calves and feet.

If you are unable to complete a small group of muscles, try again; but, this time make the group even smaller. For example, just relax your forehead and eyes. When your concentration improves, you may go through larger muscle groups until you can progress throughout the body without stopping.

Assuming A Passive Attitude

An important point related to concentration and relaxation is a principle called assuming a "passive attitude." This is a very necessary part of Deep Muscle Relaxation and of many other techniques you will learn in this book. Passive is the opposite of active. In this case, it means to be open to new experiences. An attitude is a mental disposition or way of emotionally approaching things. Thus, assuming a passive attitude is a way of allowing things to happen by adopting a quiet and open mental orientation. This will help you to become more receptive to the enjoyment of successful stress management.

Most of us have learned that we do not get anywhere without doing something. In Deep Muscle Relaxation, the doing is the assuming of a receptive attitude. This means allowing things to happen rather then trying to make anything happen. It also means acknowledging unrelated thoughts that come into our minds and letting them slip away as soon as we can. Try to have a passive, receptive attitude whether you listen to taped relaxation or guide yourself through the relaxation techniques.

Meditation

Many people are beginning to explore meditation as a form of stress management. Meditation is often associated with Eastern religions, but it can be practiced with or without a religious emphasis. Herbert Benson, M.D., a Harvard professor specializing in cardiovascular diseases and internal medicine, studied Transcendental Meditation scientifically and wrote about a meditative technique which he called the Relaxation Response. The Relaxation Response has been shown to be of significant value in the treatment of hypertension and other psychosomatic illnesses.

The basic elements of the Relaxation Response and most meditation include finding a quiet place which is free from distraction; assuming a passive attitude; getting into a comfortable position; and focusing attention on one sensory input such as a word, sound, thought, feeling or symbol. The repetition of cue words in Deep Muscle Relaxation Training can be considered a form of meditation.

If you are interested in meditation, we encourage you to explore different forms such as Yoga, Zen or Transcendental Meditation. For this purpose, we have recommended several books, including The Relaxation Response, at the end of this chapter. Some of the unique benefits of meditation beyond relaxation training, involve the self-discipline of learning to concentrate on one thing at a time, and the insights we can gain into our inner world and outer reality. However, we emphasize cue-controlled forms of relaxation for stress management because of the difficulties people may have in setting aside time for daily meditation for the rest of their lives. In addition, our goal is to help you manage stress effectively throughout your day wherever you are, rather than in special places or at special times. Zen, a Buddhist sect, envisioned an ideal personality which we feel is worth striving for. Such a person was capable of not only quiet meditation, but also of life-affirming action.

Using Relaxation Tapes Or Guiding Yourself

If you are using recorded relaxation exercises or guiding yourself, then schedule time now to rate your subjective degree of muscular tension and practice Deep Muscle Relaxation. If you are using relaxation tapes, see the recommended recordings at the end of this chapter to help select the appropriate tape.

If you will be guiding yourself through the exercises, review the directions below. If possible, tape them or ask someone to read them to you.

After you have practiced and recorded your relaxation ratings, complete the Review Questions. Check your responses and if you miss some questions or fail to understand some ideas, you may want to review this chapter. We have provided a summary at the end of this chapter for quick review.

OUTLINE FOR DEEP MUSCLE RELAXATION

I. Deep Breathing

    A. Breathe deeply and slowly.
    B. Silently say "Relax and let go" each time you breathe out.

II. Body Scanning

    A. Focus on relaxing each muscle.
    B. Feel the tension slip out with each time you breathe out.
    C. Progress from your forehead and the top of your head to your feet and toes.

III. Examine the Feelings of Relaxation.

IV. Massaging Relaxation

    A. Imagine a gently massaging relaxation flowing through your body.
    B. Feel the massaging relaxation move slowly from forehead to toes.
    C. Move to another muscle each time you breathe out.

V. Cue Words

    A. Silently say "Peaceful and calm" while continuing to relax.
    B. Silently say "I am at peace" while continuing to relax.

VI. Return To Activity -- count forward from one to three.

WORD-BY-WORD DEEP MUSCLE RELAXTION

Preparation

Spend a little time getting as comfortable as you can. While you are finding a good position, you will also want to loosen any tight clothing. Loosen your shirt or blouse at the neck. Loosen your belt. If your shoes feel a little tight, then take them off. Allow your eyes to close.

Mentally, you should begin to clear your mind of the business and rushing that may characterize your life. Allow a passive attitude to develop. Try to let the relaxation begin.

Open your mouth for a moment and move your jaw slowly and easily from side to side.... Now let your mouth close, keeping your teeth slightly apart. As you do, take a deep breath....and slowly let the air slip out.

Breathing

Take another deep breath....As you breathe
out silently say, "Relax and let go."
Feel yourself floating down. Now that you
are comfortable, let yourself relax even
further. The more you can let go, the
better it will be.

Again, take a deep breath. (Briefly pause.)
As you breathe out, silently say "Relax
and let go." Just let the air slip out
easily and automatically, and already you
may be feeling a little calmer. Now just
carry on breathing normally.

Study your own body and the feelings you
are experiencing. (Briefly pause.) As you
relax more and more, your breathing becomes
slower. You may notice that it is slower now
and you breathe more and more from the
bottom of your lungs.

It's too much trouble to move, just too
much trouble to move. All tension is
leaving you and you are so very comfortable.
Notice that you have a feeling of well-being,
as though any troubles have been set aside,
and nothing seems to matter.

Body Scanning

Now, as we continue, let's use the natural abilities of your mind and body to experience feelings of deep, deep relaxation. We will do this by going through your body from head to foot, and progressively instilling those good feelings of relaxation. Each time you breathe out, you should feel more relaxed.

Keep your eyes gently closed. Relax your jaw muscles. Keep your teeth slightly apart and your face, neck, and shoulders loose and relaxed.

As you think about each part of your body and you allow that part of your body to relax, you will feel all the tension flowing away, and that part of your body will be comfortable, calm and peaceful. Each time you breathe out you will become more relaxed and feel the relaxation spreading slowly through your body.

Head And Neck
Scanning

Now think about the top of your head. Feel
the area. As you breathe out feel the top
of your head relax more and more, as it
becomes loose and free of wrinkles. Let
tensions flow from the top of your head.
The top of your head is becoming completely
relaxed.

Think of your forehead. Feel it, the skin
that covers it. Feel your eyes, the muscles
that are around them. Feel those muscles
relaxing more and more with each breath.
Feel your forehead relaxing more and more.

Your eyelids grow heavier and quieter with
each breath. Let yourself go as you breathe
gently in and out. Let the relaxation
spread naturally as the tension flows out
each time you exhale. Your forehead, your
eyes and all these muscles are relaxing
more and more.

Feel your throat and neck. Feel them
relax. As you breathe out you "Relax and
let go." Your throat and neck are loose,
quiet and comfortable.

Shoulders And
Arms Scanning

Feel your shoulders and upper back. Be aware of the skin and muscles of your shoulders and upper back. Effortlessly, allow relaxation to spread into your shoulders and upper back. With each breath you take, each time you breathe out you become more and more relaxed. The muscles are loose and comfortable. Feel quiet in your shoulder muscles.

Feel your upper arms relaxing. Feel your arms and hands. Your arms, hands and fingers are feeling very, very relaxed. You may feel warmth or tingling in your arms and hands. Feel your arms, hands and fingers relaxing. Feel the tension dropping from your arms, hands and fingers.

Chest And
Stomach
Scanning

Now think about your chest. Feel it.
Sense the muscles under the skin around
the chest. Be deeply aware of your chest.
Feel relaxation spreading throughout
your chest and stomach area. As you breathe
out, feel the calm and relaxation in your
chest. As you breathe naturally, feel
relaxation and quiet in your chest and in
your stomach area. Tension flows from your
chest as you breathe out.

Breathing in, and breathing out. More and
more you feel calm. Feel your stomach.
Be aware of the skin and muscles in this
area. Feel these muscles relax. Feel the
tension being replaced by pleasant relaxa-
tion. As you breathe out, feel relaxation
spread to your stomach and lower back.

Hips And Legs
Scanning

Now feel your legs, your hips, your calves
and your ankles. Be aware of these parts of
your body. Feel the muscles in these areas.
Allow them to relax more and more. Let calm
flow down to your legs. feel the tension
leaving. Your hips, thighs, calves, and
ankles are becoming loose and relaxed.

Feel your feet and your toes. Become deeply
aware of your feet and each toe. Feel how
still and relaxed they are. Let all the
tension leave your feet and toes.

Body Review
Scanning

What does your body feel like? Is it
tingly? Is it heavy? Does it feel hollow?
Does it feel light, as if you were floating?
What does your body feel like?

Become aware of the tiniest feelings and try
to describe these feelings to yourself.
Now, for about 30 seconds or so, scan around
your body for any signs of tension. If you
find any tension in any muscle group, let it
slip out. Try to let the tension flow out
and the relaxation flow in to take its place.
(Briefly pause.)

Think about the ocean, as you continue to
scan your body for tension. Imagine that
each wave that rolls in brings with it
massaging and gentle relaxation and calmness.
As the wave rolls out, it pulls along with
it any tension that remains in your body.
Scan your body. If you find any tension, let
it go.

Massaging
Relaxation

Go through your body once more,
and relax even more until a
very profound relaxation finds its place
everywhere in your body.

Picture the ocean waves rolling in...and
out with each breath. And with each breath
imagine gently massaging relaxation flowing
all over your body.

Picture massaging relaxation coming
over and flowing around the top of
your head. Feel the relaxation flowing
into each part of the skin on your head,
and coming over the forehead and relaxing
the eyes. The relaxation is entering parts
of your eyelids and making your eyelids feel
heavy, and your eyes feel at rest. Just
completely relaxed.

Now the relaxation gently massages the rest
of your face and the feelings of relaxation
move down to your nose. These massaging
feelings of relaxation move over your nose
and over your cheekbones, and down through
your throat and your mouth. These waves of
gentle relaxation and massaging energy come
one after another over your head and over
your eyes. Your eyelids feel very heavy
and it's a very good feeling, a very relaxing
feeling.

Let this relaxation move on down the back of
your head and enter the very deepest muscles
of your shoulders and neck. Feel the relaxation as it seeps into the muscles of your
neck, relaxing each part of your neck. And
as the muscles of your neck relax, the
muscles of your shoulders relax, and the skin
on your neck relaxes.

If you feel any tension, just move your neck
and shoulders a little bit until you feel
more comfortable. Allow this relaxation to
continue flowing over the shoulders to the
upper arms, and to the lower arms, coming
down and relaxing the very deepest muscles
of your arms. This relaxation pours down
from your shoulders in waves of gentle massaging, over your skin, into your muscles,
even into the flow of blood.

Every part of your body is becoming perfectly
balanced, relaxed and in harmony. It is
flowing down over the shoulders into the
upper arms, the lower arms, and through the
fingers.

And, as this flow comes down from your head and neck, it also enters your back muscles, down through the neck into the back, so that you feel relaxation around each bone of your back and in all of the muscles in your back.

This energy continues through your stomach, into each part of your lungs, so that your breathing becomes low and quiet. You feel that all is well. Let it go down into the stomach and gently massage it, making it feel very heavy and warm.

Now down through the legs, the thighs, into the knees and the calves, and down to the feet and the toes. Feel wave upon wave of this relaxation pouring over your body.

Cue Words

Now let's try and deepen the relaxation still further by using some cue words. Let's use the words "peaceful" and "calm." As you relax even further, think these words to yourself. Just say to yourself as you relax, "peaceful" and "calm," and then feel the deepening, ever deepening waves of relaxation as you feel so much more peaceful and calm. Think of these words, these cue words, "peaceful" and "calm." Think very, very clearly about them as you say them over and over to yourself. "Peaceful" and "calm."

Let the words echo in the back of your mind. Just continue to relax and repeat the words "peaceful" and "calm" over and over again. In the back of your mind the words "peaceful" and "calm" echo over and over again.

Pleasant feelings of quiet have spread throughout your body. Feel your body and feel the calm. Let it relax fully. Feel at peace. Your breathing is regular and calm, calm and regular. You are now in a deep state of calm and relaxation. It is comfortable. You feel good. You feel refreshed.

"I am at peace." Say this to yourself. Feel the peace and the tranquility throughout your body. You will enjoy a good feeling everytime you do these exercises, and you will feel more and more relaxed.

Return To
Activity

If, during the rest of the day, or for that matter, if, at any time, you find yourself getting upset about something, remember the relaxation you have just enjoyed. Before you get upset, take a deep breath and, as you breathe out, think the word "relax." Just think the work "relax" as you breathe out. Then for a brief period of time, think of the words "peaceful" and "calm," and let the feelings of relaxation that you are now enjoying come back to you. This will help you to control situations rather than being controlled by them.

Now, count from one to three. When you reach three, open your eyes. You will be relaxed, but you will be alert and refreshed.

One, relaxed, but alert....
Two, mentally wide awake....
Three, eyes open, alert and refreshed.

Deep Muscle Relaxation Summary

Practice your Deep Muscle Relaxation everyday, twice a day, if possible. Be sure to mark this on your Home Practice Chart or in your appointment book. We usually recommend that a person continue to practice Deep Muscle Relaxation exercises twice daily for at least a week. If you are under the guidance of a psychologist or other professional, then follow the professional's instructions. Use the rating forms on the following pages to rate your pre- and post-relaxation. Once again, you will want to put the pre- and post-session totals on your Home Practice Chart. If you are overviewing the book first, practice reading through the Deep Muscle Relaxation instructions at least once before going to the next chapter.

After a few sessions of Deep Muscle Relaxation you will be able to relax unneeded muscles differentially, while you perform tasks with needed muscles. For example, you do not need a tight jaw or a clenched fist while writing a memo at your desk.

Be sure to use Deep Muscle Relaxation whenever you see the cues that you have set up in your home or office. If you drive to work, you may want to use stopping at a signal light as a cue to mentally scan your body. Then let your breathing become smooth and rhythmic. Allow the relaxation to replace any tension, as a wave of calm comes over your body. Try to be creative and find new places where you can practice your Deep Muscle Relaxation.

SUBJECTIVE RATINGS
OF MUSCLE RELAXATION

Directions: Before and after your relaxation sessions, rate your subjective relaxation from 0 (very relaxed) to 10 (very tense) for each muscle group. Carefully record these ratings in the spaces provided. Then add these ratings to get your total scores for before and after the session.

Be sure to transfer your total score for before and after the sessions from the bottom squares to the Home Practice Chart. Circle the muscle groups that you find particularly difficult to relax. These may need extra practice.

DATES OF PRACTICE

| | BEFORE | AFTER | BEFORE | AFTER | BEFORE | AFTER |

FOREHEAD AND EYES
Very relaxed 0   1   2   3   4   5   6   7   8   9   10 Very tense

JAW AND MOUTH
Very relaxed 0   1   2   3   4   5   6   7   8   9   10 Very tense

NECK
Very relaxed 0   1   2   3   4   5   6   7   8   9   10 Very tense

SHOULDERS
Very relaxed 0   1   2   3   4   5   6   7   8   9   10 Very tense

ARMS AND HANDS
Very relaxed 0   1   2   3   4   5   6   7   8   9   10 Very tense

CHEST
Very relaxed 0   1   2   3   4   5   6   7   8   9   10 Very tense

BACK
Very relaxed 0   1   2   3   4   5   6   7   8   9   10 Very tense

STOMACH
Very relaxed 0   1   2   3   4   5   6   7   8   9   10 Very tense

HIPS
Very relaxed 0   1   2   3   4   5   6   7   8   9   10 Very tense

LEGS AND FEET
Very relaxed 0   1   2   3   4   5   6   7   8   9   10 Very tense

TOTALS

DATES OF PRACTICE	BEFORE	AFTER	BEFORE	AFTER	BEFORE	AFTER	BEFORE	AFTER	BEFORE	AFTER	BEFORE	AFTER	BEFORE	AFTER	BEFORE	AFTER	BEFORE	AFTER	BEFORE	AFTER
HEAD																				
JAW																				
NECK																				
SHOULDERS																				
ARMS																				
CHEST																				
BACK																				
STOMACH																				
HIPS																				
LEGS																				
TOTALS																				

REVIEW QUESTIONS

Directions: Circle the letter in front of the best response to
each question. The correct answers are provided on the page
following the last question.

1. The Deep Muscle Relaxation technique is designed to help a
   person gain greater control over

   a. the same muscle groups used in Progressive Relaxation.
   b. different muscle groups than those used in Progressive
      Relaxation.
   c. anxious thoughts and feelings, rather than the muscles.
   d. muscle spasms caused by Progressive Relaxation.

2. Deep Muscle Relaxation involves much more _____ than
   Progressive Relaxation.

   a. tensing and relaxing muscles
   b. deep breathing
   c. mental awareness and suggestions
   d. control over the autonomic nervous system

3. The feelings of relaxation described in Deep Muscle
   Relaxation include

   a. coldness and tingling.
   b. coldness and numbness.
   c. lightness, heaviness, tingling or warmth.
   d. All the above.

4. Respiration should be _____ when a person is
   relaxed.

   a. regular and loud
   b. regular and calm
   c. irregular and low
   d. irregular and loud

5. _____ are important ways of dealing with
   intruding thoughts and trying too hard.

   a. Thought stopping and thought reversal
   b. Taped relaxation and thought reversal
   c. Thought reversal and taped relaxation
   d. Thought stopping and assuming a passive attitude

6. In Deep Muscle Relaxation, emphasis is placed on

   a. the muscles.
   b. the liver.
   c. the adrenal gland.
   d. All the above.

7. Deep Muscle Relaxation

   a. needs to be forced.
   b. deepens with practice.
   c. makes people tired.
   d. All the above.

8. When facing a stressful situation, a person, who is highly
   skilled in Deep Muscle Relaxation, can recall the feelings
   of muscular relaxation by

   a. using key words and phrases which are strongly
      associated with relaxation.
   b. concentrating on breathing lightly and quickly.
   c. using the energy field available at most department
      stores.
   d. tensing and relaxing muscles in a progressive way.

9. "I am at peace" and "serene and calm" are examples of

   a. stimulus or cue words.
   b. response or reaction words.
   c. visual imagery or differential relaxation.
   d. All the above.

10. It may be best to learn Deep Muscle Relaxation while
    reclining, but it is also important to

    a. always practice in the same position.
    b. try to practice at the same time.
    c. always practice in the same place.
    d. use it in everyday situations.

ANSWERS TO REVIEW QUESTIONS

1.	a	6.	a
2.	c	7.	b
3.	c	8.	a
4.	b	9.	a
5.	d	10.	d

SUGGESTED BOOKS AND RECORDINGS

BOOKS

How To Meditate by L. LeShan. New York: Bantam, 1974.

The Relaxation Response by H. Benson with M. Klipper. New York: Avon, 1975.

RECORDINGS

Relaxation And Stress Management Program -- Deep Muscle Relaxation by E. Charlesworth. Houston: Stress Management Research, 1981.

Relaxation Training Program -- Forehead And Facial Relaxation by T. Budzynski. New York: B.M.A. 1974.

Quieting Response Training -- Breathing by C. Stroebel. New York: B.M.A., 1978.

Chapter 8

Countdown
To Relaxation

By practicing Progressive, Scanning, and Deep Muscle Relaxation, you have learned how to relax your muscles and scan your body to release any residual tension. Now, you are ready to begin practicing exercises to help you produce deeper levels of relaxation very quickly. One of the major goals of this stress management training program is to show you ways of becoming deeply relaxed at will.

Handling life stress successfully often calls for several abilities. The ability to size up clearly the stressful situation, is important. Next is the skill to relax quickly. Finally, there is the ability to do calmly what is needed. If you are able to count from ten to zero and allow yourself to become comfortably relaxed, you will have the self-control to deal more effectively with many of life's difficult situations.

The idea of counting to increase self-control and regain composure is not new. When you were a child, your mother may have told you to count to ten before yelling at someone who made you angry. Counting often gives a person enough time to decide if what is happening is what the person wants to be happening. The decision may well be to get into an argument; but, enough self-control can be gained between ten and zero, to decide if the consequences were worth it.

Counting down from ten to zero for relaxation is a similar self-control technique. The brief time needed to count backward can be used to break spiraling anxiety and release growing tension. Counting forward could be used to promote the same response; but most people, with whom we have worked, prefer counting backward. One reason seems to be that reaching zero is a natural stopping place. Some people say that, when they first learned to count from one to ten, they were always asked if they knew what came next. Rarely are you asked what comes after zero.

Another reason given for counting backwards is that some people feel that each number getting smaller reminds them that the amount of tension in their body is also becoming less. Others say it is like counting down their age until they are as young and carefree as a sleeping baby. For these and other reasons, counting backward seems to work best. Try the exercises and see, if they work for you.

The Troubled World Is Shrinking

Mr. Crane, an accountant, was in a stress management program conducted by one of the authors. Mr. Crane had a history of seasonal blood pressure elevations. He worked for a large corporation and experienced many important deadlines, in addition to the usual April 15th deadline most tax payers face. After a period of years, his blood pressure remained high, even when he was not facing a deadline. For these reasons, he was taking two different medications to control his hypertension.

Mr. Crane developed a very pleasant picture in his mind when he practiced counting backward from ten to zero. As he started counting, he noticed that his breathing became slow and rhythmic. Then, he felt a gentle wave of relaxation spread over his body, from his head to his feet. Before he would get to the number five, he began to experience a good feeling that he found difficult to describe. He said it was as if "the troubled world was shrinking."

Mr. Crane went on to say that, as he counted, he imagined the piles of books, on which he was currently working, becoming smaller and smaller. Along with this image, he had the feeling that he no longer needed to worry about the work. He discovered that worry did not make him work faster, and that he could be relaxed and still work as effectively as possible.

In fact, Mr. Crane was as productive as ever; but, he now felt better and less uptight. Throughout the day, Mr. Crane would take brief 30-second breaks without leaving his desk. He would count backward from ten to zero, imagine his worries shrinking in importance, and then return to his work refreshed and relaxed. Eventually, his blood pressure began to decline and his doctor no longer had to prescribe one of his medications.

Elevators, Escalators And Stairs

Mr. Crane had a pleasant image of his "troubled world" and shrinking work. Not everyone will want to imagine their world or work when counting from ten to zero. Many people like to use the brief seconds to imagine being somewhere very pleasant.

We often suggest that people try imagining a slowly descending elevator or escalator. As they count backward, the elevator or escalator slowly moves down. Some people imagine the floor numbers lighting up on the elevator panel, as they count down. You can also imagine yourself walking slowly down sturdy stairs. Many people seem to prefer going, at their own pace, down the stairs. There seems to be a sense of control gained by slowly guiding the legs and feet.

No matter which image is used, when zero is reached, the image of arriving in a pleasant place should be triggered by the opening of the elevator door, the end of the escalator, or the bottom of the stairs.

Most people are very creative with the pleasant scene they imagine when they reach zero. Many are surprised at what "pops" into their mind's eye. One person saw herself riding a horse in slow motion through the surf. The summer sun was warm and sparkled on the beach. Another saw himself relaxing on a king-sized bed, covered with satin sheets and pillows. The morning sun filtered through his bedroom window, opening onto a flower garden. You may be surprised at what you find when you take the elevator in your mind to a pleasant place.

Deep Breathing And Counting Down

A favorite technique, for one of the authors, is to simply focus on breathing in and out while counting backward from ten to zero. Each time he breathes out, he silently says the next number. Instead of focusing on visual images, he concentrates on the breath rolling in...and rolling out. He imagines the sound as it rolls out, carrying with it all the "noise" and troubles of the day. With practice, this technique has become so effective that a very deep relaxation can be produced by counting backward from just three to zero.

Count Up To Relaxed Alertness

Diving into a pool of crystal clear water, is refreshing for many people. The cool, pleasant water relaxes and refreshes at the same time. When you are becoming fatigued, counting backward to relaxation can have a similar refreshing effect. Spend a few seconds becoming totally relaxed. Do not think about worries or work. These can be important breaks for anyone experiencing a stressful day.

After the brief relaxation, you can return to a state of relaxed alertness, by bringing your attention back to yourself and counting forward from zero to three. This time, silently count the next number as you breathe in rather than when you breathe out. Let the breaths become deeper and stronger, as you approach the number three. With each number, feel the energy and vitality flow into your lungs. When you reach the number three, open your eyes and feel alert and eager to resume your activities. Your mind will be fully alert, but your body will be calm and relaxed.

Ways To Use Countdown Relaxation

Use a countdown to relaxation any time you need a brief break from work or activities. It can be combined with scanning relaxation. First scan to see if any muscles are tense, feel these muscles relax more and more with each breath; then, deepen the relaxation by counting from ten to zero. After practicing, you may find that you can return to a very relaxed state by counting from only three to zero.

It should be evident, after practicing this and the other muscle relaxation techniques, that relaxation is not wasteful inactivity. On the contrary, relaxation is a purposeful and active state that you control. You take the breaks you need from your work, and replace the excess stress and tension with relaxation. You conserve energy so you can draw from your reserves. Be creative in finding times and ways to cultivate the habit of relaxing.

Common Problems And Their Solutions

The difficulty most frequently reported with countdown relaxation is failing to become totally relaxed after counting to zero. This can be avoided by taking several precautions. First, remember that countdown is a deepening technique. By this, we mean it should be used to deepen the relaxation, after you have already become somewhat relaxed. If you briefly Practiced Progressive, Deep Muscle and Scanning Relaxation without becoming deeply relaxed, then counting from ten to zero will probably not have a great effect. However, if you have practiced the other techniques until you experienced deep relaxation, then you are ready to start using the countdown procedure.

A second way of avoiding disappointment with the countdown technique is to make it part of your regular practice sessions. You may want to complete your sessions of Progressive or Deep Muscle Relaxation practice by counting from ten to zero. This should help you develop your ability to use the procedure at other times to become deeply relaxed.

Do not be concerned if, when you first practice Countdown Relaxation, you feel relaxed; but, not as relaxed as when you have experienced the more detailed Progressive or Deep Muscle Relaxation. Continue to practice during brief breaks in the day to see if you are able to become more and more relaxed in less and less time. Building brief relaxation breaks into your day is just as important as the longer relaxation practice you have already scheduled.

How To Do Countdown Relaxation

Countdown Relaxation is a simple and rather short technique. We are not aware of any relaxation tapes that focus exclusively on this procedure. The Charlesworth and Peiffer Progressive Relaxation and Deep Muscle Relaxation tapes use Countdown Relaxation procedures to deepen relaxation, but the exercise is only a small part of each tape.

We emphasize learning Countdown Relaxation to use during short 30-second breaks throughout the day. When the technique is used in this fashion, tapes are not really needed. You may wish to make some countdown signs that read "10-9-8-7-6-5-4-3-2-1-0" or "3-2-1-0" and add them to your relaxation reminders. On elevators, use the descending lights to remind yourself to use Countdown Relaxation.

The best way to start is to read over the outline and word-by-word instructions that follow, then attempt the procedure on your own. We have included two different word-by-word guides for Countdown Relaxation. One describes only the countdown procedure. The other uses imagery to accompany the countdown procedure. Read both techniques and select the one you prefer.

If you have difficulties with Countdown Relaxation, record and listen to your own relaxation tape using the instructions or listen to the Charlesworth and Peiffer Progressive Relaxation or Deep Muscle Relaxation tape. Also, remember to practice Countdown Relaxation at the end of your practice sessions with Progressive or Deep Muscle Relaxation.

OUTLINE FOR COUNTDOWN RELAXATION

I. Basic Technique

   A. Count backward from ten to zero while becoming progressively more relaxed.

   B. Silenty say each number as you breathe <u>out</u> and feel tension flowing out with each breath.

   C. After you reach zero, briefly experience the relaxation.

II. Countup

   A. Count from one to three to return to an alert but relaxed state.

   B. Silently say each number as you breathe <u>in</u> and feel mental alertness returning, while you remain calm and relaxed.

II. Imagery Additions

   A. Imagine yourself moving slowly down a stairway, or on a gently moving elevator or escalator.

   B. When you reach the number zero and the bottom of the stairs, elevator, or escalator, see yourself getting off in a pleasant and relaxing place.

   C. When you start to count forward from one to three, imagine yourself returning to the place where you are practicing the exercises, but imagine that everything around you is relaxed and calm.

WORD-BY-WORD COUNTDOWN RELAXATION

Counting Down

Count backward from ten to zero. Silently
say each number as you breathe out. As you
count, you will relax more deeply, and go
deeper and deeper into a state of profound
relaxation. When you reach zero, you will
be completely relaxed.

Ten, deeper and deeper....Nine, relaxing
more deeply....Eight, relaxing deeper and
deeper....Seven, serene and calm....Six,
I feel more and more relaxed....Five, deeper
and deeper....Four, becoming as limp as a
rag doll....Three, profoundly relaxing....
Two, deeper and deeper....One, very, very
relaxed....Zero, profound relaxation....

Now drift still deeper with each breath.
Deeper and deeper. Just feel that deep relaxation all over and continue relaxing.
Now, relaxing deeper and deeper, you should
feel an emotional calm, tranquil and serene
feelings....feelings of safe security....
and a kind of calm peace.

Try and get that quiet inner confidence,
this good feeling about yourself and relaxation. Study once more the feelings that come
with relaxation. Just let your muscles
switch off; just feel good about everything.
Calm and secure feelings make you more and
more tranquil and peaceful.

Return To
Activity

Now, count from one to three; silently
say each number as you take a deep breath.
Open your eyes when you count three. You
will be relaxed and alert. When you open
your eyes, you will find yourself back in
the place where you started your relaxation.
However, the environment will seem slower
and more calm; and you will be more relaxed
and peaceful.

One, relaxed, but more alert....
Two, mentally wide awake....
Three, eyes open, alert and refreshed.

WORD-BY-WORD COUNTDOWN RELAXATION

WITH STAIRWAY IMAGERY

Stairway
Imagination

Use your imagination now. In your mind's eye, imagine that you are standing at the top of a large winding staircase. See the steps in front of you. See the handrail.

You are all alone standing in front of the staircase. It's your private staircase and you know it well. You feel comfortable being there. Count backward from ten to zero. Silently say each number as you breathe out. As you count, imagine you are stepping down the stairway, very slowly.

Imagine yourself walking slowly down the staircase. You move yourself down the steps deeper and deeper. With each count you will more deeply relax, as you go deeper and deeper into a state of profound relaxation. When you reach zero, imagine you have reached the bottom of the staircase. You then find you are in a place of perfect calm.

Counting Down   *Ten, and you take your first step....*
Nine, relaxing more deeply....Eight,
deeper and deeper relaxation....Seven,
gently walking down the stairs....Six,
feel more and more relaxed....Five,
deeper and deeper....Four, serene and
calm....Three, very relaxed....Two,
deeper and deeper....One, very, very
profoundly relaxed....Zero, gently step
off the bottom step into a perfectly
relaxed and calm peace.

Now, drift still deeper with each breath.
Deeper and deeper. Just feel that deeper
relaxation all over and continue relaxing.
Now, relaxing deeper and deeper, you
should feel an emotional calm...tranquil
and serene feelings...feelings of safe
security...and a kind of calm and peace.

Try to get that quiet inner confidence,
this good feeling about yourself with the
relaxation. Study once more the feelings
that come with relaxation. Just let your
muscles switch off; just feel good about
everything. Calm and secure feelings make
you more and more tranquil and peaceful.

Return To
Activity

*Now count from one to three. Silently
say each number, as you take a deep breath.
When you reach three, open your eyes. You
will be relaxed and alert. When you open
your eyes, you will find yourself back in
the place where you started your relaxation.
However, the environment will seem slower
and more calm; and you will be more relaxed
and peaceful.*

*One, relaxed, but more alert....
Two, mentally wide awake....
Three, eyes open, alert and refreshed.*

REVIEW QUESTIONS

Directions: Circle the letter in front of the best response to each question. The correct answers are provided on the page following the last question.

1. Countdown Relaxation is designed to

   a. help you relax in 20 to 30 minutes.
   b. help you count how many days you have practiced relaxation.
   c. help you relax quickly.
   d. All of the above.

2. Counting to regain self-control and calmness

   a. is a technique that is brand new.
   b. has been used to avoid impulsive and angry acts.
   c. does not really work for relaxation.
   d. was developed for NASA astronauts.

3. Countdown Relaxation

   a. can help break spiraling anxiety.
   b. involves counting each finger.
   c. involves counting each toe.
   d. involves counting each finger and each toe.

4. Counting backward is used instead of counting forward because

   a. some people associate counting forward with counting in school and being asked what comes next.
   b. some people associate numbers that get smaller with tension that decreases.
   c. some people like to imagine becoming younger until they are as relaxed as a sleeping baby.
   d. All of the above.

5. In the example about Mr. Crane, he used Countdown Relaxation to

   a. imagine his work getting done.
   b. imagine a tropical island.
   c. imagine his "troubled world shrinking" and reduce his worry about work.
   d. All of the above.

6. Mr. Crane practiced Countdown Relaxation and

   a. lost his job because he did not seem worried enough about his work.
   b. decreased his productivity at work.
   c. was as productive as ever, but felt less uptight.
   d. was severely reprimanded at work for taking frequent 30-minute breaks.

7. Countdown Relaxation uses the image(s) of a

   a. stairway.
   b. elevator.
   c. escalator.
   d. All of the above.

8. When counting down to relaxation, you silently say each number

   a. as you breathe in.
   b. as you breathe out.
   c. as you breathe in and again as you breathe out.
   d. three times for each breath.

9. When counting up from one to three to return to an alert state, you silently say each number

   a. as you breathe in.
   b. as you breathe out.
   c. as you breathe in and again as you breathe out.
   d. three times for each breath.

10. When you begin Countdown Relaxation, you may need to

   a. practice it, after you have already relaxed, using Progressive, Scanning, or Deep Muscle Relaxation.
   b. practice during brief daily breaks to see if you become more and more relaxed in less and less time.
   c. use cues and reminders for Countdown Relaxation.
   d. All of the above.

ANSWERS TO REVIEW QUESTIONS

1.	c	6.	c
2.	b	7.	d
3.	a	8.	b
4.	d	9.	a
5.	c	10.	d

Chapter 9

Autogenic Phrases And Images:
How To Relax From The Inside

"Autogenic" means self-regulation or self-generation. This technique was developed by Johannes Schultz, M.D. and Wolfgang Luthe, M.D. It uses and builds on the passive, receptive attitude you learned in Deep Muscle Relaxation training. The power of the trained mind to influence the body in a healthy fashion is the cornerstone of this technique.

Autogenic Training is thought to help balance the body's self-regulating systems of the "homeostatic" mechanism. While a thermostat regulates temperature inside a room, the homeostatic mechanism regulates the things that go on inside of our bodies.

Our internal, self-regulating systems automatically help to control heart rate, blood circulation, breathing and many other functions needed for us to survive. If we lacked such an automatically regulated system, we would have to spend our time consciously commanding our heart muscles to pump and our diaphrams to pull air into our lungs.

These functions are also a part of the "fight or flight" system we described earlier. If you will recall, the sympathetic nervous system can automatically increase arousal to help us prepare for confronting or retreating from a potential danger. This is adaptive when the threat requires such action; but, for modern man, most threats are psychological or philosophical. For these threats, it is not adaptive to increase heart rate and breathing, nor to constrict peripheral blood vessels to help redirect blood flow to vital organs.

Reprogramming Inner Calm

Autogenic Training helps you control stress by training the autonomic nervous system to be more relaxed when you are not faced with a real need to fight or run. This follows in a natural progression after you have learned to control tension in

your major muscle groups.   It would be difficult to learn
Autogenic Training before learning to produce a general state of
relaxation in your muscles. This is because automatic nervous
system responses are difficult to recognize, except when you are
really "uptight." At these times, you may be aware, not only of
muscle tension, but also of your pounding heart, sweating, rapid
breathing, and so on. Therefore, you should be able to produce
good results with Progressive and Deep Muscle Relaxation before
attempting Autogenic Training.

Autogenic Relaxation is accomplished by "passively" paying
attention to verbal cues for relaxation. It can be thought of
as helping to reprogram the subconscious mind to create a state
of internal calm. In contrast to Progressive and Deep Muscle
Relaxation, Autogenic Training involves no direct muscle relaxation exercises. Instead, the body is conditioned to respond to
particular verbal cues which generally reduce physical arousal
and tension. Autogenic Training will emphasize smooth and
rhythmic breathing, regular and calm heart beating, and pleasant
warmth with relaxing heaviness throughout the extremities of the
body.

Passive Concentration And The Receptive Mode

You will need to assume a passive, receptive attitude even
more than you did in Deep Muscle Relaxation Training. In Autogenic Training this is called "passive concentration." In some
ways being passive and concentrating seem to be contradictory;
and this is one of the reasons that Drs. Schultz and Luthe's
work was a breakthrough in modern science. An example may help
explain the technique of "passive concentration" better than
reading a definition.

Recall an incident where your eyes began to fill with tears
or you began to cry. You may remember a relationship breaking
up or a loved one dying and the sadness you experienced thinking
of the person you were losing. You may also associate crying
with dirt or onion juice in your eyes. For a few seconds, close
your eyes and imagine a personal memory or any of the above
examples.   If you take the time to recall vividly the
experience, you will notice when you open your eyes that they
are wetter than before you closed them.

Now, if you do the same thing but actively tell yourself
that you must cry, and try to force yourself to cry, you will
probably find yourself unsuccessful. Crying is an automatic
function.   Without practice, most of us cannot do it on
command.   However, we all probably know someone that has

practiced this automatic response and seems to be able to produce "crocodile tears" at will. This may be the result of focusing on sad events and thoughts, and conditioning the tear ducts to flood the eyes.

Autogenic Training involves conditioning positive and relaxing responses. The originators of the process, Drs. Schultz and Luthe, maintain that by concentrating passively, a person can lapse into an unstructured free-floating state of mind which is relaxing in itself. The key is to focus on a relaxing phrase or image that will help to "mediate" or passively cue the automatic response you desire.

Focusing on the words "My breathing is smooth and rhythmic" or an image of gentle waves rolling in and rolling out can trigger a relaxed respiration rate. However, while the process of focusing must be deliberate,it does not involve the usual rules for human achievement. If you were to focus on "I want my breathing to be smooth and rhythmic." or "I am going to make my breathing smooth and rhythmic, or else!", you would probably not be successful.

Learning to accomplish something worthwhile by learning not to work "actively" at it, is unusual to most people. Passive concentration skills and Autogenic Training require careful practice; but if you have been successful learning Progressive and Deep Muscle Relaxation, then this technique will seem much easier.

Biofeedback - The Machines Say You Can

At first, many of the people we train do not believe that they can control "automatic" functions. Biofeedback machines show them that they can produce changes. The instruments also show them the amount of change they have produced.

The word biofeedback can be divided into three parts to make it more understandable. "Bio" refers to living organisms or tissues. "Feed" means to give or, in this case, display. "Back" refers to the direction in which this information is provided. Thus, biofeedback is simply a term for the modern technology of measuring a person's internal (bio) response and giving the person immediate knowledge (feedback) about that response.

An early form of biofeedback was taking your own pulse for a minute. Now, machines can tell you second by second exactly how many beats per minute occur and whether the beats are increasing or decreasing.

It is known that one of the common automatic responses which accompanies relaxation is vasodilation or widening of the arteries in the arms, hands, legs and feet. There is a pleasant warm and heavy sensation that occurs as the blood flow increases into these areas. With a biofeedback machine, the temperature of the hands or feet can be measured while this internal relaxation takes place.

Blood Circulation, Temperature And Biofeedback

Autogenic exercises help train the arteries and circulation system to remain in a more "relaxed" state. A way of thinking about this form of internal tension is to consider that all the blood vessels are made out of muscle -- a special form of muscle. Thus, blood vessels can tighten up (constrict) or relax and widen (dilate). If the balance between this action is "disregulated" then a person may experience physical stress responses.

Let's consider some of the disorders which can be influenced by the disregulation of this balance. For example, if the peripheral vascular system is constricted, then there is less space for the blood to flow and a person's blood pressure may increase. Constantly cold feet or hands may also reflect constriction and poor circulation. In addition, migraine headaches are thought to be caused by overdilation of the arteries of the brain, after a period of constriction.

The use of Autogenic Training and temperature biofeedback has been helpful in regulating blood flow. This has even been successful when vasoconstriction was complicated by blocked arteries. One of the authors worked for six months teaching a patient with severe arterial blockage how to increase blood flow to his legs and arms. The patient, whom we will call Allan J., was afflicted with what is known as Buerger's Disease. Allan's arteries were so extensively blocked and his circulation so poor that he previously had both legs amputated below the knees. Lack of circulation to the fingers contributed to constant pain and frequent infections.

At the time, biofeedback was a relatively new treatment and there were still many skeptics. It may have been the first attempt to use biofeedback with Buerger's Disease. Allan was willing to try anything.

When Allan began Autogenic Training and biofeedfack the temperature at the tips of his finders was below 70°F -- less than the surrounding room temperature. As the training progressed, he would come into the session with an average finger temperature of 85°F, and could increase it as high as 94°F while receiving the temperature feedback.

Although the Autogenic Training and biofeedback could not remove the blockage from his arteries, it did appear to help increase the blood flow, probably by dilating the smaller accessory arteries that were not blocked. As you can imagine, when biofeedback helped to keep Allan from further surgeries, he almost became the hospital's biofeedback salesman!

Exactly how Autogenic Training works is not completely known. The technique works for many perople and we now know that the heavy and warm feeling of relaxation in the arms, hands, legs and feet is a real phenomenon. Not only have temperature changes been reported, but, in Dr. Luthe's early research, he showed that the increase in blood to an area also contributes to an increase in weight.

The Little Girl In A Swing Who Calmed An Irregular Heart

Tachycardia is a condition with symptoms of rapid and irregular heart beats. Mary C. had experienced tachycardia for three years, before she was seen by one of the authors. Mary was 21 years old and had worked as a secretary for the same company since graduating from high school. She was a good worker, conscientious and very interested in constantly bettering her skills. She aspired to become an executive secretary, took college courses at night, and always received excellent ratings from her supervisors.

Mary presented with a complaint that when her boss said he needed a letter or report typed immediately, her heart rate would increase, feel as if it were "pounding" and become irregular. She usually was able to finish the work, but over a period of years, she became more and more distressed. The tachycardia became more frequent as Mary accepted more responsibility.

Mary began Autogenic Training after learning to use Progressive and Deep Muscle Relaxation. When she practiced Autogenic training, she was able to produce a calm and regular heart rate. With encouragement, Mary slowly began practicing in front of a typewriter at home.

Mary discovered that she could increase her heart rate control by imagining a small girl, swinging rhythmically under a tree, while the wind gently blew through her blond hair. She began practicing the Autogenic Training and using this imagery.

Eventually, Mary was able to imagine the little girl swinging while typing at work. This helped her to remain calm. Her tachycardia became less and less of a problem as she was able to regulate her heart beat by imagining the girl swinging to and fro.

When describing her success at work, she also reported that, by quickly getting this image and holding it in the back of her mind while she typed, she seemed to have a smoother rhythm to her typing. She felt this contributed to greater speed and fewer errors.

Self-Regulation And Symbolic Imagery

The use of imagery to help regulate various bodily responses is not new. A "symbol" is something that stands for or suggests something else. The little girl swinging under the tree stood for, or represented to Mary, the more rhythmic beating of her heart. This sort of symbolic imagery has been used in hypnosis since the time it was discovered, and, more recently, it has been incorporated into both relaxation and biofeedback.

Why does symbolic imagery seem to work? Why does it seem very important in trying to regulate the automatic bodily systems? One theory suggests that different parts of our brain think in different ways. The left side of the brain is very logical and verbal. "Talking" ourself through a problem or telling ourself to lift up a glass of water and drink from it may originate there. The right side of the brain seems to think more in pictures, and is less logical.

This may explain why people have counted sheep to go to sleep all through the ages. The technique probably survives because verbal counting tends to bore the left side of the brain to sleep, while the picture of the sheep jumping over the fence tends to bore the right side of the brain to sleep. With both sides of the brain occupied, we have a hard time worrying about something that might arouse us and keep us from falling to sleep.

According to another theory, the right side of the brain may control the autonomic nervous system and our automatic functions. If this theory is correct, then it would help us understand why we must both "passively" concentrate and use images to help regulate blood flow or heart rate.   If we actively and logically concentrated, we would engage our left brain. This part of the brain may not be where the control for circulation originates.   In addition, the left brain may critically evaluate a suggestion for your heart beat to become regular and decide, "I don't have control over my heart beat. It just happens automatically."

The Autogenic Training exercises will introduce you to symbolic imagery and help you to regulate your respiration and circulation.   You may discover, after practicing, that other symbols work for you.   Experiment and discover the symbols you use to imagine changes occurring in your body.

One of the authors worked with over 60 hypertensive individuals and found their symbolic imagery to be highly creative.   Some of these people would imagine the complete vascular system and see the vessels relaxing as blood flowed through.   One man saw muscles "tight as rocks" pushing against the vessels, and watched the rocks slowly dissolve.   A person who worked in gas transmission saw a pipeline system and was able to open up valves and decrease pressure or redirect flow. Others saw the heart connected to a system of flexible hoses. Another person imagined a clear plastic model of the human body and placed a thermometer at the tips of the fingers.   She visualized the blood flow increasing to the hands and also watched the temperature rising.

What are your symbols for how your body works? As you practice Autogenic Training, be creative with the images you use to help your breathing become smooth and rhythmic, your heart beat calm and regular, and your blood flow to your extremities heavy and warm.

Ways To Use Your New Skills

Many people find they are able to practice Autogenic phrases or visualize relaxing scenes briefly throughout their day to promote a calming response. Mary imagined the little girl swinging as she began to type. Several people we know relax their breathing as they go into stressful situations by thinking of the ocean waves rolling in and out. Others allow the image of a slowly ticking metronome to pace their breathing or heart rate.

We recommend that people with high blood pressure check their blood pressure at work. You may bring your own blood pressure cuff and stethoscope, or stop by the medical clinic at lunch. This helps you get exact feedback about your blood pressure, and you may decide you need to spend less time eating during your lunch break and use the time to practice some Autogenic exercises.

Often individuals suffering from migraine headaches prefer Autogenic Training over other relaxation techniques. Focusing on the continued relaxing warmth of the hands and feet seems to help prevent the onset of the headaches. Currently, research is being done to help us better understand how this works.

Certain individuals may experience cold hands or feet and can warm them by imagining the sun shining brightly on them as they work. Discover what responses you need to work with and, after practicing the Autogenic exercises, begin incorporating your new skills into your daily activities.

Scheduling And Recording Autogenic Practice

Autogenic Training should be practiced during the same times you previously practiced muscle relaxation exercises. Again, we recommend you use the same times twice daily. During the work week, use the morning coffee break or lunch hour and then practice in the afternoon after arriving home.

Occasionally, we recommend that a person practice a muscle relaxation exercise during one practice session and Autogenic Training during the other. This is done when a person is relatively confident of his ability to relax his muscles, but still has some difficulty maintaining his muscle relaxation levels throughout the day. Also, some individuals like to use muscle relaxation exercises or Autogenic exercises to help them sleep at night. This should be done in addition to the other scheduled exercise periods.

Before and after your first Autogenic Training session, complete the rating scale in this chapter. This is titled "Subjective Ratings of Autogenic Relaxation." Write in the numbers that describe your feelings of relaxation and then add them up to find your levels of relaxation before and after practice. Record these practice ratings on the Home Practice Chart on the last four pages of this book. Use the "Subjective Ratings of Autogenic Relaxation" scale as a guide to continue rating your Autogenic practice levels. Remember to record after every practice session, the technique used, how long you practiced, and how relaxed you became.

Preparing For Autogenic Training

Once again, as with muscle relaxation, plan on practicing Autogenic Training in a place that is private, quiet, comfortable and free from distractions. Be sure family, friends and co-workers will not interrupt you.

As before, the first thing to do is to get comfortable. You may wish to practice in the same place that you have been practicing your muscle relaxation exercises. We already mentioned that it is beneficial to become "conditioned" to relaxing in a special place. You may already be in a habit of immediately relaxing as soon as you sit in your favorite chair.

Be sure that all of your body is supported so that further relaxation will not cause your arms or legs to fall from the force of gravity. This is sometimes a problem with Autogenic Training. When the arms begin to feel heavy and warm, they may slip off the side of the chair if not properly positioned.

Your hands should be open, your legs uncrossed, and your clothes should be loose. Be sure your neck is supported in a high-backed chair or on pillows. If you cannot find something to support your head, you can let your head hang forward or balance it comfortably in an upright position.

Common Problems And Their Solutions

When you first start Autogenic Training, it is best to allow yourself enough time to experience the changes in respiration, heart rate and circulation. Often a person can calm their breathing and heart rate quickly; but, it takes longer to experience heavy and warm relaxation in the arms, hands, legs and feet. If you are going to have a brief period of time to practice, then concentrate only on your breathing and heart rate.

For example, let us say that you are now able to relax your whole body in five minutes during your morning coffee break. When you first start Autogenic Training, you will probably find it difficult to produce heavy and warm feelings in such a short time. It will be better if you schedule adequate time when you come home, than to discourage yourself by not producing the feelings at work. However, you may decide to calm just your breathing or heart rate during a brief period at work. After you are able to produce relaxing heaviness and warmth at home, then you may also want to begin briefer practice of this at work.

Some people find it hard to assume a truly passive attitude. Even when they are repeating the Autogenic phrases, other thoughts come to mind. Combining the Autogenic phrases with images will usually help. If thoughts still intrude, do not dwell on them or criticize yourself for having them--just gently bring your mind back to the phrases and images.

OUTLINE FOR AUTOGENIC PHRASES AND IMAGES

I.   Deep Breathing Exercises

     A. Imagine ocean waves rolling in...and out.
     B. Silently saying "Breathing, smooth and rhythmic."

II. Heartbeat regulation exercises

     A. Imagine slow ocean waves.
     B. Silently saying, "My heartbeat is calm and regular."

III. Blood Flow

     A. Right arm and hand

         1. Silently saying, "My right arm and hand are heavy
             and warm."
         2. Imagine the warm sun.

     B. Left arm and hand

         1. Silently saying "My left arm and hand are heavy
             and warm."
         2. Imagine the warm sun.

     C. Legs and feet

         1. Silently saying "My legs and feet are heavy and
             warm."
         2. Imagine the warmth flowing down from the arms and
             hands.

IV. Summing Up Phrase--"I am calm."

V.   Return To Activity--count forward from one to three.

WORD-BY-WORD AUTOGENIC PHRASES AND IMAGES

Preparation

Now, get into a comfortable position. While you are finding a good position, you will also want to loosen any tight clothing. Just become as comfortable as possible.

Let your mouth drop open for a moment and move your jaw gently from side to side. Now close your mouth slowly, keeping your teeth slightly apart. Take a deep breath.... Breathe in so that the air flows into your lungs and feels as though it's filling up your stomach area. Now, breath out slowly.... Feel yourself floating down.

Breathing -
Smooth And Rhythmic

Focus your attention completely and fully on your breathing. Imagine your breathing is as automatic as the ocean waves, rolling in...and out...in...and out.... Silently say to yourself "Breathing, Smooth and Rhythmic...." "Breathing, Smooth and Rhythmic...." "My breathing is effortless and calm...." "Breathing, Smooth and Rhythmic...." "My breathing is effortless and calm...." "Breathing, Smooth and Rhythmic...."

As you breath, imagine relaxation flowing over your body, one wave after another. Feel the waves of relaxation moving through your chest and shoulders. Down into your arms. Through your back muscles. Down into your hips and legs.

With each wave of relaxation, try to feel the heaviness and warmth in your arms and your legs. Now I want you to think, still in a passive way, about wave after wave of relaxation. Concentrate on the relaxation moving upward from your lungs in waves, up and across your face and scalp.

Tranquility And
Heart Rate Calming

Your mind is becoming more passive and tranquil, and you have a placid, relaxed awareness of the feelings of relaxation throughout your body. All of the tensions and worries will slip away from you, as you feel waves of relaxation flooding over you. There is a growing feeling of warmth and heaviness in your arms and legs, and a passive awareness of your state of relaxation.

Remember how you imagined the waves rolling in and out to help you breathe effortlessly. Try to feel that again as you now imagine your heart beating. Silently say to yourself, "My heartbeat is calm and regular...." "My heartbeat is calm and regular...." "My heartbeat is calm and regular...." "I feel very quite and my heartbeat is calm and regular...." "My whole body is deeply relaxed and my heartbeat is calm and regular...." "My heartbeat is calm and regular."

Right Arm And Hand-
Heavy And Warm

These feelings of relaxation, passivity and peace will now become more and more profound as you concentrate on just your right hand and arm. Focus all your attention on your right hand and your right arm. In fact, just to make sure you have made mental contact with your right arm and hand, lightly touch these areas with your left hand.

While you gently stroke your right hand and arm, say to yourself, "My right arm and hand are heavy and warm; warmth is flowing into my arm and down into my hand...." "My right arm and hand are heavy and warm; warmth is flowing into my arm and down into my hand...." Let your left arm return to a resting position, if you have not already done so.

Continue to silently repeat to yourself, "My arm and hand are heavy and warm...." "Warmth is flowing into my right arm, down into my right hand, and it feels pleasantly warm." Remember you do not want to try to force any of these things to happen, just allow them to happen. They will occur naturally and gently as you passively continue to focus on your right arm and hand and the feelings of heaviness and warmth. "My right arm is heavy and warm...." "Warmth is flowing into my right arm and down into my right hand."

At this time, carefully study the feelings in your arm and hand and attend to the feelings of heaviness and warmth. You may use any kind of thoughts you care to in order to imagine your right arm and hand becoming warm. You can imagine that they are in warm water, or that the warm sun is beating down on them. Continue repeating to yourself: "My right arm and hand are heavy and warm; warmth is flowing into my right arm, and it feels pleasantly warm."

Left Arm And Hand -
Heavy And Warm

Now I would like you to turn your
attention to your left hand, wrist and
arm. Just concentrate on this area of
your body and focus all your attention
there. If you need to, gently touch it as
you silently repeat: "My left arm is
heavy and warm; warmth is flowing into my
arm and down into my hand." "My left arm
and hand are heavy and warm." "Warmth is
flowing down my arm and into my hand."
"My left arm and hand feel pleasantly
warm."

The feelings of warmth may be deepened by
imagining the sun shining on your left
hand and arm. Continue saying these words
while focusing on your left arm and hand:
"My left arm and hand are heavy and warm."
"Warmth is flowing down my left arm and
into my wrist and hand." "Warmth is
flowing down my left arm and into my wrist
and hand."

Become fully aware of the feelings in your
left arm and hand, and be sure to keep out
all other thoughts as you continue to
focus on heaviness and warmth in your left
arm and hand. If other thoughts come into
your mind, you will find it possible to
let them go as quickly as they came. You
are passively concentrating on heaviness
and warmth. Simply let these things
happen; allow these feelings of heaviness
and warmth to just happen to you.
Continue to silently repeat to yourself:
"My left arm and hand are heavy and warm;
warmth is flowing into my left arm and
down into my left hand."

Can you feel the relaxation? Does your
arm feel as if you would need help to lift
it? Maybe the warmth reminds you of the
summer sun. However you describe it is
fine, as long as it is pleasant for you.
Just continue to feel the heaviness and
warmth, and feel the relaxation.

<u>Both Arms And Hands</u>
<u>Heavy And Warm</u>
- Now I want you to focus on both of your
arms and hands at the same time, as you
say to yourself: "My arms and hands are
heavy and warm, warmth is flowing into my
arms and down into my hands." "Both my
right and my left arm are heavy and warm."
"My arms and hands are heavy and warm."
"Warmth is flowing into my arms, and
gently down into my wrists, hands and
fingertips; and, they feel very pleasant."

Very good. You are relaxing all over as
your arms become very heavy and warm. As
the warmth flows into your hands, you will
feel your whole body relaxing. You are
letting everything go, all cares and
worries are far, far away. This is your
time to think only of pleasant relaxation
and the feelings it brings. It is better
for you if you think of nothing
but the way your body feels. Let all
other thoughts leave your mind.

Once again, focusing on both of your arms,
think to yourself: "My arms are heavy and
warm." "Warmth is flowing into my hands."
Continue to passively concentrate on your
arms being heavy and warm. Be sure to
gently push out any other thoughts. In
our modern society, the mind is often not
used to being quiet and relaxed; and it
tends to wander. If you find this
happening, do not become upset or
disappointed, just bring your mind back to
the thought: "My arms are heavy and warm;
warmth is flowing into my hands."

Take some time, now while you keep your
arms very heavy and warm, and check around
your body to see if there is any tension
in any muscle. Check all around. Is your
jaw loose and slack, and are your eyelids
gently closed? Be sure the muscles in
your face are relaxed.

You are becoming very relaxed, and you feel loose and limp -- just like an old rag doll. And you really are that relaxed, as you continue to practice Autogenic Relaxation.

Legs And Feet-
Heavy And Warm

Now I want you to focus on your legs. If
you need to, make contact with your legs
by touching them and becoming more aware
of them. Notice where they are touching
the surface where they are resting.
Notice that pleasant heaviness and warmth
is spreading down from your arms to your
legs. Let it happen.

Passively allow the warmth to spread as
you silently say to yourself: "My legs
are becoming heavy and warm, warmth is
flowing into my feet...." "My legs are
warm and heavy...." "My feet are warm and
heavy...."

"My legs are heavy and warm, and warmth is
pleasantly flowing into my legs and down
into my feet -- all the way to the very
tip of my toes...." "My legs and feet are
heavy and warm...." "Heavy and warm, very
pleasantly warm...."

Very good. Now I want you to focus on all
your limbs, arms and legs together.
Become very aware of your arms and your
legs. Repeat silently to yourself: "My
arms and legs are heavy and warm, warm and
heavy...." "My feet and hands are heavy
and warm, warm and heavy...."

"Warm and pleasant feelings are sinking
into every part of my arms, hands, legs
and feet...." "My arms and legs are very
limp...." "The muscles in my arms and
legs are letting go and I am becoming more
and more relaxed."

All The Limbs --
Heavy and Warm

Take a deep breath.... Breathe in so that
the air flows into your lungs and feels as
though it is flowing way down into your
stomach area. Breath very deeply down
into your stomach area and, as you breathe
out, say to yourself, "I am calm."

"I Am Calm"

This is a very important group of words that I want you to use only when you are relaxed, very deeply relaxed. These will be summing up words which you will say when you feel deeply relaxed. "I am calm...." Take a deep breath and say, "I am calm...."

Eventually you will be able to relax yourself by simply thinking the words, "I am calm." When the day is going badly or you are caught in a traffic jam, you will be able to control your stress by saying, "I am calm." You will remember the feelings of deep relaxation that you are feeling now.

Whenever things make you nervous, whether it is meeting new people, asking your boss for a raise, or talking to large groups, you will find you can relax yourself by simply thinking the words, "I am calm." But, at first, be sure to say it only when you are deeply relaxed. After practicing, you can begin to use it in everyday life.

Return To Activity   *Now as we complete this Autogenic Relaxation practice, take a deep breath, and slowly let it out. Now I want you to see yourself lying in the room where you started these exercises. Just imagine yourself back where you were when you started the exercises; safe, secure, and pleasantly relaxed. You will enjoy a good feeling everytime you do these exercises; and you will feel more and more relaxed.*

Now count from one to three. Silently say each number as you take a deep breath. When you reach three, open your eyes. You will be relaxed and alert. When you open your eyes, you will find yourself back in the place where you started your relaxation. However, the environment will seem slower and calmer; and you will be more relaxed and peaceful.

One, relaxed, but more alert.... Two, mentally wide awake.... Three, eyes open, alert and refreshed.

(If you plan to return immediately to a physical activity; then follow these suggestions. Yawn and stretch as you do in the morning. Also, if you are going to do some manual activities, shake your hands briskly.)

SUBJECTIVE RATINGS
OF AUTOGENIC RELAXATION

Directions: Before and after your practice sessions, rate your subjective experiences from 0 to 10 for each rating line. Carefully record these ratings in the spaces provided. Then add these ratings to get your total scores for before and after each session.

Be sure to transfer your total score for before and after the sessions from the bottom of each column to the Home Practice Chart.

THOUGHTS

Active thoughts | | | | | | | | Passive thoughts
0   1   2   3   4   5   6   7   8   9   10

FOREHEAD TEMPERATURE

Hot forehead | | | | | | | | Cool forehead
0   1   2   3   4   5   6   7   8   9   10

RESPIRATION RATE

Fast breathing | | | | | | | | Slow breathing
0   1   2   3   4   5   6   7   8   9   10

RESPIRATION DEPTH

Choppy breathing | | | | | | | | Smooth breathing
0   1   2   3   4   5   6   7   8   9   10

HEART RATE

Fast heartbeat | | | | | | | | Slow heartbeat
0   1   2   3   4   5   6   7   8   9   10

STOMACH

Stormy stomach | | | | | | | | Calm stomach
0   1   2   3   4   5   6   7   8   9   10

ARMS

Tense arms | | | | | | | | Heavy arms
0   1   2   3   4   5   6   7   8   9   10

HANDS

Cold hands | | | | | | | | Warm hands
0   1   2   3   4   5   6   7   8   9   10

LEGS

Tense legs | | | | | | | | Heavy legs
0   1   2   3   4   5   6   7   8   9   10

FEET

Cold feet | | | | | | | | Warm feet
0   1   2   3   4   5   6   7   8   9   10

DATES OF PRACTICE

BEFORE	AFTER	BEFORE	AFTER	BEFORE	AFTER

TOTALS

DATES OF PRACTICE	BEFORE	AFTER	BEFORE	AFTER	BEFORE	AFTER	BEFORE	AFTER	BEFORE	AFTER	BEFORE	AFTER	BEFORE	AFTER	BEFORE	AFTER	BEFORE	AFTER
THOUGHTS																		
FOREHEAD																		
RESPIRATION RATE																		
RESPIRATION DEPTH																		
HEART RATE																		
STOMACH																		
ARMS																		
HANDS																		
LEGS																		
FEET																		
TOTALS																		

REVIEW QUESTIONS

Directions: Circle the letter in front of the best response to each question. The correct answers are provided on the page following the last question.

1. The autonomic nervous system in your body is the nearly automatic system which regulates

    a. breathing.
    b. heart rate.
    c. blood circulation.
    d. All the above.

2. Autogenic refers to

    a. self-generation or regulation.
    b. relaxing in a car.
    c. self-motivation.
    d. relaxing automatically.

3. Autogenic Training helps you control stress by teaching the autonomic nervous system to _____ internal organs such as your heart and stomach.

    a. tense
    b. relax
    c. tense and relax
    d. stop

4. Autogenic Training involves a(n) _____ attitude.

    a. excited
    b. passive
    c. good
    d. bad

5. A passive attitude means that the person _____things happen rather than _____ things happen.

    a. watches; lets
    b. makes; hopes
    c. makes; lets
    d. lets; makes

6.   Autogenic Training involves

     a.   tensing muscles.
     b.   using muscles.
     c.   massaging muscles.
     d.   None of the above.

7.   All of the following phrases except one is used in
     Autogenic Training.

     a.   "My arms are warm and heavy."
     b.   "Breathing, smooth and rhythmic."
     c.   "Hold one, two, three, four, five and release."
     d.   "My heartbeat is calm and regular."

8.   Another Autogenic phrase is

     a.   "I am stronger and better every day."
     b.   "My legs are warm and heavy."
     c.   "Release and hold one, two, three, four, five."
     D.   None of the above.

9.   When other thoughts come to mind during Autogenic
     Training

     a.   gently bring your mind back to the Autogenic phrases.
     b.   dwell on the thoughts until they leave.
     c.   struggle and force them to go away by saying "go."
     d.   All the above.

10. Autogenic Training can

     a.   not be used in everyday life.
     b.   be used in everyday life.
     c.   be learned in one session.
     d.   be practiced only in one place.

ANSWERS TO REVIEW QUESTIONS

1.	d	6.	d
2.	a	7.	c
3.	b	8.	b
4.	b	9.	a
5.	d	10.	b

SUGGESTED RECORDINGS

Relaxation And Stress Management Program -- Autogenic Training by E. Charlesworth. Houston: Stress Management Research, 1981.

Relaxation Training Program -- Limb Heaviness, Arms And Legs Heavy And Warm by T. Budzynski. New York: B.M.A., 1974.

Quieting Response Training -- Relaxing Smooth Muscles by C. Stroebel. New York: B.M.A., 1978.

Chapter 10

Imagery Training:
The Windows Of Your Mind

"It's All Inside Your Head, She Said To Me"

Our thoughts, images and other mental activities can be harmful when they are upsetting to us. What does "up-setting" mean? You could say that you are pushing "up" the "setting" of your arousal. This adds to our stress.

Most of us have struggled with unwanted thoughts, only to find ourselves upset. Maybe something at work is extremely pressing, or perhaps a personal problem is troubling us. Thoughts about the problems keep spinning in our minds, almost as if they were being rolled around in a clothes dryer. One idea leads to another, and soon we find ourselves totally worked up and in a frazzle. We just keep rehashing the problem without really finding a solution. We may find that we are simply unable to pay attention to anything else during the day, or we become so aroused that we cannot sleep at night.

"I Think, Therefore I Am"

When introducing Progressive Relaxation, Deep Muscle Relaxation and Autogenic Relaxation, we made the point that these relaxation techniques work because it is almost impossible to be physically relaxed and tense at the same time. You simply cannot do both simultaneously -- at least not very well! Relaxing your mind is based on the same principle. You cannot be thinking relaxed, peaceful and calming thoughts while your mind is racing wildly up and down the stairways of your life.

"Picture Yourself On A Boat On A River"

You have read how to relax muscles that are under your voluntary control and how to calm systems of your body that are usually regulated automatically, such as heart rate and blood flow. You are now about to learn how to produce relaxing images and thoughts. These images and thoughts can be used to block out intruding and upsetting ideas. You can learn how to do this with Imagery Training. The goals of Imagery Training are to reduce and control mental anxiety.

Anxiety usually involves both physical and mental parts; but, at times, one of these may be stronger than the other. For example, one may be physically tired and yet be unable to sleep because of upsetting thoughts. This is mental anxiety.

By using pleasant visual images, we can control upsetting thoughts and enjoy a deep state of physical relaxation. Learning to control your thoughts takes knowing what you need to think about, practicing those thoughts, and then using them when you want to relax.

Once you have developed your ability to create pleasant mental images, you will be able to begin to visualize yourself being successful and meeting the goals to which you aspire. There are additional ways of learning to control and enjoy what you think and feel. Some of the additional ways will be presented in later chapters.

Imagery, Music And Your Mind

Mental imagery is a little like a daydream. You may want to start by trying to visualize, in your mind's eye, a pleasant scene you have seen many times. Try to re-experience the scene in every way you can.

The technique should use both sight and sound. We could use the term audio-visual imagery to describe the procedure.

Many people listen to music to calm themselves. It is hard to be calm to whistle a tune and think anxious thoughts at the same time.

The music on visual imagery tapes helps you to produce a state of calm. When you practice visual imagery without using a prerecorded imagery tape, we invite you to add your favorite music. You may also want to use pleasant environmental sounds, such as gentle ocean waves rolling in...and out. Appendix I lists different musical and environmental selections that you may find helpful.

Imagery And The Five Senses

As you learn imagery, you will also want to add your other senses: taste, touch and smell. Maybe mental imagery really means sensory imagery.

When you practice the imagery exercises, try to include all five of your senses. Make believe you can "see the lush green of a tropical rain forest" with your eyes, "hear the sound of the birds at sunrise" with your ears, "smell the scent of the many multicolored flowers" with your nose, "taste the salt from the sea breeze" with your tongue, and "feel the soft grass" beneath your feet.

Common Problems With Imagery Training: Intruding Thoughts

Be patient with yourself as you begin to learn mental relaxation. Complete concentration, even on pleasant images, requires a great deal of practice. Do not get upset if unwanted thoughts come to your mind. This happens even to the most practiced masters of other mental techniques like yoga and meditation.

Being forewarned is being forearmed. Knowing that unwanted thoughts may come to your mind, will help you treat these thoughts calmly. Tell yourself that the thoughts will soon pass if you do not pay attention to them and if you return to your pleasant image. Do not fight them. Let them gently pass. This is where the practice comes in. If you get upset about all these thoughts racing by, then you will be increasing your stress rather than decreasing it. Allow the thoughts to leave your mind as easily as they came into your mind. Simply refocus on the imagery once again. Every time you find yourself distracted, gently refocus on the imagery.

If you continue to have difficulty with intruding thoughts, you may want to begin using the thought stopping technique that was mentioned briefly in the Deep Muscle Relaxation chapter. Now, after saying "Stop!" quickly refocus on the imagery you were trying to visualize. This two-step technique can be used whenever you find yourself preoccupied and unable to shake a thought and return to the task at hand.

Helpful Hints To Tape And Self-Instruction Users

Make your images your own. Only you can experience and know what images are relaxing to you. Also, only you can know what images and scenes are upsetting and should not be used.

Work on having at least one personally relaxing scene that you may use for relaxation.

Practice letting your personally relaxing image come rapidly into your mind. Take a deep breath and imagine breathing in the clean air from your special image. As you breathe out, feel the relaxation spread over your body and allow yourself to be in that comfortable place for a brief moment. When you return to whatever you were doing, bring with you the feelings of relaxation from your personally relaxing scene.

Using Relaxation Tapes

If you are using recorded relaxation exercises, schedule times now and begin listening to the tape on visual imagery. Use the "Subjective Ratings of Imagery Clarity and Overall Involvement" chart in this chapter to record your ratings before and after your visual imagery practice sessions. After each practice session, remember to list your overall relaxation levels on the Home Relaxation Chart on the last four pages of this book.

Guiding Yourself

If you will be guiding yourself through the relaxation exercise, then review the directions below. You may find it helpful to read the directions several times. You may also want to ask someone to read the visual imagery instructions to you. If possible, you may want to record these instructions onto a tape, and then use the tape to practice. In either case, the instructions should be read slowly and calmly.

More Helpful Hints

Continue using Progressive, Deep Muscle and Autogenic Relaxation, whenever you can. Be sure to keep checking and decreasing your muscle tension and autonomic arousal, by using the cues and signs you have made for yourself.

OUTLINE FOR IMAGERY TRAINING

I. Basic Technique

    A. Form a clear image of a pleasant scene.

    B. Try to include images from other senses such as:

        1. Smell - "smell the scent of flowers"

        2. Touch - "feel the grass beneath your feet"

        3. Sound - "hear the birds singing in the trees"

        4. Taste - "taste the salt air on your lips"

II. Suggested Images

    A. Tropical island

        1. You are on a mountain top.

        2. Below is a tropical rain forest.

        3. The morning rains are ending.

        4. In the distance, is a white, sandy beach and palm
            trees.

    B. Cloud

        1. A cloud gently floats down.

        2. It surrounds your body and supports you completely.

        3. You are in the cloud and gently float off in a
            gentle breeze.

    C. Valley

        1. The cloud floats down to a green valley.

        2. Water laps against the shore of a small lake.

        3. You get into a small boat and begin to float
            gently.

        4. You move into a stream and drift until the boat
            washes up against a shore.

OUTLINE FOR IMAGERY TRAINING (CONTINUED)

    D. Willow tree

        1. You recline next to a willow tree.

        2. You begin to sleep and dream of other images:

            a. Sunny beach

            b. Field of wild flowers

            c. Cool forest

            d. Log cabin

            e. Clear stream

            f. Sloping hill

III. Return to activity by counting forward from one to three.

WORD-BY-WORD IMAGERY TRAINING

Preparation

Spend a little time getting as comfortable as you can. Move around if necessary, as you get into a very comfortable position.

Breathing

Close your eyes and take a deep breath.... Breathe out very slowly and easily. Take a second deep breath.... Slowly breathe out. As you do, feel yourself floating down. Concentrate on your breathing.... Allow your breathing to become smooth and rhythmic.

Island Imagery

Picture yourself on a mountain top, above a tropical rain forest on a small island. The morning rains have finished, and the wind is carrying the clouds away. The sky is clear and blue, with the warm tropical sun shining down.

You can see below you the bright green trees in the rain forest. The raindrops on the leaves are reflecting the bright morning sun. Artistically scattered within the dense greenery are bright colorful flowers: Reds, yellows, and blues.

In the far distance you can see a line of coconut palms all along the sugar-white, sandy beach. Beyond that, as far as you can see, is crystal clear, brilliantly-blue water.

Cloud Imagery

The sky is completely clear, except for one, small, fluffy cloud that drifts alone in the gentle breeze, until it is directly over you. Slowly this little cloud beings to sink down upon you.... It is a very pleasant, delightful feeling. As the small, fluffy cloud moves down across your face, you feel the cool, moist touch of it on your forehead and on your cheeks. As it moves down your body, all tension slowly slips away, and you find yourself letting go completely.

The soft cloud moves across your shoulders, your chest and upper back, and across your arms as it gently brings with it a feeling of complete relaxation. It sinks down around your waist, your lower back, your hips and your legs; and it moves down around you, bringing a deep feeling of relaxation. Then the little cloud sinks underneath you, and you are now floating on it. The cloud holds you up perfectly and safely. It is a pleasant feeling.

You are now lying back in relaxation on the soft cloud. The warm tropical sun is shining. Your body is warm from the sun, but still with the soft moist touch of coolness on your forehead and face. You are feeling very pleasant. You are held up comfortably and securely.

The little cloud begins to drift down wind; and, from your safe position on the cloud, you can see the world go by below you. There is a gentle, pleasant, rocking motion as you drift along. All your cares and concerns are left behind you. The cloud is magic and can take you any place you want to go, as it silently floats along.

Valley Imagery   In the far distance, you see a delightful,
green valley. The valley is between some
gently sloping mountains. This is a place
where you can be completely at peace and
totally happy. Gradually the fluffy
cloud takes you drifting down, through the
sky, to this beautiful place.

As you move into this valley, the cloud
gently comes to the ground and stops. You
get off the soft cloud in this beautiful
place and you are completely at peace and
alone.

Take some time to look around at the
fresh, green valley. You are next to a
lake. Listen to the birds. Feel the sun
shining on you. The scent of spring is in
the air.

<u>Lake Imagery</u>

The water is just barely lapping along the shore of the lake. You see a small boat tied there. You enter the boat and find some blankets in the bottom. Now, lying on the soft blankets, gently untie the boat. You are floating in the quiet, shallow lake. The boat is rocking gently from the motion of the water, as it drifts on and on. The boat drifts gently on and on, rocking and massaging.

As the boat carries you along, the lake lazily flows into a stream. Feel the warm sunlight once again. There is a soft breeze as you continue to drift. You feel relaxed, peaceful, and calm. The gentle rocking motion massages you with feelings of peace. All is well. Your state of relaxation will become more and more profound as the boat gently tosses, to and fro.

You drift deeper and deeper into your feelings of relaxation. As you continue to drift, become aware of the sounds of nature: the soft breeze, the lapping water, and the birds and animals on the shore. Smell the grass and flowers as the breeze brings you their pleasant scents. You are lazily drifting deeper and deeper into a profound feeling of peace and pleasantness until very slowly and gently, the small boat washes up against the shore. You remain in a very complete and total state of relaxation.

Willow Tree Imagery   Get out of the boat and take the soft
blanket with you. Walk up the slightly
sloping bank to a huge willow tree that
hangs out over the water. You feel
drowsy. The gentle, rocking motion of the
boat has made you very, very drowsy.

The old willow tree has thick, soft grass
around the base, and you find a perfect
spot to spread your blanket for a
comfortable bed. There are some roots
above the ground and you rest your head,
as you snuggle into a restful position.
The temperature is perfect, not too cool
and not too hot. Everything is restful
and peaceful.

Dream Scenes

Imagine you fall asleep under the willow tree and begin to dream. Practice a few more scenes in your imagination as you dream. This will help you know that you can go to any relaxing place you wish to, by using the power of visual imagery.

Beach Imagery

Now see yourself walking along a warm, sunny beach at the edge of crystal clear, blue water. Hear the roar of the waves. Feel the clean sand under your feet. Smell the clean salt air. (Pause)

Field of Flowers Imagery

From there, move to a picture of yourself sitting in a field of wild flowers on a spring day. The temperature is just right. The air smells fresh with wildflowers, and the sounds of birds and animals are very soothing. (Pause)

Forest Imagery

Then move to a view of yourself walking through a forest. You are under the cool shade of the tall trees, and the sunlight moves through the trees to the ground. See the ferns and small plants. Smell the clean freshness. Feel the gentle breeze blowing through the trees. Hear the birds, very high in the trees.

Stream Imagery

See yourself standing beside a clear stream, as it rushes across the rocks with a pleasant gurgle. Feel the coolness and moistness of the spray on your forehead and cheeks, as the stream splashes off the rocks, as you bend down to get a drink of the crystal clear water.

Sloping Hill Imagery

Then see yourself moving down a long, gently sloping hill in the country, with the soft feel of the wind in your hair and on your face. As you move slowly through the green grass, you are happy, smiling, very comfortable and deeply relaxed.

Using Imagery

You can use the power of your imagination to create a feeling of relaxation whenever you want. If during the rest of your day, or for that matter, if at any time, you find yourself getting upset about something, remember the feelings of relaxation you have just enjoyed. Before you get upset take a deep breath; and, as you breathe out, see yourself in whatever place you find relaxing. For a little while, let yourself enjoy all the calm feelings you have with your peaceful imagery. This will allow you to control situations, rather than being controlled by them.

Return to Activity

Now count from one to three. As you take a deep breath, silently say each number. When you reach three, open your eyes. You will be relaxed and alert. When you open your eyes, you will find yourself back in the place where you started your imagery exercises. However, the world around you will seem slower and more calm; and you will be more relaxed and peaceful.

One, relaxed, but more alert.... Two, mentally wide awake.... Three, eyes open, alert and refreshed.

SUBJECTIVE RATINGS OF IMAGERY CLARITY AND OVERALL INVOLVEMENT

Directions: Before and after your practice sessions, rate your subjective experiences from 0 to 10 for each rating line. Carefully record these ratings in the spaces provided. Then add these ratings to get your total scores for before and after each session.

Be sure to transfer your total score for before and after the sessions from the bottom of each column to the Home Practice Chart.

DATES OF PRACTICE

	BEFORE	AFTER	BEFORE	AFTER	BEFORE	AFTER

PRESENCE OF IMAGES

Dream-like images 0 1 2 3 4 5 6 7 8 9 10 Blank mind

PLEASANT IMAGES

Something delightful 0 1 2 3 4 5 6 7 8 9 10 Something unpleasant

IMAGES OF COLOR

Distinct colors 0 1 2 3 4 5 6 7 8 9 10 Black & white images

SPONTANEOUS VISUAL IMAGES

Added extra visual images 0 1 2 3 4 5 6 7 8 9 10 Tape visual images only

AUDITORY IMAGES

Heard birds & waves 0 1 2 3 4 5 6 7 8 9 10 Heard noises

SPONTANEOUS AUDITORY IMAGES

Added extra sounds 0 1 2 3 4 5 6 7 8 9 10 Heard only sounds on tape

OLFACTORY IMAGES

Clear fragrances 0 1 2 3 4 5 6 7 8 9 10 No fragrances

IMAGES OF MOTION

Felt slight motion 0 1 2 3 4 5 6 7 8 9 10 No motion

FLOW OF THOUGHTS

No interruptions of own thoughts 0 1 2 3 4 5 6 7 8 9 10 Own thoughts interrupted often

FLOW OF FANTASY

Escaped full into fantasy 0 1 2 3 4 5 6 7 8 9 10 No escape into fantasy

TOTALS

DATES OF PRACTICE	BEFORE	AFTER	BEFORE	AFTER	BEFORE	AFTER	BEFORE	AFTER	BEFORE	AFTER	BEFORE	AFTER	BEFORE	AFTER	BEFORE	AFTER	BEFORE	AFTER	BEFORE	AFTER
PRESENCE OF IMAGES																				
PLEASANT IMAGES																				
IMAGES OF COLOR																				
SPONTANEOUS VISUAL IMAGES																				
AUDITORY IMAGES																				
SPONTANEOUS AUDITORY IMAGES																				
OLFACTORY IMAGES																				
IMAGES OF MOTION																				
FLOW OF THOUGHTS																				
FLOW OF FANTASY																				
TOTALS																				

REVIEW QUESTIONS

Directions: Circle the letter in front of the best response to each question. The correct answers are provided on the page following the last question.

1. An example of mental anxiety is

    a. a student taking a test and daydreaming about going to the beach.
    b. a student taking a test and thinking "I'm a dummy," "I should have studied more last night," or "I'm certain to fail."
    c. a student whose muscles are all tensed up during a test.
    d. a student relaxing and growing calm just before and during a test.

2. An example of mental anxiety with very little physical tension is

    a. a person who is physically restless, lying in bed thinking about a hard day at the office.
    b. a person who has jogged a few miles, and goes to bed, but starts practicing what it will be like to give an important talk the next day.
    c. a person who is relaxing in a lounge chair, and is just about to fall asleep.
    d. a person watching a humorous television show.

3. The pleasant image of lying on a beach and feeling warmth from the sun is intended to promote

    a. sunburn.
    b. profound excitement.
    c. profound relaxation.
    d. stressful feelings.

4. Imagining yourself in a tropical forest after a gently falling rain, with a blue sky, vividly colored flowers and coconut palms, is an example of

    a. Imagery Training.
    b. Deep Muscle Relaxation.
    c. Progressive Relaxation.
    d. Autogenic Training.

5.   Which of the following sense(s) is(are) called upon to facilitate Imagery Training?

   a.   Sense of hearing
   b.   Sense of smell
   c.   Sense of touch
   d.   All of the above and even taste.

6.   The goal(s) of Imagery Training exercises is(are) to

   a.   enjoy a natural high.
   b.   feel calm and peaceful.
   c.   intensify your awareness.
   d.   All of the above.

7.   Imagery Training can also be used to

   a.   control disturbing thoughts.
   b.   facilitate physical relaxation.
   c.   promote growing calm.
   d.   All of the above.

8.   The Imagery Training helps a person

   a.   produce relaxing images and thoughts.
   b.   tense and relax the muscles.
   c.   relax those systems of the body that are usually regulated automatically.
   d.   a and c.

9.   Imagery Training can be used to control

   a.   physical anxiety.
   b.   mental anxiety.
   c.   fatigued muscles.
   d.   muscle cramps.

10.   When a person begins to feel tense and experience anxiety, it is helpful to

   a.   practice Progressive and Deep Relaxation.
   b.   practice Autogenic relaxing (slowing down heart rate, breathing, etc.).
   c.   practice Imagery Training.
   d.   Any or all of the above.

ANSWERS TO REVIEW QUESTIONS

1.	b	6.	d
2.	a	7.	d
3.	c	8.	d
4.	a	9.	b
5.	d	10.	d

SUGGESTED BOOKS AND RECORDINGS

BOOKS

Mind Games by R. Masters & J. Houston. New York: Dell, 1972.

The Psychology Of Consciousness by R. Ornstein. San Francisco: W. H. Freeman, 1972.

RECORDINGS

Family Relaxation And Self-Control Program by M. Lupin. Houston: Biobehavioral, 1981.

Personal Enrichment Through Imagery by A. Lazarus. New York: B.M.A., 1982.

Relaxation And Stress Management Program -- Visual Imagery Relaxation by E. Charlesworth. Houston: Stress Management Research, 1981.

Section III

Overcoming Your Special Stressors

Chapter 11

Life-Change Management

Most of the stressors we have been learning to recognize and manage are day-to-day, week-to-week stressors. These might be called the stressors of the prevailing winds -- the stressors that prevail in our daily lives.

In chapter three, we asked you to consider some stressors under a category called "change stressors." Just like weather conditions, change stressors are more intense and variable than the prevailing winds. They can range from bad weather to scorching sunlight to tropical storms.

It is said that about the only thing that we can count on in life, besides death and taxes, is change. For better or for worse, nothing ever stands still. Of all the times to be alive, modern life presents us with more change than ever before. In fact, Alvin Toffler wrote a popular book about the acceleration in the rate of change and called it Future Shock. We change everything rapidly: where we live and work, our friends and even our spouses.

Change of any sort can be scary or exciting and usually triggers our stress response. It takes energy to adapt to any change, whether the changes are for good or for bad. Thus, any change is a stressor and too much change at one time can cause stress.

Some people make a change in lifestyle to reduce stress, but it backfires. During his first interview, one of our patients described why he had moved to the Southwest. He had gone to a counselor in Florida who had listened to his problems and suggested that his anxiety might be the result of difficulties in his marriage, his job or his friendships; so he had filed for divorce, gotten fired and moved to Texas! His decisions may have shown poor judgment, but many of us make smaller decisions that inadvertently add up to just as much stress.

In this chapter, we will learn about some fascinating research that shows scientifically how too much change in too little time can be harmful to our health. You will have the chance to chart the winds of change in your life by taking a rating scale that was used in research to demonstrate a relationship between life change and illness.

The prevailing winds in our lives can be predicted and can be managed using the skills you have been learning. What about the tropical storms and heat waves you will be reading about and rating? What can we do to manage these stressors? In the last part of this chapter, you will learn ways to better manage these life changes.

From The Laboratory

Dr. Thomas Holmes and Dr. Richard Rahe, at the University of Washington School of Medicine, have made major breakthroughs in our understanding of the effects of life changes on health and disease. Convinced by their own experiences as physicians, and following up on the earlier work of Dr. Adolf Meyer at Johns Hopkins and Dr. Harold Wolff at Cornell University, Drs. Holmes and Rahe set out to measure the life changes that seem to precede illnesses.

From case histories of 5,000 patients, they gathered a long list of life events that seemed to precede major illnesses. Some of these events were positive or socially desirable, while others were negative or socially undesirable.

They then asked about 400 people to compare the amount, intensity and length of readjustment it takes for each life event on the list. The people were asked to assume that marriage had a certain numerical value, use it as a standard of comparison, and to assign a numerical value to each of the other life events on the list.

Scientists began using this scaling system to understand and predict susceptibility to illness. Thousands of individuals reported the number of times they had experienced an event. Holmes, Rahe and others multiplied the number of times an event was experienced by the readjustment valve given to the events and summed these products to find a life-change score for each person. Those who had a high life-change score were much more likely to contract an illness following the events. The illnesses ranged widely, from accidents to alcoholism, from cancer to psychiatric disorders, and from the flu to the common cold.

Look at the list of events on the Social Readjustment Rating Scale that is reprinted on the following page. It is interesting that of the 43 stressful events, only 13 are clearly negative, 6 are positive and the other 24 are so worded that one can only call them neutral. Over half of the negative events were given scores in the top 8, but it is obvious that both positive and negative changes make up the life-change scores and can be related to the onset of disease.

Charting The Winds Of Change

Follow carefully the directions on the Social Readjustment Rating Scale. Take your time and try to include any event that is similar to the one given in the scale. Sometimes a friend or a family member can help you. They may also want to take the test. When you are finished, total up your life-change units for the past year.

THE SOCIAL READJUSTMENT RATING SCALE*

Directions: Read each Life Event and indicate in the space provided the number of times you have experienced the event in the last year. Multiply the number of times you experienced the event by the points next to it and total up the products.

Life Event	Stress Value	Number of times you experienced the event last year		Your total life change scores
1) Death of spouse....................................	100	X _____	=	_____
2) Divorce	73	X _____	=	_____
3) Marital separation from mate	65	X _____	=	_____
4) Detention in jail or other institution	63	X _____	=	_____
5) Death of a close family member	63	X _____	=	_____
6) Major personal injury or illness	53	X _____	=	_____
7) Marriage	50	X _____	=	_____
8) Being fired from work..............................	47	X _____	=	_____
9) Marital reconciliation with mate......................	45	X _____	=	_____
10) Retirement from work..............................	45	X _____	=	_____
11) Major change in the health or behavior of a family member...	44	X _____	=	_____
12) Pregnancy.......................................	40	X _____	=	_____
13) Sexual difficulties.................................	39	X _____	=	_____
14) Gaining a new family member (e.g. through birth, adoption, oldster moving in, etc.)	39	X _____	=	_____
15) Major business readjustment (e.g. merger, reorganization, bankruptcy, etc.)	39	X _____	=	_____
16) Major change in financial state (e.g. a lot worse off or a lot better off than usual)	38	X _____	=	_____
17) Death of a close friend.............................	37	X _____	=	_____
18) Changing to a different line of work	36	X _____	=	_____
19) Major change in the number of arguments with spouse (e.g. either a lot more or a lot less than usual regarding childbearing, personal habits, etc.).......	35	X _____	=	_____
20) Taking on a mortgage greater than $10,000 (e.g. purchasing a home, business, etc.)................	31	X _____	=	_____
21) Foreclosure on a mortgage or loan	30	X _____	=	_____

22) Major change in responsibilities at work
(e.g. promotion, demotion, lateral transfer)............. 29 X _____ = _____

23) Son or daughter leaving home (e.g. marriage,
attending college, etc.)............................... 29 X _____ = _____

24) Inlaw troubles...................................... 29 X _____ = _____

25) Outstanding personal achievement.................... 28 X _____ = _____

26) Wife beginning or ceasing work outside the home....... 26 X _____ = _____

27) Beginning or ceasing formal schooling................ 26 X _____ = _____

28) Major change in living conditions (e.g. building
a new home, remodeling, deterioration of home
or neighborhood)................................... 25 X _____ = _____

29) Revision of personal habits (e.g. dress,
manners, associations, etc.)......................... 24 X _____ = _____

30) Troubles with the boss.............................. 23 X _____ = _____

31) Major change in working hours or conditions .... 20 X _____ = _____

32) Change in residence .... 20 X _____ = _____

33) Changing to a new school .... 20 X _____ = _____

34) Major change in usual type and/or amount of recreation..... 19 X _____ = _____

35) Major change in church activities (e.g. a lot
more or a lot less than usual) .... 19 X _____ = _____

36) Major change in social activities (e.g. clubs,
dancing, movies, visiting, etc.)...................... 18 X _____ = _____

37) Taking on a mortgage or loan less than $10,000
(e.g. purchasing a car, TV, freezer, etc.) .... 17 X _____ = _____

38) Major change in sleeping habits (e.g. a lot more
or a lot less sleep, or change in part of day when asleep)..... 16 X _____ = _____

39) Major change in number of family get-togethers
(e.g. a lot more or a lot less than usual).............. 15 X _____ = _____

40) Major change in eating habits (e.g. a lot more
or a lot less food intake, or very different
meal hours or surroundings)........................ 15 X _____ = _____

41) Vacation .... 13 X _____ = _____

42) Christmas .... 12 X _____ = _____

43) Minor violations of the law (e.g. traffic tickets,
jaywalking, disturbing the peace, etc.) .... 11 X _____ = _____

GRAND TOTAL .... _____

When To Increase Your Health Insurance Coverage

The studies that Drs. Holmes, Rahe and other scientists have conducted, provide us with a valuable way of predicting the onset of illness. If you scored below 150 points on the Social Readjustment Rating Scale, you have about one in three chances of having a serious physical or emotional illness during the next two years. If you scored between 150 and 300 points, your chances are 50-50.

If you totaled over 300 points on the Social Readjustment Rating Scale, your chances are over 80% of having a serious physical or emotional illness during the next two years. This means that if you were in a room with nine other people who had a score over 300 points, chances would be that only two of you would not have serious health problems in the next couple of years. If might be time to increase your health insurance!

How about the other illnesses that make us stay home from work, but for which we do not seek medical attention? The frequency of these illnesses has also been shown to be related to life changes. In fact, higher life-change scores have even been associated with injury among college football players. It is simple -- too much change increases our risk of illness or injury.

How To Manage Life-Change Stressors

The first step that Dr. Holmes suggests is that we all become familiar with the life events and become aware of the amount of change they require. This can be done by discussing the number of points given to each life event with a friend. You could also simply review your life and think about the changes that you have experienced.

To better familiarize yourself with the values, see if you agree or disagree with the ratings that were given by hundreds of people. Obviously, some events are easier for you to adjust to than they would be for other people. Likewise, some events are more difficult for you to cope with than they would be for other people. The points given are averages, but, in general, they apply to all of us.

Don't be fooled by the tendency to view positive changes such as marital reconciliation (45 points) or gaining a new family member (39 points) as free of stress. These also take a great deal of adaptive energy. Even "outstanding personal achievement" takes a toll of 28 points.

Dr. Holmes suggests putting the scale where you and your family can see it frequently. We often suggest to our patients that they also take a reassessment of their current life changes at the end of every month, when they pay the bills and reassess their financial changes. It is helpful to keep the rating scale with the folder where you place the bills. This will help to remind you to take a good look at your current life conditions every month.

Anticipating Life Changes

Dr. Holmes also suggests anticipating life changes, planning for them in advance and pacing yourself. Just as weather conditions change on a seasonal basis, many life changes can be predicted. Christmas and many vacations are seasonal. In addition, some events follow the seasons of life. For example, retirement from work, children leaving home (e.g., marriage, attending colleges, etc.) and beginning or ending formal schooling are all stressful changes.

Still other life events can be planned well in advance, so that we don't have to face too many life changes in too short a time. For example, we can choose the date for our marriage, we can apply for new work now or later, and we can delay buying a home or moving. In this way, if some of the things we have less control over occur, such as being fired from work, major business readjustments or major changes in financial status, we can put off making the changes over which we do have control. It is similar to taking our temperature. If we are living life at a near feverish pace, recording our change score can remind us to cool things off and put the freeze on big changes.

Seasons Of Life

Two books have recently appeared that shed light on the predictable crises that people go through in life. Daniel Levinson wrote Seasons of a Man's Life and Gail Sheehy wrote Passages. Both of these books deal with the fact that, as we go from birth to death, we are faced with different predictable crises.

An important part of your stress management training is to realize that some life crises are predictable. The evolution of our life is not determined by chance alone. We all go through a series of stable periods which alternate with transitional periods. During stable periods, we make certain crucial choices and seek to attain particular goals and values. During transitional periods, we work toward terminating previous

patterns of individual life and begin to work toward initiating
new patterns. Realizing that certain patterns of living occur
in a predictable fashion, gives us the opportunity to cope with
these life changes in a more adaptive and healthy fashion.

Early Adulthood

One of the first major transition periods that adults go
through begins at the end of adolescence. This transition may
start around the age of 17 and last until around the age of
22.   During this transition, we begin to modify existing
relationships with important individuals, groups and
institutions. We make a preliminary step into the adult world.
We begin to explore the possibilities of the adult world and to
even imagine ourselves as a participant in it.

Transition periods do not effect everyone equally. Many
individuals will remain in a student/learning capacity
throughout the chronological years of 17 to 22. By doing this,
they may postpone the transition crises of early adulthood.

Entering The Adult World

Typically, an individual will begin to enter the adult
world between the ages of 22 and 28. There is a shift from a
position of being a child in a family to the position of being a
novice adult.   Choices are made regarding occupation,
relationships, values and lifestyles.

During the transition into the adult world, a person tends
to explore the possibilitites of adult living, but also avoids
making strong commitments.   At the same time, and almost
paradoxically, a person begins to create a stable life
structure. A person tries to avoid making strong commitments
and attempts to view all their alternatives, but also tries to
settle down and become more responsible. This is a time of many
crises as a person attempts to balance out the conflict between
stability and exploration.

During this crisis period individuals may capriciously
change jobs, relationships, and places of residence. Others
find that they make a strong commitment in one sector of life,
such as work, but do not make that commitment to other sectors,
such as their personal life. Still other individuals will not
suffer a great deal from crises during this period and may
postpone exploring and questioning their values and goals.

As individuals begin to approach the years of their late twenties, they may begin to question the commitments they have previously made. They may also begin to question whether they want to keep life forever the way they have established it.

Turning Thirty

Around the age of thirty, there is a major transition period. During this transition period, a person becomes more serious, more restrictive, and more "for real." The person feels some strong need to move forward and to produce the things that they may feel are missing from their life. There is a feeling that perhaps "too soon it will be too late." During this period and this crisis, some people will build upon the past without making fundamental changes, while others will see this as more of a stressful crisis.

During this transition period around age thirty, there is a peaking of marital problems and divorce. It is often a time for changes in occupation or a time for settling down after a period of transient jobs. During the early thirties, many people enter psychotherapy as they experience the strong emotions which often accompany crises.

Settling Or Settling Down?

After going through this period of transition, a person then reaches a settling-down point that may last from the age of about 32 until the ages of 39 or 40. During this period of time, the major tasks to accomplish include establishing a place in society and "making it" in terms of vocation. There are great efforts made to build a better life and to attain certain goals.

Toward the end of the thirties, a dilemma is reached when an individual wants to be more independent and more true to their own wishes. The dilemma is that the person at this stage also wants to continue to retain the respect and reward that they have built in the world.

Mid-Life Transition

The mid-life transition, which occurs next, may last roughly from the ages of 40 to 45. At this time, a person may begin to question what they have done with their life. They try to discover their real values. They look back on their earlier dreams and ask themselves if they really want those dreams now.

According to one study of individuals going through the mid-life transition, approximately 80% of the people experience very severe struggles within themselves and the external world during this period of life. The struggles involve questioning virtually every aspect of the life they have created. The person may, at this time, test a variety of new choices out of a need to explore as well as out of confusion.

It is important to realize as you learn how to manage stress that these life changes and crises are very normal parts of development. A transition is often a crisis. But, a crisis involves both danger and opportunity. There is often the danger of losing some security, but the opportunity of discovering new and untapped, inner resources.

People, during their mid-life crisis, will often recognize that certain long-held assumptions and beliefs about themselves and the world are just not true. They will have gone through a period of seeking to accomplish various things and fulfill various dreams. However, they will find that the various dreams they have sought are, perhaps, not the true goals that they want in life.

Albert Ellis once said that experience is the only thing that we are guaranteed in life. If we set up other ultimate goals then we can find ourselves racing toward them, only to be dissatisfied when we reach them. Perhaps the best goal to strive for in life is to fully experience the richness of living.

This paradox may explain the words of a song that read "Little they know that it is so hard to find, one rich man in ten with a satisfied mind." As we seek to race toward various goals and needs that have been artificially created and may be somewhat illusionary, we may find that we grow stressed because we have set up something as an ultimate goal, other than the experiencing of life. For example, we may race toward getting certain designer blue jeans only to find out that a new designer is in favor this month. What needs are we really trying to fill with designer jeans?

We personally believe it is necessary to think seriously about our goals and the importance we place on achieving them. We hope that the time management chapter will help you in establishing your true goals. The knowledge of predictable life crises and the identification of valuable goals can help you through the changing seasons of your life.

Boredom

Earlier, we spoke about the stress of boredom. This is also a change stressor because it is really the lack of change that often brings on boredom. When we are not excited about what we are doing, we often become depressed, irritated and uptight. Variety is the spice of life, and without it our senses become dull or we become jumpy. It is during these times of boredom that we may wish to consider making some of the changes which we can control on the Social Readjustment Rating Scale.

It may be, that if your score on the Social Readjustment Rating Scale is below 50, it would be a healthy decision to increase your change score. A low score does not mean you are a boring person or that you are necessarily under a lot of stress. However, if you have a low score and you feel stressed, you could be experiencing boredom.

You may consider changes such as finding a more rewarding job, changing the number of arguments with a spouse (hopefully decreasing them), altering your responsibilities at work, changing your living conditions, revising your personal habits, or changing the usual type or amount of recreation, church activities, or social activities.

Working Hard At Staying Well

Another way of managing a high level of change stress is to work harder at staying well. What we mean by this is to apply the skills that you will learn from this book and slowly adopt other healthier living habits. The time to be sure to apply the knowledge in the chapter on nutrition, for example, is when you are experiencing the greatest amount of stress from the prevailing winds or the tropical storms.

Another healthy habit is to get the proper amount of sleep so that you are well rested to face the stress which change can bring. You should also be careful not to neglect your body. During times of change, you need to maintain good hygiene and exercise.

You certainly would not want to change your living habits radically, because you would be adding stress. After all, a revision of personal habits adds 24 points, a major change in sleeping habits adds 16 points, a major change in eating habits adds 15 points, and so on. Nevertheless, it is possible to increase slowly your healthy living habits during times of major social readjustment.

A Widow, Mrs. Jones

One of our patients experienced a great deal of social readjustment during a series of life events, and the rating scale was used to help her make a decision regarding still another change she was considering. Mrs. Jones, a 39-year-old mother of three, lived in a modest home with her husband, who was a salesman. During the previous year, her husband had contracted a malignant form of cancer and died.

Shortly after his death, Mrs. Jones had suffered from severe bronchitis and was hospitalized. The patient sought stress management and biofeedback training on the advice of a friend whose husband had also died of a chronic disease.

Many issues were discussed during the treatment, particularly her relationship with her husband and his death. In the midst of treatment, Mrs. Jones began discussing her plans for building a new home near a friend who had become ill. She asked the therapist's advice.

In order to help Mrs. Jones make her decision, the therapist had her complete the Social Readjustment Rating Scale. He suspected that her recent illness may have been partially a result of the tremendous stress which she and her family had experienced over the past year.

Mrs. Jones accumulated the following points before her recent hospitalization: Her husband had contracted cancer, thus she had a major change in the health and/or behavior of a family member (44 points). The particular form of cancer prevented their engaging in any sexual behavior. This was considered a form of sexual difficulty and added 39 points.

Her husband's illness had brought about two major changes in financial status (38 times 2 equals 76 points), when he got cancer, his income dropped off considerably and, when he died, his insurance once again made a major change in the family's financial picture. The husband's illness brought with it a major change in the number of arguments (35 points) because Mrs. Jones felt that she should not cause him any additional problems and, in some ways, began withdrawing from her husband.

The illness also brought about difficulties with in-laws (29 points) because Mrs. Jones felt they were insensitive and unwilling to help when she needed it. Other life changes included major changes in usual type and/or amount of recreation (19 points), major change in church activity (19 points), and major change in social activity (18 points). The care which her husband required imposed limitations on how much the family could leave the home for activities. The medication had to be given at night, and this brought about a change in her sleeping habits (16 points). The family experienced a sad Christmas (12 points), but experienced Christmas nonetheless.

Mrs. Jones' total life-change points were 407 before she contracted bronchitis. As you know, of those people experiencing over 300 life change units during a year, almost 80% get sick in the near future. This is a reasonable explanation, in part, for Mrs. Jones' susceptibility to her illness.

After hospitalization, Mrs. Jones' life-change units increased by 53 points as a result of illness. This brought her total to 460 points. The therapist was able to help Mrs. Jones understand how the accumulation of stress during the last year may have predisposed her to illness.

Mrs. Jones added up the increase in change points that building a new home would bring. It was a change in living conditions (25 points), a change in residence (20 points), and a change in church, as well as social activities (37 points). This would only add to her already overwhelming life-change total. Mrs. Jones decided against the move. At follow-up, she reported that she was well and had not been seriously ill during the last year.

A Volunteer, Mrs. Jackson

Another person taking stress management training as part of preparation for volunteer work with patients, counted up her points on the rating scale and had a total of 25. Mrs. Jackson had experienced a vacation and Christmas during the last year, but had not enjoyed any other life changes.

This is an example of possible understimulation. If Mrs. Jackson was not volunteering and had come for stress management help, the authors might have asked her to consider seeking out additional stimulation and changes in her life to prevent boredom. Joining the volunteer group would add 26 points to her total, as she would be beginning or seeking work outside the home. The sense of excitement and interest in the new project was evident.

An Executive, Mr. Cummings

Another student of stress management who came to us as part of a program for executives in a major industry was quite surprised to find that he had accumulated a great deal of potentially stressful life events. After all, Mr. Cummings said that nothing could be better in his life.

During the last year he had married (53 points) the girl of his dreams, who had shortly thereafter become pregnant (40 points). He had decided to get married because he had gotten a raise at work (38 points) and a promotion (29 points). His promotion had come as a result of his selling more real estate than any other man in the office (28 points). In addition, his change in status at the office had allowed him to buy the new home they dreamed of (31 points), and he had even more time away from work (20 points) to spend time enjoying his new son (39 points). Mr. Cummings saw little of his old friends at the bowling alley or the pub (18 points), but he really enjoyed his honeymoon (13 points) and the family atmosphere of Christmas that year (12 points).

You can see by listening to this man's recent experiences that he had accumulated a great deal of change stress. In fact, Mr. Cummings' total was over 300 points which suggested that he probably should slow down and make as few major life changes as possible during the next year; and to be sure and get enough good food, sleep and rest so as to protect himself from the increased probability of illness. Becoming aware of life change stress, helped this man to anticipate life changes and plan for them in advance.

Are You Sitting On A Two-Legged Stool?

Most of us are striving for a healthy, happy and meaningful life. Balance is needed to achieve and maintain such a life. Balance means that you avoid building your life around one person or one thing, no matter how great or wonderful it may seem. If you do, no matter who or what it is, the loss could be devastating.

Sigmund Freud considered work, play and love to be three major parts of life. Other psychotherapists have called these by other names, but most agree that they are important building blocks for a balanced life. If we ignore any one of them, we ask too much of the other two. It is like sitting on a stool with only two legs -- you may find yourself on the floor.

If you review the social readjustment scale you will notice
that a majority of the life events involve loved ones and love,
itself. Some have called this our interpersonal life and
community. When things go wrong at work or we are unable to
play because of illness, we are left with a great deal of
stress. Without a supportive network of friends and family, we
have no one with whom to share our troubles. Likewise, when
things go our way, we have no one with whom to enjoy it.
Loneliness is a major form of stress.

If, on the other hand, we do not know how to enjoy life and
to maintain outside interests in hobbies, sports and the arts,
we lose our ability to play and we may put too much emphasis on
work and love. This may lead to work that is draining and a
love from which we ask too much. Likewise, if we go through
life ignoring the need for contributing to our community through
work, even if we were so fortunate as to have an independent
income, the balance would be upset. Without an investment in
work or volunteer activities, we would place a burden on our
loved ones and our recreation.

What if you are not interested in one or two of these
factors? If this is the case, it may be worthwhile to review
your life situation and to pay particular attention to the
factors which you are ignoring to see if there is a conflict
which needs your attention.

Most people have very strong needs for work, play, and
love. Try to recognize and fulfill your needs in these areas.
When the unpredictable storms or heat waves of life take their
toll on one of these three areas, you will survive the stress
much better if you have spent enough time, interest and energy
on the other two.

REVIEW QUESTIONS

Directions: Circle the letter in front of the best response to each question. The correct answers are provided on the page following the last question.

1. Of all the times to be alive, this century presents us with

   a. fewer change stressors than ever before, because with automation we can do more in less time.
   b. the most rapid acceleration of change and, thus, more change stressors than ever before.
   c. about the same number of changes and, thus, the same number of change stressors as earlier in history.
   d. the most rapid acceleration of change and, thus, fewer change stressors than ever before.

2. Change of any sort can be

   a. scary.
   b. exciting.
   c. a stressor.
   d. All the above.

3. Change stressors, particularly those listed on the Social Readjustment Rating Scale, can

   a. only be socially undesirable and negative.
   b. only be socially desirable and positive.
   c. be socially desirable or undesirable.
   d. all be avoided if one plans carefully.

4. Each of the life events listed on the Social Readjustment Rating Scale were given a number in comparison to the amount, intensity and length of readjustment the life event requires in comparison to marriage. Which events are at the top (100 points) and bottom (11 points) of the scale?

   a. Foreclosure on a loan and in-law troubles
   b. Death of a spouse and minor violation of the law
   c. Death of a spouse and a divorce
   d. Christmas and pregnancy

5. If your score on the Social Readjustment Rating Scale is above 300 in one year, your chances of becoming ill are

    a. 100%
    b. 50%
    c. 80%
    d. 30%

6. One of the following ways of using the Social Readjustment Rating Scale was mentioned in the chapter. Calculate your score each month when you write bills and

    a. put off making changes that will push your score into a danger zone.
    b. avoid all changes on the list of life events.
    c. avoid seasonal changes if at all possible.
    d. increase your change score to least 150.

7. Boredom is a change stressor and the irritability or depression it often brings can result from

    a. too little change.
    b. too many changes.
    c. an average amount of change.
    d. an above average amount of change.

8. To alleviate the stress of boredom, one might first consider making life changes that are on the bottom of the Social Readjustment Rating Scale such as changing ones social activities, the number of family get togethers, or

    a. spouse.
    b. type or amount of recreation.
    c. the size of ones family.
    d. employment situation by getting fired.

9. Another way to manage a high level of change stress is to

    a. immediately give up unhealthy living habits and adopt healthy habits.
    b. add only good changes like outstanding personal achievements.
    c. go on a crash diet to lose all unhealthy weight.
    d. gradually adopt healthier living habits and slowly give up unhealthy ones.

10. A balanced life means that you do not wrap your life around one person, thing or goal. In addition, you get involved in

    a. work.
    b. play.
    c. intimacy.
    d. All the above.

ANSWERS TO REVIEW QUESTIONS

1. b	6. a
2. d	7. a
3. c	8. b
4. b	9. d
5. c	10. d

SUGGESTED BOOKS AND RECORDINGS

<u>BOOKS</u>

Passages: Predictable Crises Of Adult Life by G. Sheehy. New York: Bantam, 1977.

Pathfinders by G. Sheehy. New York: William Morrow, 1982.

The Seasons Of A Man's Life by D. Levinson. New York: Knopf, 1978.

<u>RECORDINGS</u>

How To Get An Emotional Divorce by A. Jones. Clute, Texas: Individual Success, 1980.

Passages by G. Sheehy. Waco, Texas: S.M.I., 1982.

Chapter 12

Stress In The Here
And Now

Recognizing Your Own Stress Response

Knowing how to recognize your own stress response is similar to knowing when your car sounds "funny" or when the engine is "pinging." If you drive your car every day, you may be able to tell when something is in need of repair by the way it "feels" or "sounds." If you have repaired the car yourself, you may even know what is wrong. In general, the more knowledge you have about automobiles, the more likely it is that you will notice the changes and know if a repair is needed.

The more we study our bodies and how they respond to stress, the more we will be able to prevent major stress problems. If we have been driving ourselves beyond reasonable limits, we may have the same trouble our car would have if we always drove it all day at 80 miles an hour. We may not notice the little things that are going wrong which may lead to major problems. Likewise, if we get used to a strange sound or racing motor, it may be hard to "hear," even when we listen for it.

If you have learned to ignore your personal stress response, try studying your body's response during an exciting part of a movie or television show. This is like taking a drive to "listen" to your car.

In a stress management group for hypertensive executives, one of the authors learned that many participants had increased blood pressure during T.V. programs. Several executives began to monitor their blood pressures during the half time of football games on television. Their blood pressures were significantly higher than prior to the game. The executives then began using half times for their Sunday afternoon practice sessions. Realizing that stressful situations at work and home were having similar effects, they started monitoring their blood pressure levels and analyzing the stressors in their life. They began using coffee breaks and lunch hours to assess their stress levels and practice relaxation.

Your body's response to an exciting show will help teach you what happens to your body when you are "uptight." Much of the pleasure associated with watching a show is your emotional involvement as the actors realistically portray the drama. If you take time to notice, you may find your heart pounding during a chase scene, or your stomach full of butterflies during a horror picture.

The Habit Of Being Uptight

Being uptight in the real world cannot only produce discomfort, but may produce feelings of terror even greater than when viewing a horror film. Think of common everyday stressors such as traffic jams, deadlines, problems at work, or quarrels at home. This is not an easy world in which to relax.

In an unusually stressful situation, you may notice your "emergency response" as your heart beats faster, muscles tense, and blood pressure soars. But all too often, our stress is slowly and steadily grinding away at us. Many people stop listening to their stress warnings, and may not realize how tense they have been until their daily headache starts pounding.

An active executive may have 250 blood pressure peaks during each day, until eventually his blood pressure stays up permanently. The habit of being uptight is something we cultivate, but relaxation can also be cultivated.

Another Habit: Quiet Confidence

Imagine your heart slowing down, your breathing becoming smooth and rhythmic, and all tension slowly slipping away. Now, imagine someone rushing in to ask for an important decision. You slowly breathe in and slowly breathe out. As you do, your body relaxes and your mind clears of distractions; you make the decision calmly. This moment of relaxation is often seen by others as a sign of quiet confidence. Imagine how good it must feel to have cultivated such a habit.

One of the first steps to making this kind of relaxation a habit is to recognize the habit of being uptight. Each of us respond to different stressors, and stressors vary in the amount of response they trigger. For example, a student may experience a great deal of stress when taking an examination in a subject he finds difficult or uninteresting. Before, during, and after the test he may experience constant worry.

The same student may respond in a totally different fashion to a test in his favorite subject. He may still experience stress in preparing for this test, but the intensity will be less. He may go through the same activities to prepare for each test, but the emotional and mental stress will be different.

In modern life, stress from emotional frustration is more likely to produce disease than physical stress. One famous cardiovascular surgeon works 18 to 20 hours a day. He is often on his feet, and usually takes the stairs instead of the elevator to insure he gets exercise. Although his schedule is hectic and demanding, he seldom becomes ill or experiences the effects of chronic stress. Why? Because he is not experiencing "distress" from a job he finds frustrating. He is doing things he enjoys and finds meaningful.

In our complex world, we may realistically find that not everything about our lives and jobs is as rewarding as we would like. Sometimes jobs are frustrating. Retirement is sometimes boring. Work may be good if you achieve something meaningful by doing it. It may wear you out if you never seem to get anything done or what you get done is not important to you. Marriage and family life are also frustrating and stressful at times. By learning how you currently respond to the stress in your everyday living, you will be able to learn how to respond differently in the future. First, we must learn to recognize the stressors in our life.

Charting Your Stress

The chart on the following pages is entitled "List of Current Stressors." Follow the directions and write down all the stressors you are currently experiencing, how much they affect you, and whether you would benefit from being more relaxed in response to the stress. The examples at the top of the list may help you to begin writing down your own. Try to become more and more aware of your stressors. As you do, your list should grow.

In the next chapter, we will use the list of your current stressors to practice stress management techniques for each of the major stressors in your life. Update your list frequently by adding, removing or changing stressors. If you need additional space, continue recording the stressors you are experiencing on a blank piece of paper.

LIST OF CURRENT STRESSORS

Directions: Write down a one or two word label and a brief description for each stressor you are currently experiencing. Indicate by the following codes the category of the stressor:

Ch	Change (moving, new house, etc.)	Fm	Family (births, divorce, etc.)
Cl	Chemical (Caffeine, drugs, ets.)	Pb	Phobic (fear of flying, fear of heights, etc.)
Cm	Commuting (distanct to work, traffic, etc.)		
De	Decision ("Should I change jobs?" "What if I went back to school?", etc.)	Ph	Physical (pregnancy, lack of sleep, etc.)
Ds	Disease (diabetes, dermatitis, etc.)	Pn	Pain (trauma, headaches, etc.)
Em	Emotional (attitudes, anxieties, etc.)	Sc	Social (parties, dating, etc.)
En	Environmental (noise, heat, etc.)	Wk	Work (deadlines, frustrations, etc.)

Quantify how much current stress you experience by labeling it from 0 to 10 SUDS (Subjective Units of Distress) with 0 being no stress and 10 being the maximum you could imagine. Also indicate(x) if relaxation and controlling your body's stress response would be helpful. You may not experience stressors such as noise or pregnancy as distressful. List stressors to help you understand all areas of stress in your life. Other stressors you face may benefit from relaxation by helping you feel more calm, in control, or in less pain. Comment in the last column on how you may reduce the stress.

STRESSOR LABEL	BRIEF DESCRIPTION	CODE	SUDS (0-10)	RELAXATION HELPFUL	COMMENTS
Example: *Pregnancy*	*3rd month of Pregnancy*	*Ph*	*2*	*x*	*Relaxation may help nausea*

STRESSOR LABEL	BRIEF DESCRIPTION	CODE	SUDS (0-10)	RELAXATION HELPFUL	COMMENTS
Example: *Bro's Anger*	*Trying to explain what I've done*	wk	5	x	*Relaxation calms me so I explain better*
Example: *Cold Office*	*Federal Temperature Control too low for me*	Env	2	x	*Best to just dress for it*
1.					
2.					
3.					
4.					
5.					
6.					
7.					

STRESSOR LABEL	BRIEF DESCRIPTION	CODE	SUDS (0-10)	RELAXATION HELPFUL	COMMENTS
8.					
9.					
10.					
11.					
12.					
13.					
14.					
15.					
16.					
17.					

REVIEW QUESTIONS

<u>Directions</u>: Circle the letter in front of the best response to each question. The correct answers are provided on the page following the last question.

1. Knowing your own stress response is similar to

    a. racing your car down the street without watching the oil pressure.
    b. filling your car up with gas without checking the oil and water.
    c. knowing when your car sounds "funny" or the engine is "pinging."
    d. None of the above since your body is not a vehicle that needs to be periodically checked or listened to.

2. One way to help recognize your body's stress response is to

    a. study your body's response to exciting movies or shows.
    b. measure your blood pressure before and after stressful situations.
    c. become more aware of your body and its response to different stressors.
    d. All of the above.

3. Being uptight in the real world can be

    a. more terrifying than watching a horror movie.
    b. related to traffic jams, deadlines, problems at work, or quarrels at home.
    c. a sign you are a weak person, since the world is an easy place in which to relax.
    d. A & B.

4. We may often stop listening to our stress responses, since

    a. it takes too much time to monitor our responses.
    b. it is impossible to recognize them without equipment.
    c. we can learn to ignore them and they can build up without our awareness.
    d. All the above.

5. An active executive may have _____ blood pressure peaks during the day.

    a. 5
    b. 50
    c. 250
    d. 0

6. If the blood pressure increased dramatically enough times per day

    a. the heart would become healthier, because of the exercise.
    b. there would be less chance of a stroke, since the blood vessels would be stronger.
    c. it may eventually remain high; a condition called essential hypertension.
    d. A & B.

7. The habit of being uptight is cultivated, but

    a. relaxation cannot be cultivated.
    b. relaxation is natural, and if you cannot relax now, you will never be able to.
    c. relaxation should not be cultivated, since it will make a person lazy.
    d. relaxation can also be cultivated.

8. Stress from emotional frustration

    a. will seldom produce disease.
    b. is not as bad as physical stress.
    c. should not be a concern, since it is "all in your head."
    d. can lower resistance of the body and lead to physical illness.

9. In order to eliminate stress from your life

    a. make everything about your life and job totally rewarding.
    b. retire, live alone and cancel your newspaper subscription.
    c. stay single, child-free and on unemployment payments.
    d. None of the above. It is not possible, practical or beneficial to eliminate all stress from your life.

10. By learning how you currently respond to stress in your everyday living

    a. you will become depressed.
    b. you will be able to change how you respond in the future.
    c. you will no longer need to examine your stress response.
    d. All of the above.

ANSWERS TO REVIEW QUESTIONS

1.	c	6.	c
2.	d	7.	d
3.	d	8.	d
4.	c	9.	d
5.	c	10.	b

Chapter 13

Mental Simulation:
Rehearsing Stressful Scenes

You have now learned Progressive and Deep Muscle Relaxation to relax muscles that you have voluntary control over. You have also learned Autogenic Training to help you relax and regulate those parts of your body that are usually not under your voluntary control. In addition, you know how to relax by using visual images of pleasant scenes. Now you are ready to apply these skills in new ways to deal with some of the major stressors in your life.

Choosing A Target Stressor

Most of us have some areas of our life that are particularly stressful. In the last chapter, you began to list your personal stressors. We would like you to go back to this list and group them into a few difficult situations. These will be called your target stressors. Choose one of these to work on.

Some people choose talking with a person of the opposite sex, others, taking an examination. Many people select a difficult work stressor. On the other hand, if you have a phobia, such as a fear of heights, air travel or closed spaces, you may choose this as your target stressor. If you are reducing your weight, you may want to focus on your eating behavior in difficult situations. If you are stopping smoking, you may want to work on scenes where the urge to smoke is strong. It is often stressful to resist urges when you are modifying harmful habits.

Each of us has our own particular stressors. Pick one which is not the most difficult for you, but still gives you a good deal of trouble in your life. Use the SUDs (Subjective Units of Distress) rating to decide on the stressor's level of difficulty. It is best to pick a mild to moderate stressor so as to increase the likelihood of success, before you tackle your most upsetting stressors. At the same time, pick one that is important enough to you to make your efforts seem worthwhile and keep your level of motivation high.

Research and clinical work has shown that if we imagine stressors while feeling calm and relaxed, we can gain control and mastery over them. In this way, the techniques of relaxation that you have learned can be transferred to any situation you find upsetting. But first, we need to build a twenty-step stress ladder.

A stress ladder is a list that goes from the smallest or lowest stressor to the largest or highest stressor. In this case, we want you to take small steps in dealing with one of these stressors. For example, if you have a good deal of trouble with examinations, you may have picked examinations as your mild-to-moderate stressor. You probably find certain parts of taking an examination less upsetting than others. Studying for an exam that is three months away, is not as upsetting as studying the night before an exam or sitting down to take the actual examination.

Before you build your own stress ladder, turn to page 230 and study the ladder constructed by a student with test anxiety. Notice that the closer he got to the exam time, the more stress he experienced and the higher he placed the stressor on his ladder. Notice, also how each step is clear and specific.

Next turn to page 232 and study the ladder constructed by a patient who was afraid of needles and injections. Notice that the larger the needle and the closer the patient got to taking an injection, the more stress she experienced, and the higher she placed the stressor on her ladder.

Building a useful stress ladder is not as easy as it looks. Therapists spend a good deal of time with patients tailor-making the ladders. There are "prefabricated" ladders for some stressors, but the best ones reflect the person's real life experiences and individuality. What is very stressful for one test anxious person may be only mildly stressful for another. Another important aspect of a good ladder is that the steps between rungs are very small and about the same distance.

To help you organize your own ladder into small, equal steps, use 3x5 filing cards or cut paper into small strips. Start writing down one step of a stressor on each card or slip. Write as many as you can up to about twenty. Think of a two-or three-word code for each card and write it on the top of the card. Take these cards and arrange them from the least to the most stressful. Then read the directions and fill in the blank Twenty-Step Ladder on page 234.

Stressor: _Tests_

TWENTY-STEP STRESS LADDER

Directions: To create your twenty-step stress ladder, write a
two or three word code and a full description of each level of
the stressor on the ladder. The least stressful level or form
of the stressor should be numbered one. The most stressful
should be numbered twenty. The list should read from the least
(1) to the most (20) stressful situations.

Code Words for Stressor   Full Description of Stressor

1. _Teacher announces final_   : Teacher announces final exam
                                   in three months

2. _Buying text books_   : Buying books for the course and
                                   thinking about the exam

3. _Studying, month before_   : Studying when the final exam
                                   is one month away

4. _Talking, month before_   : Talking with friends about the
                                   exam one month before.

5. _Studying, week before_   : Studying when the final
                                   exam is one week away

6. _Talking, week before_   : Talking with friends about
                                   the exam one week before

7. _Studying, day before_   : Studying when the final
                                   exam is the next day

8. _Talking, day before_   : Talking with friends about
                                   the exam the next day

9. _Studying night before:_   Studying the night before the final exam

10. _Laying in bed night before:_   Laying in bed the night before the final exam

11. _Talking, hour before_ :   Talking with friends about the exam one hour before

12. _Walking to building_ :   Walking to the building where I will take the exam

13. _Entering building_ :   Entering the building where I will take the exam

14. _Entering classroom_ :   Entering the classroom where I will take the exam

15. _Finding a seat_ :   Finding a seat where I will take the exam

16. _Watching teacher hand out:_   Watching the teacher hand out the exam

17. _Reading directions_ :   Reading the directions on the examination

18. _1st question not understood_ :   Not understanding the first question on the exam

19. _Forgetting and guessing:_   Not remembering and having to guess on the exam

20. _Rushing to finish_ :   Rushing to finish the exam when others have left early

Stressor: _Needles_

TWENTY-STEP STRESS LADDER

Directions: To create your twenty-step stress ladder, write a two or three word code and a full description of each level of the stressor on the ladder. The least stressful level or form of the stressor should be numbered one. The most stressful should be numbered twenty. The list should read from the least (1) to the most (20) stressful situations.

Code Words for Stressor	Full Description of Stressor
1. Picture of small needle :	Looking at a picture of a small needle with a shield on it
2. Someone else picture medium size :	Someone else looking at a picture of a medium sized needle with shield on it
3. Medium needle across room :	Looking at a medium sized needle with a shield on it from across the room
4. No shield medium size :	Looking at a medium sized needle without a shield on it from across the room
5. Large needle across room :	Looking at a large needle with a shield on it for a minute from across the room
6. Large needle close :	Looking at a large needle without a shield for five minutes a foot away
7. Nurse filling needle :	Sitting in a nurse's station as a needle is filled
8. Husband awaits shot :	Sitting in a doctor's office while husband is waiting for an injection

9. *Husband's arm prepared*: Sitting in a doctor's office while husband's arm is prepared for an injection

10. *making appointment for shot* : Making an appointment for a visit involving an injection

11. *waiting for shot* : Sitting in a doctor's office while waiting for an injection

12. *In doctor's office* : Being called from the waiting room into the doctor's office for an injection

13. *Nurse fills needle* : Watching the nurse fill the needle for my injection

14. *Doctor takes needle* : Watching the nurse give the doctor the needle for my injection

15. *wiping off skin* : Feeling the nurse wipe off my skin to prepare it for the injection

16. *Doctor squirts needle*: Watching the doctor squirt the needle to clear oxygen

17. *Doctor takes arm* : Watching the doctor lean over and take my arm when he is ready to give the injection

18. *Doctor pinches skin*: Watching the doctor pinch my skin and hold my arm

19. *Feel prick of shot* : Feeling the needle prick my skin as it enters

20. *Doctor injects fluid*: Watching the doctor inject the fluid and remove the needle

Stressor: _____

TWENTY-STEP STRESS LADDER

Directions: To create your twenty-step stress ladder, write a
two or three word code and a full description of each level of
the stressor on the ladder. The least stressful level or form
of the stressor should be numbered one. The most stressful
should be numbered twenty. The list should read from the least
(1) to the most (20) stressful situations.

Code Words for Stressor   Full Description of Stressor

1. _____ :   _____

                            _____

2. _____ :   _____

                            _____

3. _____ :   _____

                            _____

4. _____ :   _____

                            _____

5. _____ :   _____

                            _____

6. _____ :   _____

                            _____

7. _____ :   _____

                            _____

8. _____ :   _____

                            _____

9. _____: _____

_____

10. _____: _____

_____

11. _____: _____

_____

12. _____: _____

_____

13. _____: _____

_____

14. _____: _____

_____

15. _____: _____

_____

16. _____: _____

_____

17. _____: _____

_____

18. _____: _____

_____

19. _____: _____

_____

20. _____: _____

_____

Now that you have created your twenty-step stress ladder, find the upcoming form titled, "Ratings of Relaxation and Imagery on the Four-Step Ladder". Read the directions closely. Carefully transfer the first four code words from your twenty-step stress ladder onto this four-step ladder. Be sure that these are the least upsetting steps of your twenty-step stress ladder.

Using Relaxation Tapes

If you are using recorded relaxation exercises, schedule times now and begin listening to a tape on Image Rehearsal or Stress Management. The tape you listen to will help you use the four-step stress ladder you just created to desensitize yourself to four mildly stressful situations. After you listen to the tape, rate your level of relaxation and the clarity of the visual images you created on the four-step hierarchy form.

You can also use a tape recorder to tape and later present sounds associated with the steps of your stress ladder. For example, one flight-phobic executive asked his wife to take a flight and tape the sounds of the airplane on the runway and in the air, as well as the voices of the ticket clerk and the pilot over the intercoms. He then played the four-step relaxation tape on one recorder and turned it off to listen to these air travel sounds on the second recorder when the instructions were given to visualize those steps of his stress ladder.

Guiding Yourself

If you will be guiding yourself through these exercises, then review the directions below. You may find it helpful to read the directions several times. You may also want to ask someone to read the image rehearsal instructions to you. Be sure they read the instructions slowly and calmly. If possible, you may want to record those instructions onto a tape and then use the tape to practice. Set aside about thirty minutes for each practice session.

Helpful Hints For Tape And Self-Instruction Users

During the next week, practice once or twice a day on your four-step stress ladder. Be sure to get a firm footing and become fully relaxed on the first four steps of your ladder before you use a new four-step ladder. One way of doing this is to make sure your ratings of relaxation and image clarity are as good or better than the ratings you made of your responses to the earlier tapes. This should take only one or two practice sessions.

Sometimes the first step of a stress ladder is too anxiety provoking. If this is the case, you may find it helpful to lower the stress of the whole ladder. The test anxiety student whose original ladder appeared on page 230 did this by using the ladder for an easy subject before applying it to his most difficult subject. Another way of dealing with the problem of getting started is to add easier steps prior to the original first step. Practice these before trying the original first step again.

Occassionally, people get stuck on one step of a ladder and can't go up to the next one without a lot of anxiety. The problem may be the distance between the two steps and the solution is to add more steps between the step you are on and the next one.

When you have succeeded in desensitizing yourself to the first four steps, you can replace them with additional stressful situations from your twenty-step stress ladder. Continue doing this once or twice a day, during the next week, until you have climbed all the way up the stress ladder for the stressor you have been working on. When you finish one stress ladder, choose another, more challenging stressor. Build another stress ladder for the stressor you choose. You can continue this process until you have conquered your most difficult stressors.

It is often helpful to practice with a friend. You can help each other build your stress ladders and guide one another using the word-by-word instructions which follow.

Mental Simulation And Rehearsal

You may also want to use your imagination to rehearse acting in a skillful and relaxed manner, in the face of your life challanges. You will not only become less anxious, but you will build up your confidence and your ability to handle the situation. The winners in life practice and rehearse every situation that they find difficult. Make it your goal to experience your stressors in a calm fashion.

RATINGS OF RELAXATION AND IMAGERY ON THE FOUR STEP LADDER

Directions: Write in the code words of the steps you plan to work on today. The *least* stressful level or form of the stressor should be numbered one. The *most* stressful should be numbered four. The list should read from the least (1) to the most (4) stressful level.

After you practice, circle the number on the Relaxation Scale that best describes your total feelings of relaxation during the presentation of the image you created for each code word. Then circle the number on the Imagery Scale that describes the intensity of the image you created for each code word. Do this one line at a time for each of the four levels you worked on.

Level	Code Words of Stressor	Relaxation Scale										Imagery Scale									
		Tension								Relaxation		Unclear Interrupted Images								Clear Uninterrupted Image	
1	_____	10	20	30	40	50	60	70	80	90	100	10	20	30	40	50	60	70	80	90	100
2	_____	10	20	30	40	50	60	70	80	90	100	10	20	30	40	50	60	70	80	90	100
3	_____	10	20	30	40	50	60	70	80	90	100	10	20	30	40	50	60	70	80	90	100
4	_____	10	20	30	40	50	60	70	80	90	100	10	20	30	40	50	60	70	80	90	100

Date of Practice: _____

Name of Major Stressor: _____

Relaxation Scale Imagery Scale

Level	Code Words of Stressor	Tension								Relaxation		Unclear Interrupted Images								Clear Uninterrupted Image	
1		10	20	30	40	50	60	70	80	90	100	10	20	30	40	50	60	70	80	90	100
2		10	20	30	40	50	60	70	80	90	100	10	20	30	40	50	60	70	80	90	100
3		10	20	30	40	50	60	70	80	90	100	10	20	30	40	50	60	70	80	90	100
4		10	20	30	40	50	60	70	80	90	100	10	20	30	40	50	60	70	80	90	100

Name of Major Stressor: _____ Date of Practice: _____

Level	Code Words of Stressor	Tension								Relaxation		Unclear Interrupted Images								Clear Uninterrupted Image	
1		10	20	30	40	50	60	70	80	90	100	10	20	30	40	50	60	70	80	90	100
2		10	20	30	40	50	60	70	80	90	100	10	20	30	40	50	60	70	80	90	100
3		10	20	30	40	50	60	70	80	90	100	10	20	30	40	50	60	70	80	90	100
4		10	20	30	40	50	60	70	80	90	100	10	20	30	40	50	60	70	80	90	100

Name of Major Stressor: _____ Date of Practice: _____

Level	Code Words of Stressor	Tension								Relaxation		Unclear Interrupted Images								Clear Uninterrupted Image	
1		10	20	30	40	50	60	70	80	90	100	10	20	30	40	50	60	70	80	90	100
2		10	20	30	40	50	60	70	80	90	100	10	20	30	40	50	60	70	80	90	100
3		10	20	30	40	50	60	70	80	90	100	10	20	30	40	50	60	70	80	90	100
4		10	20	30	40	50	60	70	80	90	100	10	20	30	40	50	60	70	80	90	100

Name of Major Stressor: _____ Date of Practice: _____

To strengthen your stress management skills, you may also wish to practice stress reduction while watching a movie or a show on television. When you are in the middle of a tense scene, use your training to relax. You may be surprised at how calm you can become after a while. This is very good practice for the stress reduction you will want to use in your everyday life.

"Taking It To The Streets"

Once you have desensitized yourself to a stressor in your imagination, it is time to try out your new skill. The most common mistake people make in applying what they have learned, is to first try their most difficult stressor. Practice relaxing and being calm, first with your easier situations. Go slowly up the ladders in order of their difficulty. Get a good firm footing on one step before moving up to the next. If the going gets rough and your anxiety is too great, alternate between imagination and real life practice or add more steps to your ladders. With practice, you will be surprised how easily you handle your stressors and your self-confidence will grow.

WORD BY WORD LADDER CLIMBING AND SCENE REHEARSING

Getting Comfortable

Let's begin by getting totally relaxed all over. Spend a little time getting as comfortable as you can. Move around, if necessary, as you get into a comfortable position. Become as completely relaxed as possible.

Focusing On Breathing

Focus your attention completely and fully on your breathing. Imagine your breathing is as automatic as the ocean waves, rolling in...and out...in...and out. Silently say to yourself, "Breathing, smooth and rhythmic." "Breathing, smooth and rhythmic." Become aware of the air flowing in and out of your lungs.

Relaxation

As you breathe, imagine air moving through your body in massaging waves of relaxation. Feel the waves of relaxation moving through your chest and shoulders, down into your arms, through your back muscles, down into your hips and legs. With each wave of relaxation, feel the growing heaviness and warmth in your arms and legs.

Ten To Zero

Now, I am going to count from ten to zero. Each time I move from a higher number to a lower number, you will feel more relaxed, even more relaxed than you feel right now. When I reach the number zero, you will feel profoundly relaxed. Ten...more and more relaxed. Nine..."I am calm." Eight...relaxing deeper and deeper. Seven...calm and peaceful. Six...peaceful and calm. Five...heavy, warm and comfortable. Four...more and more relaxed. Three...feeling very quiet. Two...muscles like jelly. One...deeper and deeper. Zero...profound relaxation.

Limp Rag Doll

You are becoming as relaxed and limp as an old rag doll, and you really are that relaxed. Just see yourself in your imagination. Lying back, warm, comfortable, calm, peaceful and relaxed. Totally relaxed. Just as limp and loose as a rag doll.

In A Meadow

You might want to imagine that you are lying in a beautiful meadow. You may know of a place such as this; and, if so, imagine you are there. If you don't know such a place, then use your imagination to create it. A beautiful meadow with the temperature just right, not too hot, and not too cool. Try to see yourself there in the meadow. You are perfectly comfortable on a bed of very soft, green grass. Feel a beautiful and warm sense of relaxation all around your body. Nothing to be worried about. Just let go and feel the relaxation.

Continue to stay in a peaceful, safe imaginary meadow and try to keep the feelings of peace and calm as we now imagine some scenes that may be slightly stressful (anxiety-producing or anger-provoking). Try to see the scenes as clearly as you can, but know in your mind that if, at any time, the scene makes you uncomfortable, you can immediately return to the pleasant image of yourself lying peacefully in your meadow.

Success Rehearsal

See yourself very much in control, confident, and the master of the scene. See yourself very successfully meeting the problems head on, with confidence and control. Now begin.

Scene One

Look at the first scene. See yourself in control. Master the scene. Pause 30 seconds and visualize the scene in your mind.

Return To The Meadow And Relaxation	*Now leave that scene behind and return to your peaceful meadow. Think to yourself: "Face relax. Neck relax. Shoulders relax. Arms relax. Chest relax. Stomach relax. Hips, legs and feet relax." Remember the relaxation you have felt before and let it flow back into your body. You are safe and comfortable. Deeply relaxed.*
"I Am Peaceful And Calm"	*Say to yourself, "I am peaceful and calm." "I am calm and peaceful." Once again begin to imagine the same scene. (You can go on to another scene if the last scene did not trigger a lot of stress or tension). Picture yourself in total command of the situation.*
Scene Two	*Pause 30 seconds and visualize the scene in your mind.*
Back To The Meadow	*Now, in your mind return to the meadow. See yourself there, very comfortable, very much at peace. Say to yourself, "I am calm" each time you breathe out. "I am calm." "I am calm." You are alert and awake, but fully at ease. Now pay attention to your body and use the natural abilities of your mind to relax. Focus on feelings of deep, deep relaxation. You feel good. You feel refreshed. "I am at peace." Say this to yourself. "I am at peace." Feel the peace and calm throughout your body.*
Scene Three	*Now once again, imagine the scene you are working on. Begin seeing it now, and try to make it as clear as possible. This is your time to be master of that scene. You are in control. Pause 30 seconds and visualize the scene in your mind.*

Return to The Meadow Leave that scene now, and return to the image of yourself lying comfortably in the pleasant meadow. The temperature is just right and you feel very deeply relaxed. Concentrate on waves of relaxation moving through your body. Waves of relaxation flood into every part of your body, as you are lying in your meadow.

If you find any tension, any tension at all, let that part of your body relax. Try to remain mentally alert, and don't let yourself get tired or fall asleep; because you need to see the scenes as clearly as possible.

Scene Four Try another scene, scene four, if you are ready. See it clearly and stay in control of it. Pause 30 seconds and visualize the scene in your mind.

Return To The Meadow Now, in your mind, return to the meadow and relax.

More Scenes (You may wish to go through more scenes. If not, then complete the following exercises.) Your practice is over for today, but spend a few more minutes being as relaxed as possible. As you practice thinking of stressful life areas (anxiety or anger scenes), and seeing yourself in command and relaxed, you will continue to gain more and more control. Soon you will be able to face real-life situations with greater confidence. You will control these situations, rather than allowing them to control you. You will have the power to imagine yourself in your relaxing place. You will be able to do this quickly and easily, getting control of yourself and then facing life's challenges.

Awakening Safely ....   *Now, see yourself safe and secure, exactly where you started these exercises. Remove yourself from the meadow. I will count forward from one to five. Open your eyes on five. One, still profoundly relaxed. Two, very relaxed. Three, relaxed, but more alert. Four, eyes open. Five, wide awake. Before getting up, stretch your muscles. Take a deep breath, and you will feel confident, alert and refreshed.*

REVIEW QUESTIONS

Directions: Circle the letter in front of the best response to
each question.   The correct answers are provided on the page
following the last question.

1. Rehearsing stressful scenes, at each step on a stress ladder,
    while you are relaxed, will help you

    a. relax even more fully than you have relaxed to earlier
        exercises in the program.
    b. work on particularly upsetting life stressors or phobias
        you may have.
    c. eliminate stress from your everyday life.
    d. relax differentially, that is to stay calm when you can
        and manage things when you cannot stay calm.

2. The stressors you will work on by climbing a stress ladder
    will come from

    a. remembering the three most upsetting situations you have
        ever been in.
    b. the lists you wrote in the last chapter.
    c. your imagination of the most upsetting situations you
        could ever face.
    d. the standard list given on tapes and in books.

3. You should start with the stressor that is

    a. the most upsetting to you.
    b. not upsetting to you.
    c. somewhat upsetting to you.
    d. a little relaxing for you.

4. Research and clinical work has shown that, if we imagine
    stressors, while feeling calm and relaxed, we

    a. will be less able to relax in the future.
    b. will gain control and mastery over these stressors.
    c. will feel less in control, but relax more when we think
        about these stressors.
    d. will feel more in control, but not be able to face these
        stressors.

5. A stress ladder is a(n) _____ that goes from the smallest or lowest stressor to the highest or largest stressor.

    a. feeling
    b. animal
    c. situation
    d. list

6. To form a stress ladder for a stressor, you put the least _____ situation at one end and, step by step, add situations until you get to the most _____ situation.

    a. upsetting; relaxing
    b. relaxing; upsetting
    c. distrubing; relaxing
    d. disturbing; threatening

7. Each situation on the stress ladder should be _____ the one before it.

    a. a good deal more stressful than
    b. somewhat more stressful than
    c. about twice as stressful as
    d. about three times as stressful as

8. If we use our imagination to rehearse acting in a skillful and relaxed manner in the face of life's stressors, we will not only become less anxious, but also build our

    a. confidence and ability to handle these situations.
    b. fear and ability to escape these situations.
    c. stress ladders almost twice as high.
    d. hopes in a useless way.

9. When you climb a stress ladder

    a. get a firm footing on each step before progressing any higher.
    b. be sure you are fully relaxed on one step before you try the next.
    c. try to make the steps small and your climb easy.
    d. All the above.

10. Rehearsing skillful and relaxed actions in stressful scenes
    will help you

    a. transfer the relaxation skills you have learned to the
        more stressful life pressures you may face.
    b. relax some muscles while tensing others.
    c. eliminate the more stressful life pressures you may face.
    d. None of the above.

ANSWERS TO REVIEW QUESTIONS

1.	b	6.	d
2.	b	7.	b
3.	c	8.	a
4.	b	9.	d
5.	d	10.	a

SUGGESTED BOOK AND RECORDINGS

BOOK

I Hurt Too Much For A Band-Aid by K. Olson. Phoenix: O'Sullivan Woodside, 1980.

RECORDINGS

Relaxation And Stress Management Program -- Image Rehearsal Practice by E. Charlesworth. Houston: Stress Management Research, 1981.

Relaxation Training Program -- Stress Management by T. Budzynski. New York: B.M.A., 1974.

Taking The 'Ouch' Out Of Headaches by J. Miller. Atlanta, Georgia: Atlanta Headache Clinic, 1981.

Quieting Response Training -- Ten Steps To The Integrated Quieting Response by C. Stroebel. New York: B.M.A., 1978.

Section IV

Attacking Your Stressful Behaviors, Thoughts And Attitudes

Chapter 14

The Help Your Heart Report Card:
When Is A "B" Better Than An "A"?

Coronary Heart Disease

Heart disease is the major cause of death in the United States. This has not always been the case in America; and it is not true of many other countries in the world. The rate of death from heart disease, in the United States, has increased dramatically since the turn of this century. A large percentage of these deaths occur between the ages of 35 and 50, and are classified as "premature" deaths. Unless a cause and cure can be found, the World Health Organization predicts that coronary heart disease may well become the "greatest epidemic mankind has ever faced."

Coronary heart disease results from damage to the arteries that supply blood to the heart muscle itself. The damage to the coronary arteries is called atherosclerosis. The heart is a muscle and, without oxygen and nutrients from the blood, it cannot survive. Angina pectoris involves brief periodic attacks of chest pain caused by insufficient delivery of blood to the heart. A heart attack occurs if the lack of oxygen is extended and part of the heart muscle actually dies. This is called a myocardial infarction.

Physical Risk Factors

Research suggests that many factors increase the risk of coronary heart disease. Men, who are aging and have high levels of cholesterol in their blood, high blood pressure, diabetes, a history of heart disease in their families, and unusual heart beat rhythms, are at higher risk than other people. In addition, those people who smoke, become obese, or fail to get sufficient exercise are also at risk. However, physical risk factors cannot be found in nearly half of all new cases of coronary heart disease.

Psychological Risk Factors

As early as 1892, physicians were aware of the distinct personality traits of coronary patients. In the late 1950's, Drs. Meyer Friedman and Ray Rosenman led the field of cardiology into a study of what they later called Type A behavior, a coronary-prone behavior pattern. Originally, these doctors were investigating the role of dietary cholesterol in heart disease. In the midst of reviewing the contradictory evidence for this risk factor, they found themselves listening to the then-president of the San Francisco Junior League.

The evidence was not contradictory for this outspoken woman. "I told you right from the first," she said, "that you would find that we are eating exactly as our husbands do. If you really want to know what is giving our husbands heart attacks, I'll tell you." When the doctors asked, she said, "It's stress, the stress they receive in their work that's what's doing it."

Drs. Friedman and Roseman investigated the relationship between stress and coronary heart disease as had other scientists; but they discovered a particular pattern of behavior with which they could explain a great deal of what was happening to men in this country. In the book, Type A Behavior and Your Heart, Drs. Friedman and Rosenman introduced to the public the differences between Type A and Type B behavior.

From Theory To Fact

The strongest evidence for the importance of Type A behavior came from a very well-controlled study known as the Western Collaborative Group Study. In 1961, Drs. Friedman and Rosenman examined through interviews three thousand healthy middle-aged men for certain behavior patterns. They were also medically examined for coronary heart disease. About half these men were classified as Type A.

Eight and one-half years later, the Type A men had twice the coronary heart disease of those men who were orginally judged as Type B. Other researchers have documented greater blockage of the coronary arteries among Type A individuals than Type B individuals. Of course not all Type A men suffer coronary heart disease; but who wants to gamble when we only have one life? It looks like this is one of the few situations where a grade of "B" is better than a grade of "A"! Complete the following exercise to find out your grade.

THE A/B LIFE-STYLE QUESTIONNAIRE

Directions: As you can see, each scale below is composed of a pair of adjectives or phrases. Each pair represents two kinds of contrasting behavior. Choose the number that most closely represents the type of person you are and put it under the column labeled YOUR SCORE. Add your scores to get your total score.

RATING SCALE

YOUR SCORE

1. Work regular hours	0 1 2 3 4 5 6 7 8 9 10	Bring work home or work late	_____
2. Wait calmly	0 1 2 3 4 5 6 7 8 9 10	Wait impatiently	_____
3. Seldom judge in terms of numbers (How many, how much)	0 1 2 3 4 5 6 7 8 9 10	Place value in terms of numbers	_____
4. Not competitive	0 1 2 3 4 5 6 7 8 9 10	Very competitive	_____
5. Feel limited responsibility	0 1 2 3 4 5 6 7 8 9 10	Always feel responsible	_____
6. Unhurried about appointments	0 1 2 3 4 5 6 7 8 9 10	Frequently hurried for appointments	_____
7. Never in a hurry	0 1 2 3 4 5 6 7 8 9 10	Always in a hurry	_____
8. Many interests	0 1 2 3 4 5 6 7 8 9 10	Work is main interest	_____
9. Try to satisfy self	0 1 2 3 4 5 6 7 8 9 10	Want to be recognized by others	_____
10. Not very precise	0 1 2 3 4 5 6 7 8 9 10	Careful about detail	_____
11. Can leave things temporarily unfinished	0 1 2 3 4 5 6 7 8 9 10	Must get things finished	_____
12. Satisfied with job	0 1 2 3 4 5 6 7 8 9 10	Striving on the job	_____
13. Listen well	0 1 2 3 4 5 6 7 8 9 10	Finish sentences for others	_____
14. Easygoing	0 1 2 3 4 5 6 7 8 9 10	Hard driving	_____
15. Do things slowly	0 1 2 3 4 5 6 7 8 9 10	Do things quickly	_____
16. Do one thing at a time	0 1 2 3 4 5 6 7 8 9 10	Think about what to do next	_____
17. Rarely angry	0 1 2 3 4 5 6 7 8 9 10	Easily angered	_____
18. Slow speech	0 1 2 3 4 5 6 7 8 9 10	Forceful speech	_____
19. Express feelings easily	0 1 2 3 4 5 6 7 8 9 10	Bottle up feelings	_____
20. Rarely set deadlines	0 1 2 3 4 5 6 7 8 9 10	Often set deadlines	_____

YOUR TOTAL A/B SCORE _____

What Your Total A/B Score Means

If your total score was 160-200, and especially if you are over 40 and smoke, you may have a high risk of developing cardiac illness.

If your total score was 100-159, you are in the direction of being prone to cardiac disease. You should pay careful attention to the advice given to Type A's.

If your total score was 50-99, you are a mixture of A and B patterns. Beware of any potential for slipping into A behavior.

If your total score was less than 50, your behavior is generally relaxed and you express few of the reactions associated with cardiac disease. You probably have a Type B pattern.

Your score should give you some idea of where you stand in the discussion of Type A behavior. Even Type B persons occasionally slip into Type A behavior. It is important to remember that any of these patterns can change over time.

Type A Behaviors

Friedman and Rosenman described Type A behavior as "an action-emotion complex that can be observed in any person who is aggressively involved in a chronic, incessant struggle to achieve more and more in less and less time, and, if required to do so, against the opposing efforts of other things or persons." It appears that the mechanism involved is related to what we have called the stress response.

In the course of struggling against time and other people, the fight-or-flight response is triggered repeatedly and chronically. As a result of the abnormal discharges of adrenalin and cortisol, most Type A people have an increase in the cholesterol and fat in their bloodstream, have a more difficult time in getting the cholesterol out of their bloodstream, and have an increase in clotting within the arteries.

Friedman and Rosenman include the following behaviors in their description of the Type A, coronary-prone individual. The Type A individual always moves, walks, eats and talks rapidly.

They tend to emphasize words in their speech like a machine gun. They tend to hurry to the end of their sentences. The Type A individual is impatient with the rate that things happen. They tend to interrupt others and finish the sentences of people who are speaking slowly. They find it difficult to wait for others to do things which they might be able to do faster. They hurry themselves in every activity they can.

The Type A individual tries to do two or more things at one time. They may think about business difficulties while they are driving to work or playing a game. They may try to eat and read at the same time. When others are saying something that does not relate to what they want to talk about, they always struggle to bring the conversation back to their interest. They have a difficult time relaxing or doing nothing, even if it is on a vacation. They are often so preoccupied that they do not appreciate things around them which do not have to do with their main goals.

They are more interested in getting things done than getting enjoyment from doing them. They try to schedule more and more in less and less time. Often, they find themselves having scheduled more than can be accomplished, and having allowed little time for unexpected interruptions or emergencies.

The Type A personality is extremely competitive and they try to achieve more than others. Their goals are more money, more possessions, more friends, more activities, more, more, more. They tend to judge themselves by the number of successes they have rather than the quality of their successes. In addition, they look upon their successes as the result of their ability to get things done faster than others, rather than as a result of their abilities. They often have gestures which suggest constant struggle, such as grinding their teeth or clenching their fists.

In summary, the Type A individual is the person who is hard-driving, competitive, impatient and aggressive. They tend to be achievement-striving and hostile. Another way to put it is to say that the Type A's slogan is "we try harder."

Type B Behaviors

On the other hand, the Type B individual is free of all the habits which are described above. They seldom feel any sense of time urgency or impatience. The Type B individual is not preoccupied with their achievements or accomplishments, and seldom find themselves angry or irritable. They tend to enjoy their recreation, finding it fun and relaxing. They are free of any guilt about relaxing and work calmly and smoothly.

Take A Second Look At Yourself

It is important to note that these are the extremes. Nevertheless, remember that half of the three thousand healthy men, whom Drs. Friedman and Rosenman studied, were identified as Type A. If you were familiar with the Type A behavior pattern before you took the exercise, another way to grade yourself is to imagine which group your wife, husband, children or friends would put you in if they had to choose between one or the other.

If you find yourself to be a Type A individual, you will want to decrease your risk for coronary heart disease by taking a good look at your lifestyle and making some of the changes we are about to suggest. If you are a Type B, read over these suggestions, use the ones that seem to apply to you, and continue your healthy behavior.

But I'm Healthy

If you have had no signs or symptoms of heart disease, you may wonder why you should try to change. According to Friedman and Rosenman, the Type A's are often the hardest to convince. In 1978, the National Heart, Lung, and Blood Institute reviewed the evidence and determined that Type A behavior was a risk factor for cornary heart disease of the same magnitude as serum cholesterol.

A statistic that is often helpful in deciding to change, is the fact that, during 1973 alone, two hundred thousand Americans died suddenly of heart disease without any previous symptoms. This is why heart disease and in particular, hypertension, are called the silent killers. Another reason to decide to change is to become more efficient and more effective through setting priorities and using other stress management skills. Still another reason to change and, perhaps one of the most important, is to improve the quality of your life.

More Recreation?

Trying to change Type A behavior does not just mean taking more time for recreation. Gary Schwartz, a noted Yale psychologist, pointed this out by recounting the time he observed three fishermen. It was a beautiful spring day, with a blue sky and a calm lake. While sipping cold drinks, two of the fishermen were enjoying the scenery and their companionship. They hardly ever checked their fishing hooks to see if the bait was taken. They were drifting along quietly in a row boat.

The third fisherman was alone in a boat with a very high powered motor. He had five different rods, all rigged up with lines, positioned off both sides of the boat. This third fisherman ran frantically back and forth checking the hooks to see if the bait was off and yelling wildly down stream, "Did you catch anything?" He moved his boat with determination from spot to spot.

The first two fishermen are Type B and the third Type A. They were all fishing and might all have been taking their doctor's advice. However, the very different effects on their bodies should be clear by now.

You might wonder if Type A's can change. The experience of hundreds suggests that they can. The gains are substantial while the losses they feared seldom occur. You too can change!

Now That I Know That I'm A Type A, How Can I Become A Type B Without Losing The Things I Want?

Part of the answer to this question is to decide if the things you are doing will bring you the things that you want. Most Type A individuals are achievement oriented and committed to vocational activities. It is not clear, from some of the research conducted subsequent to the work of Drs. Friedman and Rosenman, whether achievement-oriented activity is a critical element in the Type A behavior. It is our opinion that many of the behaviors which Friedman and Rosenman described can be engaged in without triggering the stress response.

You may wonder if people who earn more money in higher status jobs are more likely to be Type A individuals. This is true, in part; but, if you look at successful people, there are many who have succeeded without struggling against time. There are Type A's and Type B's at every rung of our society's ladders. Impatience may not lead to success and success is often found in spite of impatience!

When we try to do things too fast, we invite error and tend to adopt a rigid approach to what needs to be done. Repetitive thinking and acting tend to impede progress. When we are rushed, we are less likely to find creative and effective solutions to our problems. Thus, it is not only possible, but more likely that we will succeed if we adopt some Type B behaviors. In fact, there is a very surprising thing Type A's learn from what they are taught and later from what they experience. They discover that Type A behavior is really inefficient and that they can be more successful than ever before, after they start using stress management skills to achieve what they want.

What Do You Want?

Most Type A individuals want things that can be quantified. They want to acquire more things or more money, or to produce more. The things are almost as numerous as people. The artist may want to produce more paintings in less time, the carpenter more homes, the researcher more publications, the broker more sales, the physician more cures, and so forth.

These quantitative accumulations may lead to outward success, but a preoccupation with them can lead to an inner void. By concentrating on the things worth having, we may miss out on the things worth being or enjoying. After all, when we die, all that is left is the way we have lived our lifes. As the saying goes "you can't take it with you." Set aside some time to examine your goals and your abilities.

Much of the Type A's behavior is an attempt to store up accomplishments to overcome a general sense of insecurity and to control what is often not controllable. We need to take time to know who we are and where we are going. One way of doing this is to imagine yourself five, ten and twenty years from now. Set aside time and use visual imagery to look back at the goals you are striving for and the ways you are going about it. At times, it is helpful to remember that life is not a destination, but a road to be enjoyed.

While some research has not supported the importance of an achievement-orientation, two parts of the Type A behavior pattern have been confirmed over and over. These are time-urgency and aggressive competition. While it would not hurt to decrease the other behaviors described above, we will concentrate on these two.

Time-Urgency: Setting Priorities And Slowing Down

One of the best ways to decrease your sense of time-urgency, is to manage your time better and work more efficiently. We will spend a chapter on this later; but some of the suggestions that follow many be particularly helpful to the person with Type A behavior.

Using A Calendar Instead of A Stop Watch

Most Type A's try to do too much in too little time. They find themselves fighting time. It is as if they are using a stop watch every minute of their day. One of the best ways to throw away an invisible stop watch is to substitute a calendar as a time line to success. Think in terms of years and months rather than minutes and seconds. For most people this also involves setting weekly priorities that are realistic and that will take you efficiently from where you are to where you want to be. Read the time management chapter to help establish your priorities.

Slowing Down

Be sure to schedule time every day for the unexpected. Remember Murphy's law. If something can go wrong, it will. By leaving yourself extra time for each task, you will allow yourself to relax and enjoy the work. Schedule some time during the day between activities for relaxation. Avoid procrastination. It can lead to a rush just before the end of the day or a deadline.

When you start to feel impatient with someone or a task, use your impatience as a cue to relax. One of the tendencies Type A individuals have, is to interrupt conversations. When you feel the urge, or find yourself interrupting, use this as a signal to scan your body for tension and relax. Try not to assume that others are as impatient as you are. If you are late for a meeting, accept this human fallibility and avoid catastrophizing what the other person will do or say.

At the office, have someone screen all of your visitors and telephone calls. If you allow everyone to reach you at any time and even when you have someone in your office, you will probably try to hurry the caller or the person that you are with. This struggle will trigger the stress response. If your calls are not screened, try to screen them yourself. Indicate that you are in conference and will call the party back. This is particularly important for homemakers. You have to show that you have enough belief in your right to decide what you will do, to express your wishes to the caller.

Try to clear your desk of reminders of things to do. A list of "To Do's For Today" can be left inside a drawer or an appointment book. This way you can concentrate on the task at hand and have sense of security.

We all have a limited amount of time in life; and, in the words of Kenneth Grooms, "There is more to life than increasing its speed." Rather than trying to hurry everything, try to choose the things you will do and the people you will talk to. If someone is chewing off your ear, assert your right to end the conversation politely. Be firm and clear. You may want to read the chapters on Assertiveness Training to help you in keeping conversations from getting out of hand. When a telephone call is dragging out and you have things to do, let the other person know and, if necessary, hang up.

Part Of The Uncontrollable Is Controllable

A number of researchers have determined that the most stressful situations, and those which are most likely to elicit or trigger Type A behavior, are those that are uncontrollable. Whenever you feel you cannot influence or change a situation, look carefully at your options and your goals. Many times, assertiveness can help you regain the control you will need so that the situation will not trigger your Type A behavior. In those situations that cannot be controlled, remind yourself that, while you cannot always control the world, you can control your body's response to the world.

When you find yourself rushing to get something done, ask yourself "Has anything ever failed because it was done too well, too slowly?" If you sense that you are trying too hard to get closure on something by finishing it, it may help to remember that only a corpse is completely finished! Perhaps this is part of the reason why we use the term "deadline."

In many jobs, the worker is the one who decides when the work is done. Too many Type A's never make that decision. If you always choose to work late, time will never make the decision that your work is done until it's too late. Practice deciding when your work for the day is finished.

These changes are not easy to make and you will need to remind yourself. "Hurry up" sickness is a chronic illness. Be patient, even about making these changes. Leave yourself messages to slow down. When you do slow down, reward yourself in some way. If you put a project aside at the end of a day rather than pushing yourself to complete it, congratulate yourself. Keep a record of these successes. You could be adding days and years to your life.

Aggressive Competition Or Calm Confidence

People with Type A behaviors tend to be hostile and competitive. Read the chapter on anger management and when you start to get angry, remember to use it as a cue to relax and to strive for calm confidence. Use your thinking and your self-talk to work on the false perceptions you may have of threats, demands and challenges. When you are starting to get angry at someone because they are not doing something quickly enough, check your beliefs. You may be saying something like, "If I don't get this person to do this in time for the deadline, I will loose my job and look like a fool." Plan time for the unexpected and remember, "If at first you don't succeed, you're running about average."

Apply skills from the assertiveness chapters when you feel irritated or hostile. Be aware that some people may try to trigger your aggressive response. Try to avoid those who trigger your hostility, particularly other Type A individuals. If you get into an argument, ask yourself if winning the argument will really bring you what you want.

Developing Your Type B Behaviors

In the coming weeks, try to set aside time to expand your interests and your friendships. Take your lunch breaks if you usually work through them. Find people to share new experiences with. Try to find Type B individuals and increase your time with these people. They will help you appreciate the things which you may have left behind in your rush toward accumulating numbers and accomplishments. Rather than rushing past things on your way through life, become more receptive to the world around you.

Try to delegate work. If you think no one else can do your job, imagine what would happen if you died. Most companies would find a substitute. If you own your company, consider delegation as life insurance for your family.

Friedman and Rosenman point out the importance of rituals and traditions as ways of enjoying our lives and bringing new meaning to them. If you have moved away from traditions, and you have become preoccupied with work, you may find it enjoyable to create new family traditions or revive old ones.

One of the few things we are guaranteed in our travel through life is experience. Try to expand and enrich your experiencing through hobbies, reading, the humanities and nature. It is interesting that you cannot compete for these sorts of experience, because you are the only one who can have and enjoy them. If we move through life trying to get more things done in less time, the days will pass all too quickly. We may end up having sold our right to experience and having received very little in return.

To begin enjoying new experiences, you may need to consciously give yourself permission to use time for them. You may find yourself saying "Tomorrow, I'll let myself enjoy that." Remember, life is fragile and tomorrow may not be yours to count on. There is an old saying that applies to many things, but especially to changing Type A to Type B behaviors: If not now, when?

Social Insecurity

A recent study of heart disease patients showed that it was possible to differentiate between those patients with more serious coronary artherosclerosis and those who have less serious coronary artherosclerosis. The differentiation could be made using not only Type A behavior patterns, but also measures of social insecurity. In fact, of the 58 men having greater amounts of artherosclerosis, only 25% of those in the serious group had neither Type A behavior pattern nor social insecurity. The frequency of severe artherosclerosis in those patients having both characteristics was 91% of the cases.

Social insecurity was indicated by those patients reporting bashfulness, low-self confidence, sensitivity to criticism, difficulty thinking of things to say in groups, difficulty trusting people and self-consciousness. They also tended to answer "no" when asked if they were "good mixers" or enjoyed many different kinds of play and recreation.

This study suggests that those Type A behavior individuals who are also socially insecure may have more heart disease. Perhaps their striving for success and their striving to increase their attractiveness to others via accomplishments was a compensation for a lack of social security. Thus, those who are socially insecure may tend to spend more of their time pursuing success impatiently and aggressively. If you are socially insecure, you may spend more time at work and your hard driving characteristics may be rewarded, but you may never have time to enjoy the social rewards for which you are striving.

Think about your own social insecurity. If you find yourself anxious at parties and with other people, use the stress ladders in Chapter 13 to desensitize yourself. If you are less fearful of others, you will find it easier to spend more time in Type B behaviors and enjoy the company of others.

REVIEW QUESTIONS

<u>Directions</u>: Circle the letter in front of the best response to each question. The correct answers are provided on the page following the last question.

1. Since the turn of the century, the rates of death from coronary heart disease in American have

    a. decreased.
    b. increased.
    c. leveled off.
    d. remained the same.

2. Smoking, obesity, cholesterol, diabetes, genetics, or a sedentary life style _____ new cases of coronary heart disease.

    a. can be found in all
    b. explain 90% of all
    c. are absent in nearly half of the
    d. explain only 10% of all

3. In the Western Collaborative Group Study, Drs. Friedman and Rosenman found that the Type A men had _____ rate of coronary heart disease of the Type B Men.

    a. one-half the
    b. twice the
    c. a fourth the
    d. the same

4. All of the following behaviors are Type A <u>except</u>

    a. moves, walks, eats and talks rapidly.
    b. aggressively competitive.
    c. tries to achieve more and more in less and less time.
    d. relaxing with their families.

5. Type A behavior is often inefficient because when we rush we can

    a. make many more mistakes.
    b. become rigid and try the same thing over and over again.
    c. become less creative and effective in problem solving.
    d. All the above.

6. To give up Type A behavior, it is helpful to concentrate on

    a. the things worth having.
    b. the things worth being or enjoying.
    c. the things worth accomplishing.
    d. All the above.

7. In setting priorities, it is important to look at your

    a. lifetime goals.
    b. short-term goals.
    c. immediate goals.
    d. All the above.

8. To slow down, all but one of the following is helpful.

    a. Schedule time every day for the unexpected and for
        relaxation.
    b. Avoid procrastinating and rushing to achieve closure.
    c. Use a stop watch not a calendar.
    d. Use your anger and impatience as cues to relax.

9. Two skills are particularly useful in decreasing
    aggressive competitiveness.

    a. Anger Management and Assertiveness Training
    b. Progressive Relaxation and Deep Muscle Relaxation
    c. Progressive Relaxation and Time Management
    d. Exercise and Time Management

10. To develop Type B behaviors, people can

    a. spend more time with Type B people and be more receptive
        to the world around them.
    b. delegate work.
    c. enrich their experience through hobbies, reading and
        nature.
    d. give themselves permission to enjoy all the above
        activities.

ANSWERS TO REVIEW QUESTIONS

1.	b	6.	b
2.	c	7.	d
3.	b	8.	c
4.	d	9.	a
5.	d	10.	d

SUGGESTED BOOKS AND RECORDINGS

BOOKS

The Living Heart by M. DeBakey & A. Gotto. New York: McKay, 1977.

Type A Behavior And Your Heart by M. Friedman and R. Rosenman. New York: Knopf, 1975.

RECORDINGS

How Long Will I Live? by L. Galton. Waco, Texas: S.M.I., 1980.

Shyness: What Is It? What To Do About It? by P. Zimbardo. New York: B.M.A., 1980.

Chapter 15

How Beliefs Influence Experience:
Thinking And Feeling Better

If Names Will Never Hurt You, What Causes Bad Feelings?

Are you ready to learn something about emotions that surprises many people? Feelings and emotions we experience are not caused by the events that precede them. For example, if someone calls us a name or if we lose money in the stock market, we might say that this made us angry or brought us disappointment. Our reasoning may seem to be true, but it is faulty.

The same events can lead to very different feelings in different people. If you wanted to make someone angry at you and they called you a name, you might be pleased. If you needed a stock market loss as a deduction for your income tax, such a loss might make you feel good. Feelings are not caused by events, otherwise everyone would have the same feelings after any given event. Another example may help clarify these ideas.

One Event, Many Feelings

One of the authors was teaching an introductory course in psychology. About a week after the mid-term examination, his lecture was on emotions. The author arrived with a stack of exams and told the class that the mid-term grades could not be used because widespread cheating had been brought to his attention. He explained that because of this, he was giving the test again.

You can imagine what people felt. Think of yourself in this situation. What would you feel? Anxiety? Anger? Confusion? Most people felt these negative feelings. It might surprise you to learn that some people were very happy, some doubted the teacher, and others claimed they did not feel anything! Different people had very different reactions to the same event. It was clear that the event did not cause all these different feelings. In fact, if the author's wife was sitting in the audience, she might have had another feeling. She might have feared for the life of the teacher! How could the same event cause so many different feelings?

The ABC's Of Emotions

Dr. Albert Ellis, a renowned psychologist, developed a theory to answer this sort of question. He reasoned that the true causes of feelings are not the events, but the beliefs we have about these events. Dr. Ellis proposed a simple model to help us better understand emotions. The ABC's of emotions are:

"A's" are the activating events. In the above situation, the teacher's announcement was the activating event.

"B's" are the beliefs. In the above case, these were what each student believed about what the teacher said.

"C's" are emotional consequences. In the above example, these were all the different feelings that the students were having.

Most of the students who felt anger or anxiety had done well on the first exam, and were concerned about doing poorly on the second exam. Most of those who were pleased, had failed the exam and were happy to get a second chance. Others might have been pleased if they thought there had been widespread cheating and the cheaters were about to get their "due." Most of those who claimed that they did not feel any strong emotions, did not believe the author's announcement. The author's wife might have believed that someone would throw something at her husband!

This way of understanding our feelings is not new. As Dr. Ellis points out, the famous stoic, Epictetus, wrote "Men are disturbed not by things, but by the views which they take of them." William Shakespeare later rephrased this concept in Hamlet, "There's nothing either good or bad but thinking makes it so."

The Boss And Your Beliefs

Take another example. If your boss calls you into his office, his intent may be to compliment your work. But, before you go into his office, you wonder why he wants to see you. You may decide that he wants you to work late again and you may be irritated about the amount of work you are already doing. By

the time you get into his office you may be really angry that he
would ask more of you. In this example, "A" is the boss calling
you into his office, "B" is the belief that he wants you to do
more work, and "C" is the anger which you feel boiling up inside
of you.

You may have prejudiced your feelings, actions, and your
physiological reactions with your belief about the purpose for
being called into the boss's office. If you knew that the boss
was going to compliment you, the activating event (A) would have
been the same (boss calling you into his office), but your
belief system (B) would have been different. In turn, the
emotional consequence (C) would also have been different -
perhaps pleasure or even excitment.

If beliefs cause the feelings we experience, we should be
able to change our feelings or emotions by changing our
beliefs. False and irrational beliefs may cause harmful,
self-defeating and unnecessary feelings. To change irrational
beliefs, it is necessary to examine our beliefs and dispute
them.

Can't Stand-itis, Awfulizing, Musterbation, And Other Stressful Habits: Anger

Four irrational statements can be related to feelings of
anger. These are the beliefs that may cause you to feel the
stress response in many situations for which it is
inappropriate. Do you think one or more of these irrational
thoughts when you are angry?

(1)   "How awful for you to have treated me so unfairly."
      This can be called awfulizing. How often do you find
      yourself taking one thing and exploding it out of
      proportion into being "awful" instead of just
      unpleasant?

(2)   "I can't stand your treating me in such an
      unreasonable and unjust manner." These are the "can't
      stand it" type of beliefs that many of us suffer
      from. "I can't stand-itis" is the pain that come from
      "can't standing" something.

(3)   "You should not, must not behave that way toward me."
      This is sometimes called "musterbation" and often
      leads to the stress response and to anger.

(4)   "Because you have acted in that manner toward me, I
      find you a terrible person who deserves nothing good

in life, and you should get punished for treating me so." This is sometimes called undeservingness and damnation thinking.

All these statements tend to exaggerate our view of situations and upset us.

Can't Stand-itis, Awfulizing, Musterbation, And Other Stressful Habits: Anxiety

If you have difficulty with public speaking, you may find yourself using four similar statements that are related to feelings of anxiety.

(1) "How awful if I can't manage things." This is another form of awfulizing. It may be unfortunate if you can't manage something, but it is not awful.

(2) I couldn't stand my poor methods of coping with this situation." You stood it, or you wouldn't be able to upset yourself about it!

(3) "I should have the ability to deal with the situation better." Who says you should? Do you have enough training to do it better? Where is it written that you should?

(4) If I can't cope as well as I must cope, I am an inferior person, and I deserve what I get for not handling the situation." Perhaps you will have another chance. Why should you be punished for trying? Are you an inferior person or a person lacking skills in a particular area?

As you can see, anxiety statements can exaggerate the situation. Such statements tend to equate an evaluation of your actions with an evaluation of your whole being. These are irrational and unhealthy beliefs. The only way you can evaluate yourself or another person is to evaluate all of his or her actions over an entire lifetime. Few of us have the time to do so or the desire to take that responsibility!

Finding The Enemy Beliefs

How can we attack and dispute these irrational beliefs so we can remain calm and avoid the anger or anxiety that can trigger the stress response? First, we must discover our main irrational beliefs.   We can do this by looking for the "shoulds," "musts" and "have to's" in what we say and think. We can listen for words like "awful," "terrible" and "impossible." Finally, we can listen for words like "I can't stand that."

Common Problems: Finding The Sharks Under The Fins

Sometimes, the irrational beliefs are difficult to find. We may be thinking them so quickly that they are almost automatic. In this case, one has to trace his or her thinking step-by-step, backwards and forwards, to figure out where the irrational beliefs are lurking.

Helpful Hints

Another way of uncovering the self-defeating beliefs you may suffer from is to go through a list of beliefs which Dr. Albert Ellis and his colleague, Dr. Robert Harper, introduce in their book, A Guide to Rational Living. Most irrational ideas concern either ourselves and our self-worth or the people and events around us. For this reason, we have divided the list into those beliefs which seem to be primarily about ourselves and those beliefs which are primarily about other people and other things. As you go through these lists, check off those which seem to be ones which may be causing you some pain and problems in living, so you can return to them later.

Self-Directed Irrational Beliefs

The first five are those which have to do with yourself:

1. I need everyone's love and approval for just about everything I do.
2. I should be able to do everything well.
3. If something bad might happen, I had better worry about it.
4. It is easier to avoid difficult things than to try them and risk failure.
5. I will enjoy life more if I avoid responsibilities and take what I can get now.

Other-Directed Irrational Beliefs

Five other irrational beliefs, which Drs. Ellis and Harper describe at length, are equally important to recognize. These five have to do with beliefs we may have about the way things or other people "should" be.

1. Some people are bad and should be punished.
2. When things aren't going well in my life, it is terrible.
3. If things go wrong, I'm going to feel bad and there's very little I can do about those feelings.
4. What has happened to me and what I have done in the past, determines the way I feel and what will happen to me now and in the future.
5. People and things should be different, and perfect solutions should be found for everything.

Categorize Some Common Irrational Beliefs

To help you begin to identify irrational beliefs and categorize them as those which come from thoughts about ourselves or thoughts about other people, read through the following statements and underline only those which are about ourselves. The thoughts you do not underline are about other people or events outside yourself.

The world is unjust. My parents should not boss me around. It would be awful if I wasn't popular. I deserve to be punished the rest of my life. People should not get divorced. Because I work hard people should love me. If I ask her and she refuses, it's going to be awful. Because I have suffered, people should be kind to me. If I fail, I am worthless. My parents should love me and approve of what I do. If he doesn't like me, I am worthless and valueless. If I can't find a solution, I must be dumb or stupid. You just can't trust anyone. I was born a loser.

A Case Example: Mrs. Williams

Another way to review these ten commonly held unhealthy beliefs is to consider the following problems that a secretary can get into if she holds these beliefs about her job.

One of the authors treated a secretary. We will call her Mrs. Williams. Mrs. Williams was referred by her gastroenterologist for a nervous stomach. She worked for two executives who were very demanding; and yet, they seldom spoke to her other than to point out corrections that needed to be made.

Mrs. Williams began worrying that she was incompetent and that she might lose her job. She began typing faster, making more mistakes, and avoiding difficult tasks for fear of failing. At the same time, she was angry at her bosses for not being different, and she felt they should be called on the carpet by their superior. Life seemed terrible. Mrs. Williams just knew she would feel badly everyday she continued working.

It became clear in our interviews that Mrs. Williams' central irrational belief was that without approval for her work, she "would just die." By slowly disputing this and other beliefs, she was able to accept the conditions at the office until she could apply for a transfer. For example, she came to realize that, although gaining the approval of everyone she worked for would be very nice indeed, it was an unrealistic expectation and that she was more likely to get the approval of her friends and family than her bosses.

Mrs. Williams also saw how trying to be a faster typist and avoiding difficult tasks were making the problem worse. She began to reason that it would be great if her bosses would get reprimanded, but they were, in fact, getting the work done satisfactorialy. It was unlikely that they would be reprimanded or change their ways. She then learned how to express her feelings and her needs from the assertiveness skills that she was also learning in therapy. In addition, Mrs. Williams realized that, no matter what happened at work, part of her life might be unpleasant, but life itself was not terrible.

As a result, her stomach was less upset. At follow-up, she stated that, in the end, she had decided to get a new job. However, Mrs. Williams said that she was also pleased because she could take the "ups and downs" better now because her happiness did not depend as much on what happened in the office.

Role-Related Irrational Beliefs

Each of us has a variety of roles in life that can hook us into suffering the emotional consequences of irrational beliefs. One good example is the super mom who may believe that she has to be all things to all the people in her family and at her job. Take some time to look at your roles and some of the irrational beliefs you may have about them.

Attacking Your Irrational Beliefs

The next step is to debate your irrational beliefs actively and vigorously. Ask "What makes it awful?" (or "terrible," "horrible," etc.), "Why can't I stand it?", "Why must they never do that?" and "Where is it written that they must not do that or that I must do that?" Finally, ask "Why should I judge the whole person or myself on the basis of one or even several acts?" You will have to attack your irrational beliefs vigorously and repeatedly to get the full benefit of thinking and feeling better.

Exposing Your Inner Enemies: ABC Charts

To help you detect and dispute your irrational beliefs, complete the chart below. First, identify the stressful emotions you are experiencing. Write those in on the lines next to emotional consequences. Then, fill in the activating event that seems to be triggering your stress response under "A" for activating event.

Now, go back and try to figure out the beliefs that you hold and fill those in under "B" for beliefs. You may want to check the lists of beliefs just presented. Do this for most of the anger-arousing or anxiety-producing events that you encounter. Then begin to dispute the irrational beliefs by using the questions that we just reviewed. Finally, identify the new, healthier feelings that come with better thinking.

RATIONAL-EMOTIVE A TO E CHARTS

A. Activating Event (Example): *Boss pointing out my errors*

B. Irrational Belief (Example): *I must be totally incompetent and I am sure I will loose my job*

C. Emotional or Stressful Consequence (Example): *Anxiety, terror*

D. Dispute Your Irrational Belief (Example): *It would be nice if I did not make any mistakes, but I am not totally incompetent, just human*

E. New, Less Stressful Emotion (Example): *Some appropriate concern motivated to get the work finished*

xxxxxxxxxxxxxxxxxxxxxxxxxxxxxxxxxxxxxxxxxxxxxxxxxxxxxxxxxxxxxxxxxxxxxxxx

A. Activating Event _____

B. Irrational Belief _____

C. Emotional or Stressful Consequence _____

D. Dispute Your Irrational Belief _____

_____

E. New, Less Stressful Emotion _____

xxxxxxxxxxxxxxxxxxxxxxxxxxxxxxxxxxxxxxxxxxxxxxxxxxxxxxxxxxxxxxxxxxxxxxxx

A. Activating Event _____

B. Irrational Belief _____

C. Emotional or Stressful Consequence _____

D. Dispute Your Irrational Belief _____

_____

E. New, Less Stressful Emotion _____

xxxxxxxxxxxxxxxxxxxxxxxxxxxxxxxxxxxxxxxxxxxxxxxxxxxxxxxxxxxxxxxxxxxxxxxx

Common Problems, Uncommon Sense

Below are some anger and anxiety-management principles which you may find helpful in applying what you have been learning. Some people can easily see themselves in each of the principles. Other people are more involved with one or another or just a few of them. Circle or underline the ones that might be of help to you.

Uncommon Sense For Self-Doubt

For many people, becoming angry has something to do with doubting themselves, being unsure or feeling threatened by someone else. It's important to remember that you are a fallible human being, but, nonetheless, a worthy person and one with many good qualities. To be fallible means to be able to make mistakes. We are sure you realize that you are bound to make mistakes; but many of us have the irrational belief that we should be perfect. In addition, be sure that you understand your worth, not in terms of your accomplishments or your appearance. All of these will fade in time. You are worthwhile in terms of your natural ability to experience life and to share it with others.

Uncommon Sense For Anger

Sometimes we get angry because we take things personally when there is no need to. When someone is being directly offensive to you, you can control and contain your anger by staying with whatever you are doing. This is called staying "task-oriented." Stay focused and stick to what must be done in the situation to get the outcome you want. When you begin taking insults personally, you get distracted from your tasks and get caught up in unnecessary feelings. Recognize that the other person may be deliberately provoking you. By realizing what the other person is doing, you may find it easier to stay task-oriented.

Sometimes we get angry or anxious simply because it is what we have always done in a certain kind of situation. As you learn alternate ways of reacting to provocations or demanding situations, you will be less inclined to react with anger or anxiety. Try to catch yourself if you are saying self-defeating and irrational things like "I was born that way," and "You can't teach an old dog new tricks." These are irrational, self-defeating beliefs.

One of the most important things you can do to control your anger is to recognize the signs of arousal or the stress response as soon as they occur. As you become more and more sharply attuned to the signs of tension and upset inside of you, you will achieve greater ability to short circuit the anger process. You will be able to turn it off before it gets too strong. Intense anger can make you agitated and impulsive. As you learn to relax more easily, and quickly dispute your irrational beliefs, your ability to regulate anger will improve.

Anger As A Useful Signal

Your anger can serve a very useful function. It can be an alerting sign that you are becoming upset and that effective action is called for. Knowing that you can short circuit your anger or anxiety, you will be less agitated and impulsive. When we are agitated or impulsive, we can make more mistakes and this leads to still more anxiety and anger. Stay task-oriented and instruct yourself to relax and dispute your irrational beliefs.

Sometimes we get angry because things look like they are getting out of hand and we want to take charge. Sometimes we get concerned that things will not go the way we want them to, so we get angry trying to control them. We can learn ways of managing our anger and, thus, we can be in better control of situations. Dispute your belief that you "have to" get angry to change something. One of the best ways of taking charge of the situation is remaining calm when most people expect you, or even want you, to be upset.

Sometimes we get annoyed, upset and angry because we have spent more time being conscious of our failures than conscious of our successes. We sometimes forget or dismiss the good things that we do and, yet, we never let ourselves get away with the mistakes and short-comings that we have.

Now that you are learning to recognize and dispute irrational beliefs, be careful not to berate yourself when you have irrational beliefs and when you forget to dispute them! Remember, it's irrational to think you'll learn these skills overnight or become perfect. Beware of the belief "I should be able to relax and stay calm in all situations!"

Try to remember to congratulate yourself whenever you accomplish something, particularly if you have been able to relax or manage your anger. Let yourself feel good about all of these successes. Enjoy each step in your evolution toward your goals.

REVIEW QUESTIONS

<u>Directions</u>: Circle the letter in front of the best response of each question. The correct answers are provided on the page following the last question.

1. You have invited someone over for dinner. The person is an hour late and you are angry.

    a. The person's lateness made you angry.
    b. If the person had called, it would have made you less angry.
    c. If the person had been late before, it would have made you more angry.
    d. None of the above are true. What the person did or did not do is not the cause of your anger.

2. If what the person who is late did or did not do is <u>not</u> the cause of your anger, what is the cause?

    a. The hour you lost by waiting for the person to arrive or call.
    b. Your beliefs about why the person is late and what it means to you.
    c. How long it has been since you have seen the person.
    d. How much time you will be able to visit.

3. According to Dr. Ellis, what leads to what?

    a. An event leads to a feeling. The feelings lead to belief.
    b. An event leads to an event. The event leads to a feeling.
    c. An event leads to a belief. The belief leads to a feeling.
    d. A feeling leads to a belief. The belief leads to the event.

4. Stressful feelings of anger may arise from one or more irrational statements. Choose the statement(s) that often lead to stressful feelings of anger.

    a. "How awful for you to have treated me so unfairly. I can't stand you treating me that way."
    b. "You must not and should not treat me like that."
    c. "You are a terrible person who should be punished for treating me like that."
    d. All the above.

5. Stressful feelings of anxiety may arise from one or more irrational statements. Choose the statement(s) that often lead to stressful feelings of anxiety.

   a. "This is an unpleasant situation and one which I would like to change."
   b. "How awful it is if I can't manage things."
   c. "It would be nice if I could deal with this situation better, but it is okay if I can't."
   d. "I've made a mistake. I am as human and as fallible as anyone else."

6. If a person changes his _____ beliefs, he can change his _____ feelings.

   a. rational; stressful
   b. false; true
   c. irrational; stressful
   d. true; false

7. To use the ABC's of emotions for stress management you must first _____ your irrational beliefs and then _____ them.

   a. find; dispute
   b. hide; find
   c. find; hide
   d. hide; dispute

8. It is important not to take things personally and not to doubt ourselves. To do this:

   a. Remember, you are a fallible human being, but that this is okay because each of us is worthwhile in terms of our natural ability to experience life and share it with others.
   b. Stay focused and stick to what must be done to get the outcome you want.
   c. Keep practicing. Learning new ways of reacting takes time.
   d. All of the above.

9. All of the following statements are irrational beliefs except:

   a. "I need everyone's love and approval."
   b. "If something bad might happen, I had better worry about it."
   c. "When things aren't going well in my life, it is unpleasant."
   d. "People and things should be different."

10. In our haste to criticize our failures we often

   a. overlook all the good things we do.
   b. get more annoyed, upset, and angry than is healthy.
   c. forget to congratulate ourselves and to feel good about our successes.
   d. All the above.

ANSWERS TO REVIEW QUESTIONS

1.	d	6.	c
2.	b	7.	a
3.	c	8.	d
4.	d	9.	c
5.	b	10.	d

SUGGESTED BOOKS AND RECORDINGS

BOOKS

I Can If I Want To by A. Lazarus & A. Fay. New York: Warner, 1978.

A New Guide To Rational Living by A. Ellis & R. Harper. Los Angeles: Wilshire, 1975.

RECORDINGS

Controlling Depression Through Cognitive Therapy: Self-Management Guide And Clinical Procedure by G. Emery. New York: B.M.A., 1982.

Rational Emotive Self-Help Techniques by A. Ellis. New York: B.M.A., 1980.

Chapter 16

The Movies
Of Your Mind:
Anxiety

In the last chapter, we described how our thinking affects what we feel. You learned how irrational beliefs can lead to self-defeating feelings and unhealthy stress. In this chapter, we will go beyond irrational thinking by replacing it with positive talking. The work we are about to present comes from a new area of psychology called cognitive behavior modification.

Many psychologists have proposed that what we think is really best understood as self-talk. These psychologists have helped us understand that what we silently say to ourselves about the events we experience influences us in many profound ways. What we say to ourselves changes what we see and hear around us, what we feel within us, and what we remember when we look back on our experiences. In this chapter, we will be concentrating on the ways in which the things you say to yourself can help you to overcome anxiety. First let's examine how we can create anxiety by what we say.

What We Say Often Influences What We See, Hear, Feel and Remember

When we go to a haunted house at a carnival, what we say to ourselves can influence what we will see, hear, feel and remember about the experience. If we tell ourselves that we are alone in a real spooky house, we will see things as threatening and scary. When things loom or leer at us, we will tell ourselves that we are in danger. Likewise, if we hear the sounds that are being played in the haunted house, and tell ourselves that they are real, we are likely to feel chills running up and down our spines.

On the other hand, if we constantly tell ourselves that all of the things in the haunted house are fake and try to figure out how they were made to look real, we will probably not see ghosts or goblings, but bed sheets and paint. Likewise, we will hear sheets of metal being fluttered up and down, rather than thunder from lightening. If we say that it is all special effects, we probably will enjoy it and not feel anxious. When we look back on the experience, we will remember it as an interesting and fun show, rather than a frightening experience.

Take the example of what many of us say to ourselves when we interview for a job. If we are looking through the newspaper for a job advertisement and constantly say to ourselves that there is nothing there for us, we may be overlooking certain sections or jobs in the classifieds, because self-talk is affecting the way we see what is in front of us. Should we finally make an appointment, and walk in saying to ourselves that we do not have any skills and no one wants us, we may hear the interviewer's remarks somewhat differently than the way he says them.

If we are critical of our skills, we may not hear the interviewer's encouragement to see an associate who might be of help in finding a job. We may hear questions as attempts to find out what we cannot do, rather than what we can do. When we start to do this, we are likely to feel inadequate and anxious. If, upon returning home from such an interview, we say to ourselves that we will never get a job, then we are likely to remember only the negative things in the interview and not remember the positive ones.

All of these experiences are likely to give us, what some of our patients have called, the "screaming meemee's." It is clear from this example and from what we have learned about irrational beliefs in the last chapter, that negative thinking and self-talking can upset us and interfere with what we are doing.

Whistling A Happy Tune

One of the ways people deal with the anxiety of their self-talk is to whistle a happy tune. Any sort of distraction can help break the connection between our negative talk and the "screaming meemee's." Some people chew gum, smoke a cigarette, tap their fingers on a desk or shuffle their feet on the floor. Most of these things can lower our anxiety, but they can be annoying, and there are other, more exciting options.

The Power Of Positive Talking

The power of positive talking is very similar to the power of positive thinking that has been popularized by Norman Vincent

Peale. In this chapter, we will provide you with things to tell yourself that have been shown to improve performance and decrease the "screaming meemee's." The goal is to cope with anxious feelings so that you can concentrate on what you are doing, and remain in a relaxed state of mind and body.

To manage a stressful situation, we need to take steps at four major time periods. These phases can overlap, but usually they follow one after the other.

We need (1) to prepare for the stressful situation, (2) to cope with feelings as they start to build, (3) to cope with feelings as they start to overwhelm us, and finally (4) to cope when the feelings have passed. Each step is important in helping you to enjoy coping. By breaking an experience into four parts and learning ways of coping with each, a potentially frightening experience can become interesting and challenging, rather than overwhelming and unbearable.

One of the problems with positive talking occurs when we get stuck and don't know what to say to ourselves. Some of us have this problem in the early phases and others in the later phases of frightening or anxiety-provoking situations. This chapter will help you with each phase by providing clear, positive things to tell yourself each step of the way.

The Talkies

Some of our patients have found it helpful to think of their anxiety-provoking events as part of a scary movie. In an earlier chapter, you learned how to start using imagery for relaxing and rehearsing. Up until now, these have been silent movies. It is time to turn these silent "home movies" into talkies.

In this chapter, you will concentrate on the horror movies of your life. In the next chapter, you will deal with the situations where anger can get out of hand. So, when you are finished with the horror movies, you can turn to the war movies.

Waiting In Line For A Ticket To A Horror Movie

Preparing for a stressful situation that evokes anxiety is the first phase in maintaining a relaxed state of mind and body. We need to rehearse what we plan to do, and we need to replace negative thinking with positive thinking. Imagine this rehearsal as what you say while waiting in line for a ticket to the horror movie.

If you are scheduled to give a speech in front of a business group in a half hour, what you say to yourself will affect what you will do and feel. Some of the ways of reducing anxiety while you wait for your turn at speaking can be memorized or even written on a piece of paper to review.

One of the most important things to say, is to ask yourself "What is it that I have to do?" This helps to focus us on the task at hand rather than all of the fears that we may have about doing it. You can tell yourself to think about what you will have to say so that you will have less time to upset yourself with thoughts of failure. You may review your outline of what you will say and even jot down a few notes about issues to address. Do not, however, begin to make major changes in your presentation.

You have learned several ways of reducing your stress response and you could say "This may be difficult, but I know some ways to deal with it." You may want to tell yourself "Time for a few deep breaths and relaxation. I feel more comfortable, relaxed and at ease. I know this material very well and I have worked hard at preparing it." Another thing to say is, "No putting myself down; I'll just think about what I need to do." If you start to worry, you can tell yourself "Stop worrying; I can do it."

Concentrate on your past successes rather than your past failures. Thinking about your successes will lead to calming self-confidence. You may say that you have never succeeded. This is highly unlikely and usually comes from an irrational belief that what we do is either all good or all bad. In reality, almost everything we do involves some successful actions -- concentrate on these and you will decrease your anxiety while you build your self-confidence.

Many times, when we are waiting to do something that has caused us anxiety in the past, we can work ourselves into a frenzie before it even starts. If we tell ourselves that we will never be able to do it or that people are going to laugh at us, we may loose sleep the night before and fail to prepare adequately for our talk. By saying the positive things we have just reviewed, you can help keep yourself in a calm state and prepare for the event while you wait for it.

The things you tell yourself are often self-fulfilling prophesies. Let's strive to make the prophesies those of calmness and coping, rather than those of gloom and doom.

As The Plot Thickens

The next part to learn for coping with anxiety is what to say when the feelings start to build. In a film, this corresponds to the section created to build tension in the audience. Many of us hope that we will not feel any anxiety, and then get even more anxious, when we begin to feel scared. We start to catastrophize and tell ourselves that, since we are feeling a little anxious, we will be overwhelmed before we know it. These sorts of pessimistic ideas only increase our anxiety. They are also self-fulfilling prophesies.

Many people are anxious when they are going to meet new people at a party. They may cope well on the way to the party, but become very anxious as they walk toward a group of new people. This is when "the plot thickens," and we need to know what to say to ourselves.

You can tell yourself that the anxiety is a good reminder to begin using the relaxation skills you have mastered. You might say "My muscles are starting to feel a little tight. Time to relax. Time to slow down." As the anxiety builds, you may want to say "I can meet this challenge." As you are walking across the floor, each step seems longer than the next, and you don't know what you are going to do when you finally reach the new people, you can say "One step at a time; I can handle the situation."

Of course, you also need to have a plan for approaching any situation. Much fun is made of standard or "pat" greetings, but they can help open conversations. On the other hand, you may overcome the anxiety that prevents you from entering a conversation, but still lack the social skills to carry on a conversation. The classic book, How To Win Friends and Influence People by Dale Carnegie, is a good guide for learning some of these skills.

As your anxiety rises, you can say, "I'll just think about what I have to do." Once again, this helps us to remember that it is best to concentrate on the task at hand. In this case, you may wish to observe the people you are meeting, what they are wearing and what they are doing, so that you can ask some appropriate questions and express interest in them. The next thing you might say is, "Relax; I'm in control. I'll take a slow, deep breath." These positive statements should help you cope better and enjoy meeting people.

On The Edge Of Your Seat

When you are in the middle of an event and you are concerned that your anxiety might overwhelm you, it is similar to sitting on the edge of your seat during a scary movie. Knowing what to say to yourself can make a big difference. Some of us expect ourselves to be super cool and do the impossible. When our feelings start to overwhelm us, we are tempted to give up, escape the situation or try avoiding the next task.

Take the student who is in the middle of an examination and begins to sweat, shake and feel dizzy. Giving up, escaping or avoiding will not help to pass the exam. One of the best things the student can say is, "I'm not surprised I'm anxious. That's okay. I can handle it."

In many situations, like examinations, it is possible to take a break and say to yourself, "I'll label my fear from 0 to 10. Five is motivating, but I'll pause and relax if it reaches 8." In addition, a person can say, "When fear comes, I'll just pause," or "It's okay to be anxious. I can handle it." The student may need to remind himself "I won't try to eliminate the feeling totally: I'll just keep it manageable." Finally, the student may find it helpful to say, "I'll pay attention to the present: I'll answer one question at a time. I'll take a deep breath between questions."

All of these positive statements can help you when your feelings start to overwhelm you. You can see where they turn irrational beliefs around by helping us to accept our fallibility and to keep us task oriented.

Studies of anxiety have shown that there are facilitative and debilitative levels of anxiety. In the case of a student taking an examination, there needs to be enough anxiety so his attention does not wander and he is motivated to read the questions and answer them. Too little anxiety would actually be self-defeating. This would be almost as debilitating as when the student is so anxious he cannot concentrate.

Somewhere in the middle of two little and too much is just the right amount of anxiety. This applies, not only to examinations but, to most activities in life. Many people find trying to do new activities to be scary. It is good to remember that some of this anxiety is helpful and that it will help us to concentrate and to learn. In addition, in many areas of sports the anxiety can help us excel. The positive thinking and talking we have just reviewed help us to keep our anxiety in the right ball park for all of life's games.

A Sigh Of Relief

One of the most important phases of anxiety and anxiety management is the final phase, after the event has been concluded and the curtain goes down. We need to know what to do to optimize coping when it's all over and the feelings have passed.

This is a very unique opportunity for positive talk. It helps us to put things in perspective and to reward ourselves for our accomplishments. When we get a reward for something we have done, we are more likely to do it again. In this case, if we reward ourselves for positive talking, we are more likely to use the skill again in similar situations.

Take the example of a couple who is cleaning up after entertaining friends for the first time in a new neighborhood. Some of the guests may have had a good time, and others may not have. It is helpful to put things into perspective by saying, "We didn't do everything that we wanted to do for our guests, but that's okay. We tried and that is what really counts," or "We can only do so much and then it's up to them to enjoy themselves." The couple might also say, "That wasn't really as hard as we thought."

To help themselves to continue using their stress management skills, the couple might say, "We are doing better at this! We are making progress!" They might spend some time reviewing how they felt and what they did about those feelings. Finally, they might say "We can be pleased with our progress."

Common Problems: But It's Too Scary To Think

Sometimes it seems we are so scared that we can not think positively. This is why it is very important to memorize the coping statements for each phase of the event. If we are anxious, it is more difficult, at times, to remember things. This is why we must really master and over-learn the phrases so they will be available quickly when we are anxious.

Some people find that the phrases we use are not quite right for their own problems. In this case, we suggest that you write down personal coping phrases. Be sure to include some phrases that will prepare you for the event, some to help remind you to relax as the feelings begin to build, some statements to help you cope when the feelings start to become stronger, and some statements to keep things in perspective after the event and encourage yourself in the future. Each of the four charts on pages 298 to 301 include spaces for your personal phrases.

Learning Your Lines

It is very important that you put the things you have been reading about into practice. This means that you will need to memorize the phrases and practice them systematically.

Helpful Hints

Many people feel too busy to memorize these phrases. Try to use periods during the day when you are waiting for a bus or checking out in a supermarket, or have other "free" times. These are good times to relax and review your new self-talk. Keep these phrases on a slip of paper in your wallet or pocketbook for review during your free time.

Do not try to learn all the statements at one time. It is useful to read all of them in the beginning, but choose only a few to memorize each day. It is often best to learn these statements just before you go to sleep and, for this reason, we recommend that you leave the list on your night stand.

When you practice, remember to avoid negative thinking. Negative thinking will only lead to avoidance or additional distress. Stay on guard against statements like "I always loose control when I get into arguments" or "I just can't cope with that, and I know I will get upset."

If you find that you are unable to remember the words in real life, try to remember at what times you have the most difficulty remembering your new self-talk. Then, go over the statements for these times again. Continue doing this and you will find yourself better and better able to cope with the feelings you have in stressful situations.

You may also want to use a movie or a television show to practice these statements. Most shows have a beginning, a middle, a climax and an ending. To practice, get prepared for the excitement, lower your arousal as feelings start to build, cope when feelings start to overwhelm, and, finally, reward yourself when the show is nearly over. You may get caught off guard, but that is not bad preparation for the way stress sometimes catches us napping in real life.

You may find it easier to start practicing with reruns of your favorite adventure shows before practicing this with new ones. Of course, you will not want to practice these skills all the time, because part of the fun of watching a show is the excitement we experience. This is also true of life!

Introduction To The Talkies

One of the ways to motivate yourself to learn the positive self-talk is to review the list of anxiety-provoking situations, which you prepared in Chapter 12. It is helpful to think about some of the things you tell yourself in those situations. Compare your personal self-talk to our suggested positive self-talk. List some of your anxiety situations below.

My Anxiety Situations

Situations	Self-Talk
Example: *Giving a talk in front of a large audience*	Example: *I hope I do well*
1.	
2.	
3.	
4.	

Counting Your Talks (Are You Talking To Yourself Enough?)

Spend a little time each day going through a different stressor and the four phases for coping with anxiety. If you have a few major stressors, you may want to spend more than a day on some of them. Go slowly, and use your skill of visual imagery so that, when you begin working on these things in real life, you will recall the statements and be able to cope more successfully. Make your "talkies" as clear and provoking as you can. It's helpful to exaggerate the fearful events to test your skills and to stretch them.

Each time you go through the exercise of imagining a stressor and applying each of the four phases, fill in the blanks on the chart at the end of this chapter. All this takes practice. The more you practice in your imagination, the better you will be able to cope with the feelings in real life.

The Positive Self-Talk of Winners

Dennis Waitley in his book, The Psychology of Winning, emphasizes that we are motivated by our current dominant thought. We move in the direction of what we are thinking of most. Positive self-talk should focus on solutions and goals. It is much more effective to focus on what we want to achieve, than on moving away from our fears. If you focus on your fears, or even on trying to move away from your fears, then that is your dominant thought and you will be motivated by fear. If your focus is on a positive goal or achievement, then you will be motivated by it and you will move in that direction.

Let's look at what happens when we change the dominant thought from a goal to a fear. Imagine that we placed a 16-foot-long plank on the floor with a $10 bill at the end, and asked you to walk the plank to get the money. You would probably be more than happy to walk 16 feet for $10. Your current dominant thought is the goal of $10. If we used the same plank, but put it between two 20-story buildings and placed a $100 bill at the end, then the game would be changed. Now, would you walk the plank? Would your current dominant thought be the money or the fear of falling?

When you practice your positive self-talk, be sure to emphasize your goals and what you want to achieve. Use the following guidelines to help you practice and enjoy positive, goal-directed talking.

OUTLINE FOR POSITIVE TALKING

A. **Your new scripts.** Read slowly over the word-by-word positive talk on the following pages. Become as familiar as you can with each of these phrases.

B. **When to audition.** After you have read the words several times, try to think of each of the four time phases and write down the statements that belong in each section. Use the lines and the spaces provided on pages 302 to 303.

As in many of the other parts of this book, we suggest that you first go through the script in your imagination. This is like an audition for a film. Read your lines out loud several times. In addition, use each of the anxiety-provoking situations that you wrote down in Chapter 12, and talk yourself through each of the four time phases.

C. **Cameras, action!** When you have memorized your lines and practiced them in your imagination, choose the least anxiety-producing event on your list and begin to apply your new lines. You usually will not have time to use all of them, and for most situations, one or two positive sentences repeated a few times will help lower your anxiety. Be sure to use positive talk before the event, as the feelings begin to grow, when your anxiety becomes stronger and after the feelings have passed.

D. **Maintaining the action.** The winners in life can find something positive about everything. We know an extremely successful executive who always says "That's great!" when his employees bring him "bad news." Then, he and his employees find the silver linings. Eddie Cantor went broke during the depression, but turned bad into good by writing a best selling joke book that helped millions laugh their way through those difficult times.

Don't let others contribute negative self-talk that can interfere with your positive self-talk. If someone says how bad things look, either ignore their comment, or turn it around. Help the other person see the positive side of the situation.

E. **Use personal pronouns.** Use such words as "I", "my," and "me." This helps to personalize your self-talk.

F. **Present tense self-talk.** Self-talk should be in the present tense. Keep your self-talk in the present tense and avoid referring to the past or the future. Talk about what you are doing now, not what happened before or what may happen next.

G. <u>Give your self-talk positive direction.</u> Focus on what you want to achieve, not what you fear or want to avoid.

H. <u>Keep your self-talk non-competitive.</u> Focus on what you will do, rather than comparing what you do to what others do.

TALKING CALMLY WORD-BY-WORD TO COPE WITH ANXIETY

Preparing For Anxiety In Stressful Situations.

<u>Effective Self-Talk</u>	<u>Less Effective Self-Talk</u>
What is it I have to do?	There's so much to do.
I choose to do it.	I have to do it!
If I do the thing I fear, the fear is sure to die.	This is always frightening, but I'll do it.
I know ways to deal with this.	I think I can handle it.
I am well organized and efficient.	I can't forget what I need to say.
I have succeeded in situations like this one before. I am confident.	I won't worry anymore.
Time for a few deep breaths and relaxation. I am comfortable, relaxed and at ease.	Usually the deep breathing lessens the anxiety.

PERSONAL PHRASES TO PRACTICE

1. _____

_____

2. _____

_____

3. _____

_____

Coping When Anxiety Starts To Build.

Effective Self-Talk	Less Effective Self-Talk
My muscles are partially relaxed. Time to relax even more.	My muscles are getting tense I have to relax.
I can meet this challenge. Coping is my middle name.	This is frightening, but I think I'll be all right.
One step at a time. I can handle the situation.	I can't handle it unless I take one step at a time.
I'll just think about what I have to do.	Don't get distracted. Just do what you have to.
I'm in control. Relax and take a deep breath.	Don't get nervous, you are in control.

PERSONAL PHRASES TO PRACTICE

1. _____

_____

2. _____

_____

3. _____

_____

Coping When Anxiety Starts To Overwhelm.

Effective Self-Talk	Less Effective Self-Talk
Right now I feel nervous. However that's not like me. I'm also calm and confident.	Don't get nervous. You'll blow it.
If I do the thing I fear, the fear is sure to die.	I can't get afraid. I have to be cool.
I'll just pause. I _can_ handle it.	Don't slow down. You've just got to beat this.
I'll label my relaxation level from 0 to 10, so I keep it in a good range.	I'll label my fear from 0 to 10, so I can watch it rise.
It's okay to feel some fear. It motivates me to do my best.	I shouldn't be afraid.
I'll pay attention to the present.	I shouldn't let my anxiety show.
I won't try to eliminate fear totally. I'll just keep it manageable.	I've got to stop being afraid.

PERSONAL PHRASES TO PRACTICE

1. _____

   _____

2. _____

   _____

3. _____

   _____

Coping When It's All Over And The Anxiety Has Passed.

Effective Self-Talk	Less Effective Self-Talk
I didn't get everything I wanted. That's okay. I tried and that's what really counts.	I didn't get everything I wanted. I should have done better.
I have succeeded in some ways and I'll have these successes to draw on next time.	I wasn't a total success -- maybe next time.
I did the right things for myself. The other person may be a little angry or sad, but that's okay.	I shouldn't have hurt the other person's feelings.
That wasn't as hard I as thought. Next time it will even be easier.	I didn't think I would make it. I hope next time is easier.
I'm doing better at this. I'm making progress.	I'm not doing as well as I should.

PERSONAL PHRASES TO PRACTICE

1. _____

_____

2. _____

_____

3. _____

_____

STRESSFUL SITUATIONS AND POSITIVE SELF-TALK

Directions: Write in a description of several stressful situations involving anxiety. Each time you practice the coping statements, rate your degree of competence from 1 (total control) to 10 (loss of control) with 5 as anxious, but okay. Fill in one of the blanks until you have practiced doing this five times for each of the situations and phases listed.

Description of Anxiety- Arousing Situation	Cognitive Behavior Modification Statements:	Degree of Competence
Example: _giving a talk in front of a large audience_	I. Before _I am well prepared and I can relax_	7 5 6 3 2
	II. Beginning _I am in control. Relax, deep breath_	9 7 5 6 3
	III. Middle _I'll pay attention to making what I say easy to understand._	7 5 3 3 3
	IV. After _I'm doing better at this. That's progress_	3 3 2 3 1
1. _____	I. Before _____	_ _ _ _ _
_____	_____	
_____	II. Beginning _____	_ _ _ _ _
_____	_____	
_____	III. Middle _____	_ _ _ _ _
_____	_____	
_____	IV. After _____	_ _ _ _ _
_____	_____	

Description of Anxiety-Arousing Situation	Cognitive Behavior Modification Statements:	Degree of Competence
2. _____	I. Before _____	_ _ _ _ _
_____	_____	
_____	II. Beginning _____	_ _ _ _ _
_____	_____	
_____	III. Middle _____	_ _ _ _ _
_____	_____	
_____	IV. After _____	_ _ _ _ _
_____	_____	
3. _____	I. Before _____	_ _ _ _ _
_____	_____	
_____	II. Beginning _____	_ _ _ _ _
_____	_____	
_____	III. Middle _____	_ _ _ _ _
_____	_____	
_____	IV. After _____	_ _ _ _ _
_____	_____	

REVIEW QUESTIONS

<u>Directions</u>: Circle the letter in front of the best response to each question. The correct answers are provided on the page following the last question.

1. Cognitive behavior modification is a recent development. It can be used to help us cope with feelings by improving

    a. our surroundings.
    b. what we do.
    c. what we say to ourselves.
    d. our food.

2. The talkies involve coping with anxiety before we have it and

    a. as it starts to build.
    b. as it starts to overwhelm us.
    c. after it has passed.
    d. All the above.

3. It is not necessary to know how to cope with anxiety when it starts to overwhelm us

    a. because if we learn what to do, it will never start to overwhelm us.
    b. because we can usually escape such situations.
    c. because we can usually avoid such situations.
    d. None of the above is true. We need to know how to cope with anxiety when it starts to overwhelm us.

4. A cognitive behavior modification approach to feelings of anxiety can

    a. help remind us to use relaxation skills.
    b. eliminate feelings of anxiety entirely from our lives.
    c. be learned in one reading of the statements we need to use.
    d. None of the above.

5. Statements like: "I just can't cope with that," and "I know I will get upset," are to be

    a. memorized until easily remembered.
    b. practiced daily in imagination.
    c. dismissed and avoided.
    d. used in all stressful situations.

6. Positive self-talk should include the word

    a. "they".
    b. "I".
    c. "help".
    d. "you".

7. The winners in life can

    a. fight fear away.
    b. sense when they are about to win.
    c. find something positive about almost any situation.
    d. always avoid any situation where they may become anxious.

8. Which of the following negative statements should you add to your self-talk?

    a. "Sure is a lousy day, isn't it?"
    b. "This is going to be awful."
    c. "The company doesn't care what happens to us."
    d. None of the above.

9. What can you do to avoid being influenced by other's negative self-talk?

    a. Ignore it.
    b. Help the other person see the positive side of the situation.
    c. Call for help.
    d. a and b.

10. When we forget the things we need to say in an anxious situation

    a. we should give up.
    b. we should practice the lines we forgot.
    c. we should avoid these situations.
    d. we should plan to escape from these situations in the future.

ANSWERS TO REVIEW QUESTIONS

1.	c	6.	b
2.	d	7.	c
3.	d	8.	d
4.	a	9.	d
5.	c	10.	b

SUGGESTED RECORDING

Self-Modification Of Anxiety: Client Instructions by M. Goldfried. New York: B.M.A., 1975.

Chapter 17

The Second Feature:
Anger

We have introduced some techniques of positive self-talk for reducing anxiety. Positive self-talk can also help us manage the stress of other emotions. Anger is a very common source of such stress.

Anger can lead to destruction of property, disruption of important interpersonal relationships, and termination of employment. There are many ways of dealing with anger, and in the next few chapters, we will help you learn some assertiveness skills. For many people, however, it is first necessary to temper our aggression or violence so that we are able to put assertiveness skills to use. Changing our self-talk can help us temper our aggression.

Don't "Put Up" But Don't "Shut Up" Either

You have been learning new ways of dealing with anxiety by positive self-talking. Our goal for this chapter will be to help you learn sentences and statements that will help you avoid impulsive and negative responses to anger-provoking situations. We will show you ways to avoid "putting up your dukes" and fighting. At the same time, as you will see, we don't want you to "shut up" either. At first, you will be learning things to say to yourself. In the chapters on assertiveness training, you will be learning things to say to others that will help you feel more competent and meet more of your goals.

Some people do not have difficulty with "the shoot 'em ups." Everyone experiences anger, but some have been taught in childhood never to fight with either their fists or their words. There are some advantages to this style of life in that we avoid landing in jail, but unless we learn assertive ways of getting our needs met, we may experience frustration and stress-related psychosomatic disorders.

In the last chapter, you learned to talk yourself through anxiety by breaking most events into four time phases. These include:(1) preparing for the feelings we may have, (2) coping when some feelings start to build, (3) coping when some feelings start to ovewhelm, and (4) coping when it's over and the feelings have passed. These same phases are important in controlling our aggression.

There are some situations where anger is the best signal to fight because fighting is necessary. However, as discussed in the early chapters of this book, we encounter very few situations in modern life that would make good use of our ability to physically overcome other people or objects.

Getting In Line For The Shoot 'Em Ups

A good example of how talking to ourselves effects us involves a salesman that had a flat tire. He was in the country, far from any service stations. He had a spare tire, but he lacked a jack to help change the tire. The salesman began to walk until he came to a farm house. He began to talk to himself as he approached the farm house. "I bet the farmer won't want to help me. He probably has been plowing all day and is tired. Farmers don't like city folk anyway. He's going to think I'm really stupid for not having a jack. He'll probably laugh at me and tell me to go to town. Farmers can really be resentful."

The salesman got to the door of the farm house and knocked loudly. You can imagine the surprise on the farmer's face when he came to the door and the man in front of him turned and yelled, "I didn't want your old jack anyway." There is really a difference between positive self-talk or negative self-talk.

To prepare for stressful situations that may provoke aggression, we need to rehearse what we will do and to replace negative thinking with positive thinking. You can think of this as things to talk about while you get in line for the shoot 'em ups. If you are going home and you know that the people in the apartment above you may play loud music and you have gotten into several fights in the past, your self-talk will effect what you do and feel. Some of the ways of reducing your anger can be reviewed and practiced during red lights on your ride home. Memorize your lines or write them on a note card for use at red lights.

One of the most important things to ask yourself is, "What is it that I have to do?" Also, it is helpful to say "This may upset me, but I know some ways to deal with it." Other useful things to say include, "I'll try not to take it too seriously," and "There is not any need for an argument." As you approach the situation, remind yourself, "Time for a few breaths and relaxation. I feel more comfortable, relaxed and at ease." As you get out of your car, you may say "Easy does it. Remember, I need to keep my sense of humor." The last phrase is a very important one. It is hard to be angry when one is laughing.

In this sort of an example, we could prepare for an encounter with people who are not respecting our rights and find that they are not home. Many times, what we expect never happens. By saying the positive things we have just reviewed, you can keep yourself in a calm state while you wait and prepare for the potential event.

The things you tell yourself before you enter anger-provoking situations are just as self-fullfiling as the things you may say before anxiety-evoking situations. We need to strive to make our prophesies full of calm assertiveness, rather than blood and guts.

And In This Corner...

Next we can learn to cope with aggressive feelings by knowing what to say if our anger starts to build. In a boxing match this build-up may start when the announcer says "and in this corner...." At this point, we start to feel tense and ready to fight. We may get still more angry when we wonder if we will be disqualified, or our opponent will not show up at the last minute. These sort of pessimistic ideas not only increase our anger, but also can become self-fulfilling prophesies.

Take the example of someone who is accusing us of something we did not do. As we start to feel tense, it is helpful to say "My muscles are starting to feel a little tight. Time to relax. Time to slow down." In addition, we might repeat the words "My anger can remind me of what I need to do. Time to help myself." If a person begins to tell us all the wrong things they think we have done, it is easy to get angry. It is more helpful to say "Let's take this point by point." As a person goes into a tirrade, you can often help your own anger from getting out of hand by saying "Maybe we are both right, let's try a cooperative approach."

As the person's behavior begins to get under our skin and we begin to think of some words to put the other person in their place, it is useful to say to oneself "Arguments lead to more arguments. Let's work constructively." On the other hand, sometimes we feel our self-esteem is on the line and we have difficulty admitting that we are wrong. This can come from the irrational belief that we need to be perfect or right all the time. Remember, usually it is a question of "what is right" not "who is right." Sometimes it is also helpful to remind the other person of this fact.

Often it is best to let the other person run out of steam before taking up a discussion. By taking this time to relax, we can decrease our stress and allow the other person to become more receptive to discussion and arbitration.

In some situations, people may provoke us in order to show that we have poor self-control. Even if this is not the case, many people have helped themselves by saying something like "He may want me to get really angry. Well, I'm going to try to disappoint him." These positive statements should help you cope better when your feelings start to build.

When Your Back Is Against The Wall

When someone is provoking or insulting, you may find your feelings starting to overwhelm you. At times, we are all caught off guard. For example, a driver can cut in front of us in traffic or someone may damage something that is important to us. In some of these instances, our feelings may start to overwhelm us before we have had a chance to prepare or even recognize that they are starting to build. In other situations, we may have been preparing for our feelings as they started to build, but in the middle of the event our feelings may start to overwhelm us. Just as in anxiety management, we need to know some things to say to manage anger.

One of the best things to say is "The more I keep my cool, the more I'm in control." Often we may believe our anger will help us control the situation, but it usually does just the opposite. In addition, others will respect your ability to keep cool and stay in control.

When someone insults us, it is important to remember that we don't have to prove or defend ourselves. Some positive talking will help remind us. Try using "I don't need to prove myself." It will be helpful to have the following phrase at the tip of your tongue, "I don't want to make more out of this than I have to." Another way to deal with insults is to say "No need to doubt myself -- what he says may not matter."

There are a number of relevant situations that do not involve insults or provocations. If someone is cheating us in business or had sold us poor quality merchandise, our feelings of anger may become strong. In these cases, it's often helpful to say "I'll think of what I want to get out of this." This sort of self-talk helps us to focus on what we need to do in order to get what we hope for. Often it's helpful to remind ourselves "Look for the good parts of this. I don't want to assume the worst and jump to conclusions."

One of the advantages of anger, is that it alerts us to our need to change the situation. If we are getting cheated, it is better to know about this now than later, so that we can protect our property or investment. However, if we jump to conclusions because of our anger, we may later regret having disrupted an opportunity or a relationship. If a girl friend seems to be paying a great deal of attention to another man, it is important not to assume the worst and jump to a conclusion that she is going to leave. It is best to say to ourselves "Let me get more information. Perhaps she is speaking to her cousin or her friend."

And The Winner Is...

After the situation is over and your anger has passed, it is important to know how to reward yourself. Just as in anxiety management, this is a very unique opportunity for positive self-talk. It helps us to put things in perspective and to reward ourselves for our accomplishments. When we get a reward for doing something, we are more likely to meet future challenges in the same way. In this case, if we reward ourselves for positive self-talking, we are more likely to use this skill again and avoid blowing up in other situations.

Take the situation in which someone fails to pay back a loan or return something they have borrowed. You have coped successfully with your anger and asserted your needs to this person. The final step is to reward yourself by saying "I'm doing better at this! I'm making progress!" If you've done well, but not as well as you had hoped, remember to say "I can be pleased with my progress." If you have done even better than you had expected, you might say "That wasn't really as hard as I thought."

Most of the time, there are still some small feelings left over or some difficulties that are not quite resolved. In these cases, it is helpful to say "I will try not to take it personally. These are difficult situations. They take some time to straigten out."

Common Problems: "I Always Have And I Always Will"

Just as in managing your anxiety, managing your anger requires that you try something new. One of the common problems is to get angry, blow up, and say "I always have and I always will." This rewards the old ways, and is not a productive way of managing your anger.

Just as in anxiety management, sometimes it seems that we are so angry that we can not think positively. This is why it is very important to memorize the coping statements for each time phase of the event. If we are angry, it is often more difficult to remember things. This is why we must really master and overlearn phrases so that they will be at our fingertips when we are angry.

Just as in anxiety management, some people find the phrases we suggest are not quite right for them. In this case, write down personal phrases for the situation in which you are hoping to improve your coping. Again, be sure to include some phrases that will prepare you for the event, some to help remind you to relax as your anger builds, some statements to help you cope with the anger when it starts to overwhelm you, and some statements to keep things in perspective and encourage yourself for the future. Each of the four charts on pages 318 to 321 include spaces for your personal phrases.

Learning Your Lines

It is very important that you put the things you have been reading about into practice. This means that you will need to systematically learn the phrases and practice them.

Helpful Hints

Try to use periods of time during the day when you are waiting for a bus or checking out in a supermarket, or have other times. These are good times to relax and review your new self-talk. Keep these phrases on a slip of paper or card in your wallet or pocketbook for review during your free time.

Do not try to learn all the phrases at one time. It is useful to read all of them through in the beginning, but it is best to practice only a few each day. Again, it is often helpful to learn these just before you go to sleep and, for this reason, we recommend that you leave the list on your night stand.

If you still have difficulty with a situation, break it into its time phases, pick the phase you have the most trouble with, and go over the statements for that phase again. By continuing to do this, you will find yourself better and better able to cope with the anger that some situations evoke.

Introduction To Peace Talks

Turn back to the stressful events which you prepared in Chapter 12. If none of these involve anger, review the last week and find a few frustrating situations. It is important to think about the things you tell yourself in these situations. Compare your self-talk to our suggested positive self-talk. List your personal anger situations below.

Personal Anger Situations

Situations   Self-Talk

Example: *Reckless driver   Example: *That guy is try-*
cuts in front of me   *ing to kill me*

1. _____   _____

   _____   _____

2. _____   _____

   _____   _____

3. _____   _____

   _____   _____

Counting Your Talks (Are You Talking To Yourself Enough?)

Spend a little time each day going through the four phases for coping with anger on a different stressor. If you have just a few major stressors, you may want to spend more than a day on some of them. Go slowly, and use your skill of visual imagery, so that when you begin working on these things in real life, you will recall the statements and be able to cope more successfully. Make your "talkies" as clear and provoking as you can. It's helpful to exaggerate the anger-provoking events to test your skill.

Each time your go through the exercise of imagining a stressor and applying each of the four phases, fill in the blanks on pages 322 and 323. The more you practice your self-talk, the better you will be able to cope with feelings in real life.

OUTLINE FOR POSITIVE TALKING

A. <u>Your new scripts</u>. Read slowly over the word-by-word positive talk on the following pages. Become as familiar as you can with each of these phrases.

B. <u>When to audition</u>. When you have read the words several times, try to think of each of the four time phases and write down the phrases that belong in each section. Use the lines and the spaces provided on pages 322 to 323.

As in many of the other parts of this book, we suggest that you first go through your script in your imagination. This is like an audition for a film. Read your lines out loud several times. In addition, use each of the anger-provoking situations for you that you wrote down from Chapter 12, and talk yourself through each of the four time phases.

C. <u>Cameras, action</u>! When you have memorized your lines and practiced them in your imagination, choose the least anger-producing event on your list and begin to apply your new lines. You usually will not have time to use all of them and, for most situations, one or two positive sentences repeated a few times will help lower your level of anger. Be sure to use positive talk before the event, as the anger begins to grow, when your anger becomes stronger and after the feelings have passed.

D. <u>The supporting cast</u>. Don't let others contribute negative self-talk that can interfere with your positive self-talk. If someone says how bad things look, either ignore their comment, or turn it around. Help the other person see the positive side of the situation.

E. <u>Use personal pronouns</u>. Use such words as "I", "my," and "me." This helps to personalize your self-talk.

F. <u>Present tense self-talk</u>. Self talk thouls be in the present tense. Keep your self-talk in the present tense and avoid referring to the past or the future. Talk about what you are doing now, not what happened before or what may happen next.

G. <u>Give your self-talk positive direction</u>. Focus on what you want to achieve, not what you fear or want to avoid.

H. <u>Keep your self-talk non-competitive</u>. Focus on what you will do, rather than comparing what you do to what others do.

TALKING CALMLY WORD-BY-WORD TO
COPE WITH ANGER

Preparing For Anger In Stressful Situations

Effective Self-Talk	Less Effective Self-Talk
What is it that I have to do?	I have to win this one.
This may upset me, but I know some ways to deal with it.	This is going to make me angry.
There may not be any need for an argument.	I know there will be an argument.
I'll try not to take it too seriously.	This one's for real.
Time for a few deep breaths and relaxation. I feel more comfortable, relaxed and at ease.	I'm really ready for him.
Easy does it. Remember, I need to keep my sense of humor.	He's going to find out I'm serious.

PERSONAL PHRASES TO PRACTICE

1. _____

_____

2. _____

_____

3. _____

_____

4. _____

_____

Coping When Anger Starts To Build

Effective Self-Talk	Less Effective Self-Talk
My muscles are starting to feel a little tight. Time to relax. Time to slow down.	I'm really getting up-tight.
My anger can remind me of what I need to do. Time to help myself.	This makes me mad.
Let's take this point-by-point.	He's wrong.
Maybe we are both right. Let's try a cooperative approach.	He's against me.
Let's remember, it's not who is right, but what is right.	Only one of us is right, and it's me.
Arguments lead to more arguments. Let's work constructively.	Now, he's in for an argument.
He may want me to get really angry. Well, I'm going to try to disappoint him.	I'll show him.

PERSONAL PHRASES TO PRACTICE

1. _____

_____

2. _____

_____

3. _____

_____

4. _____

_____

Coping When Anger Starts To Overwhelm

Effective Self-Talk	Less Effective Self-Talk
The more I keep my cool, the more I'm in control.	He can't do that.
I'll think of what I want to get out of this.	I'll get even.
I don't need to prove myself.	I can't let him get away with that.
I don't want to make more out of this than I have to.	I'll take it to the top.
No need to doubt myself. What he says may not matter.	He can't say that to me.
Look for the good parts of this. I don't want to assume the worst and jump to conclusions.	This is going to be awful.

PERSONAL PHRASES TO PRACTICE

1. _____

_____

2. _____

_____

3. _____

_____

4. _____

_____

Coping When It's All Over And The Anger Has Passed

Effective Self-Talk	Less Effective Self-Talk
These are difficult situations. They take some time to straighten out.	That always happens.
I will try not to take it personally.	He still didn't see my point.
That wasn't really as hard as I thought.	That was awful.
I'm doing better at this! I'm making progress!	I should have said more.
I can be pleased with my progress.	I'll win the argument next time.

PERSONAL PHRASES TO PRACTICE

1. _____

_____

2. _____

_____

3. _____

_____

4. _____

_____

STRESSFUL SITUATIONS AND POSITIVE SELF-TALK

Directions: Write in a description of several stressful situations involving anger. Each time you practice the coping statements rate your degree of competence from 1 (total control) to 10 (loss of control) with 5 as angry, but okay. Fill in one of the blanks until you have practiced doing this five times for each of the situations and phases listed.

Description Of Anger Arousing Situation	Cognitive Behavior Modification Statements:	Degree Of Competence
Example:	I. Before *The traffic is bad.* *Time to relax*	3 3 2 3 1
Reckless driver cuts in front of me	II. Beginning *He wants me to get angry. He'll be disappointed*	8 7 5 6 4
	III. Middle *I don't need to prove myself*	7 7 5 5 4
	IV. After *I can be pleased with my progress*	3 2 2 1 2
1. _____	I. Before _____	_ _ _ _ _
_____	_____	
_____	II. Beginning _____	_ _ _ _ _
_____	_____	
_____	III. Middle _____	_ _ _ _ _
_____	_____	
_____	IV. After _____	_ _ _ _ _
_____	_____	

Description of Anger-Arousing Situation	Cognitive Behavior Modification Statements:	Degree of Competence
2. _____	I. Before _____	_ _ _ _ _ _
_____	_____	
_____	II. Beginning _____	_ _ _ _ _ _
_____	_____	
_____	III. Middle _____	_ _ _ _ _ _
_____	_____	
_____	IV. After _____	_ _ _ _ _ _
_____	_____	
3. _____	I. Before _____	_ _ _ _ _ _
_____	_____	
_____	II. Beginning _____	_ _ _ _ _ _
_____	_____	
_____	III. Middle _____	_ _ _ _ _ _
_____	_____	
_____	IV. After _____	_ _ _ _ _ _
_____	_____	

REVIEW QUESTIONS

Directions: Circle the letter in front of the best response to
each question. The correct answers are provided on the page
following the last question.

1. Learning anger management helps us prepare to

    a. apply assertiveness training.
    b. avoid all difficult situations.
    c. escape from all difficult situations.
    d. frighten other people.

2. Using positive self-talk to cope with anger is

    a. similar to using it to cope with anxiety.
    b. entirely different from using it to cope with anxiety.
    c. easy to learn in one session.
    d. None of the above.

3. The talkies involve coping with anger before we have it and

    a. as it starts to build.
    b. as it starts to overwhelm us.
    c. after it has passed.
    d. All the above.

4. A cognitive, positive self-talk approach to feelings of
    anger can

    a. help remind us to use relaxation skills.
    b. eliminate angry feelings from our lives.
    c. help us escape from situations evoking anger.
    d. None of the above.

5. Statements like, "I have always blown up and I always will"
    should be

    a. memorized until easily remembered.
    b. practiced daily in imagination.
    c. dismissed and avoided.
    d. used in all stressful situations.

6. Read the following three statements:

    (1) "He may want me to get really angry. Well, I'm going
         to try to disappoint him."
    (2) "Let's take this point-by-point."
    (3) "My muscles are starting to feel a little tight. Time
         to relax. Time to slow down."

These statements come from one of the four phases of coping
with anger. Which one?

    a. Preparing for the angry situation and the feelings we
        may have.
    b. Coping when anger starts to build.
    c. Coping when anger starts to overwhelm.
    d. Coping when it's all over and the anger has passed.

7. Read the following three statements:

    (1) "What is it that I will have to do?"
    (2) "There may not be any need for an argument."
    (3) "Easy does it. Remember, I need to keep my sense of
         humor."

These statements come from one of the four phases of coping
with anger. Which one?

    a. Preparing for the angry situation and feelings we may
        have.
    b. Coping when anger starts to build.
    c. Coping when anger starts to overwhelm.
    d. Coping when it's all over and the anger has passed.

8. Read the following three statements:

    (1) "I don't need to prove myself."
    (2) "The more I keep my cool, the more I'm in control."
    (3) "No need to doubt myself. What he says may not
         matter."

These statements come from one of the four phases of coping
with anger. Which one?

    a. Preparing for the angry situation and feelings we may
        have.
    b. Coping when anger starts to build.
    c. Coping when anger starts to overwhelm.
    d. Coping when it's all over and the anger has passed.

9. Read the following three statements:

    (1) "That wasn't really as hard as I thought."
    (2) "I can be pleased with my progress."
    (3) "These are difficult situations. They take some time
         to straighten out."

These statements come from one of the four phases of coping
with anger. Which one?

    a. Preparing for the angry situation and feelings we may
        have.
    b. Coping when anger starts to build.
    c. Coping when anger starts to overwhelm.
    d. Coping when it is all over and the anger has passed.

10. When we forget the things we need to say in an anger-
    provoking situation

    a. we should give up.
    b. we should practice the lines we forgot.
    c. we should avoid these situations.
    d. we should plan to excape from these situations in the
        future.

ANSWERS TO REVIEW QUESTIONS

1.	a	6.	b
2.	a	7.	a
3.	d	8.	c
4.	a	9.	d
5.	c	10.	b

SUGGESTED BOOK

Anger Management: How To Live With -- And -- Without Anger
    by A. Ellis. Pleasantville, New York: Reader's Digest
    Press, 1977.

Section V

I Can Relax Now, But Will the Bully Stop Kicking Sand In My Face? Communicating Your Needs And Feelings

Chapter 18

What Is Assertiveness?

We have practiced a number of techniques for stress management. Some involved relaxing our bodies. Others involved changing our thoughts and feelings so we could better cope with stressful situations. Another way of managing stress involves assertiveness training.

Sometimes we fail to "draw lines," "set limits," "speak up," or say "no" to people and demands in our lives. This difficulty can lead to procrastination, suffering in silence, half-heartedness, sloppiness or forgetfulness as we say "no" in unconscious or dishonest ways.

If we cannot refuse the requests of others, we can end up living our lives according to other people's priorities rather than our own. This can lead to additional stress that can be harmful and unnecessary. If we fail to assert ourselves, we can stock pile anger, and find ourselves mentally and physically "uptight."

Sometimes we feel that the only way to get our needs met and keep from being pushed around is to fight for our rights. When we feel bullied or fear that we will be bullied, we may try to bully others. This can lead to a continuous and desperate struggle with a lion's share of stress from guilt and loneliness.

In living and communicating with others, we behave in many ways. It is helpful to look at the things we do and group them into three main ways of behaving. We can be assertive, aggressive or passive. What do we mean by these words?

Passive Behavior

Passive behavior means giving up your own rights by not expressing your honest feelings, thoughts and beliefs. It often involves permitting others to "walk all over" you. It can also

-331-

mean expressing yourself in such an apologetic way that you are overlooked. A person is behaving passively when he does what he is told, regardless of how he feels about it. When we act passively, we often feel helpless, anxious, resentful and disappointed with ourselves. The goal of passivity is usually to please others and to avoid conflict or rejection.

Not too long ago, one of the authors found himself slipping into what would have clearly been passive behavior. He was attending a convention with his wife, who is also a psychologist. They were given a room directly beneath the disco bar. The music was loud enough that, if his wife were not pregnant and tired from a long drive, they might have enjoyed live entertainment in their room!

The author wanted to do something about the situation, but he hesitated, thinking: (1) he was given the convention rate, (2) someone had to use the room, (3) the hotel staff would think he was pushy, and (4) they would not change the room at 9:00 p.m. Inside, he felt a little angry, anxious and powerless.

Then, he laughed at himself. He realized that if he did not do something, he would be practicing passive behavior. He would not be getting what he paid for and not expressing his feelings. He would be preaching wine, but drinking water! One of the alternatives he considered next was aggressive behavior.

Aggressive Behavior

When we are aggressive, we stand up for our personal rights and express our thoughts and feelings. However, we do this in dishonest ways which are not usually helpful and almost always step on the personal rights of other people. Examples of aggressive behavior are blaming, threatening, and fighting.

When we are aggressive, we usually feel angry, frustrated or self-righteous at the time. We often feel bitter, guilty or lonely afterwards. The usual goals of aggressive behavior are dominating, protecting, winning, humiliating and forcing other people to lose.

The author, in the example above, thought about going upstairs and yelling at the band leader or pulling the plug to the amplifiers. This behavior would have violated the rights of the band to make a living and the patrons to enjoy the music they came to hear. If the author had gone upstairs, he might have felt guilty or his wife might have been so embarrased that he might feel very lonely. Finally, he might still be stuck in the noisy room or be thrown out altogether. At this point, he thought about assertive behavior.

Assertive Behavior

Assertive behavior means standing up for your personal rights and expressing your thoughts, feelings and beliefs in direct, honest and helpful ways, which do not violate the rights of others. Assertiveness means respecting yourself, expressing your needs, and defending your rights. It also means respecting the needs, feelings and rights of other people.

When we are assertive, we usually feel better about ourselves and more self-confident. Assertiveness does not guarantee "winning," but it does increase the chances of a good compromise or a better result without making others angry.

The author decided to countdown to relaxation and review his rights. He was able to relax and clarify in his own mind that he had paid for a comfortable place to sleep. He then called the desk, stated the problem, and expressed his discomfort. The operator answered that she would have the bass turned down.

The author hesitated, and then realized that he was skeptical about the effectiveness of this measure. He scanned his body for tension, and made his need for another room clear. There was a brief silence before the clerk gave him a new room. The author was pleased, the hotel gained a satisfied customer, and the couple got a good night's rest.

The first step in assertiveness training is learning to recognize passive, assertive and aggressive behavior. Read slowly through the charts on pages 335 to 340. Notice that the first two charts clarify the verbal and non-verbal characteristics of the three types of behavior.

About 60 percent of all communication is non-verbal, so pay attention to these characteristics. To become aware of potential double messages, try to imagine using the verbal part of one type of behavior with the non-verbal part of another.

The third and fourth charts reveal what our goals, feelings, and payoffs may be. How do you feel most of the time? What are your goals and what are your payoffs?

The fifth chart shows the effects of the three types of behavior on others. What effects do you want to have on your family, friends, and fellow workers?

The last chart on page 340 reveals the outcomes we can expect from such behaviors. Think of some recent events and their outcomes. Did your outcomes match the type of behaviors you used?

These charts can help you see meekness, withdrawal, attack and blame for what they are, sadly inadequate strategies of escape that create more pain and stress than they prevent. Before you can achieve assertive behavior, you must really face the fact that passive and aggressive behaviors have often failed to get you what you want.

A COMPARISON OF PASSIVE, ASSERTIVE, AND AGGRESSIVE BEHAVIORS

* * * * * * * * * * * * * * * * * * * VERBAL BEHAVIORS *

Passive

You avoid saying what you want, think, or feel. If you do, you say them in such a way that you put yourself down. Apologetic words with hidden meanings are frequent. A smoke screen of vague words or silence. Frequent use of "you know," "Well...;" "I mean...," "I guess," and "I'm sorry." You allow others to choose for you.

Assertive

You say what you honestly want, think, and feel in direct and helpful ways. You make your own choices. You communicate with tact and humor. You use "I" statements. Your words are clear and objective. They are few and well chosen.

Aggressive

You say what you want, think and feel, but at the expense of others. You use "loaded words" and "you" statements that label or blame. You are full of threats or accusations and apply one-upmanship. You choose for others.

A COMPARISON OF PASSIVE, ASSERTIVE, AND AGGRESSIVE BEHAVOIR

* * * * * * * * * * * * * * * * *NON-VERBAL BEHAVIORS* * * * * * * * * * * * * * * * * *

Passive

You use actions instead of words. You hope someone will guess what you want. You look as if you don't mean what you say. Your voice is weak, hesitant and soft. You whisper in a monotone. Your eyes are to the side or down-cast. You nod your head to almost anything another person says. You sit or stand as far away as you can from the other person. You don't know what to do with your hands and they are trembling or clammy. You look uncomfortable, shuffle and are tense or inhibited.

Assertive

You listen closely. Your manner is calm and assured. You communicate caring and strength. Your voice is firm, warm, and expressive. You look directly at the other person, but you don't stare. You face the person. Your hands are relaxed. You hold your head erect and you lean toward the other person. You have a relaxed expression.

Aggressive

You make an exaggerated show of strength. You are flippant. You have an air of superiority. Your voice is tense, loud, cold, or demand-ing. You are "deadly quiet." Your eyes are narrow, cold, and staring. You almost see through the other people. You take a macho fight stance. Your hands are on your hips and you are inches from the other people. Your hands are in fists or your fingers are pointed at the other person. You are tense and angry appearing.

YOUR APPARENT GOALS AND FEELINGS

* * * * * * * * * * * * * * * * * * GOALS *

Passive	Assertive	Aggressive
To please, to be liked.	To communicate, to be respected.	To dominate or humiliate.

* * * * * * * * * * * * * * * * * * FEELINGS * * * * * * * * * * * * * * * * * * *

Passive	Assertive	Aggressive
You feel anxious, ignored, hurt, manipulated and disappointed with yourself. You are often angry and resentful later.	You feel confident and successful. You feel good about yourself at that time and later. You feel in control, you have self-respect and you are goal-oriented.	You feel self-righteous, controlling and superior. Sometimes you feel embarrased or selfish later.

YOUR APPARENT PAYOFFS

* * * * * * * * * * * * * * * * * *PAYOFFS* * * * * * * * * * * * * * * * * *

Passive

You avoid unpleasant situations, conflicts, short-term tensions, and confrontation. You don't have to take responsibility for your choices.

Assertive

You feel good. You feel respected by others. Your self-confidence improves. You make your own choices. Your relationships with others are improved. You have very little physical distress now or later. You are in touch with your feelings.

Aggressive

You get some anger off your chest. You get a feeling of control. You feel superior.

THE EFFECTS ON OTHERS

* * * * * * * * * * * * * * * * *THEIR FEELINGS* *

Passive	Assertive	Aggressive
They feel guilty, superior, frustrated or even angry.	They feel respected or valued. They feel free to express themselves.	They feel humiliated, depreciated, or hurt.

* * * * * * * * * * * * * * * * * THEIR FEELINGS TOWARD YOU * * * * * * * * * * * * * * * * * *

Passive	Assertive	Aggressive
They feel irritated. They pity and depreciate you. They feel frustrated or disgusted with you. They loose respect for you because you are a pushover and someone who does not know where he stands.	They usually respect, trust and value you. They know where you stand.	They feel hurt, defensive, humiliated or angry. They resent, distrust and fear you. They may want revenge.

PROBABLE OUTCOMES OF EACH TYPE OF BEHAVIOR

Passive

You don't get what you want. If you do get your own way, it is indirect. You feel emotionally dishonest. Others achieve their goals at your expense. Your rights are violated. Your anger builds up and you either push it down or redirect it toward other people who are less powerful. You may find yourself procrastinating, suffering in silence, doing things half-heartedly, being sloppy, or becoming forgetful. You get maneuvered. Loneliness and isolation may become part of your life.

Assertive

You often get what you want if it is reasonable. You often achieve your goals. You gain self-respect. You feel good. You convert win-lose to win-win. The outcome is determined by above-board negotiations. Your rights and other's rights are respected.

Aggressive

You often get what you want, but at the expense of others. You hurt others by making choices for them and infantilizing them. Others feel a right to "get even." You may have increasing difficulty with relaxing and "unwinding" later.

REVIEW QUESTIONS

Directions: Label each of the following as either assertive (AS), passive (PS), or aggressive (AG).

The situation you might be in: What you say and do:

___1. You are watching a movie, but people seated in front of you are making it hard to hear the sound.

You sit and fume, clearing your throat occasionally.

___2. At a meeting one person often interrupts you when you're speaking.

You look at the person and say firmly, "Excuse me, I'd like to finish what I'm saying."

___3. You'd like a raise.

You shuffle into your boss' office and say, "Do you think that, ah, you could see your way clear to giving me a raise?"

___4. You have talked with your boss about a helpful suggestion for organizing the work in the office. He says that he thinks this is a good idea and that he will ask someone else to put the change into effect.

You put your hands on your hips and shout, "This was my suggestion, and I'll not stand for someone else getting all the credit for it."

___5. You are looking forward to a quiet night alone. A relative calls and asks you to babysit.

You communicate caring, but strength as you say, "I put aside tonight for myself and I won't be able to babysit."

___6. Your parents or in-laws call and tell you they are dropping by. You are busy.

In a loud voice you say, "You always call two minutes before you are here and expect me to drop everything."

___ 7. Two workers in your office have been talking about personal matters. The work has been piling up. Others have been complaining. You are their supervisor.

You call the offenders together, lean towards them and say, "I know how easy it is for time to slip by when you are relaxing and talking to your friends. But your work is piling up and I would like you to use the 20-minute break for personal conversation."

___ 8. A good friend is always late for things you plan to do together. You have not said anything for several weeks.

When your friend arrives, you look like you are ready to explode. You say, "You're never on time!"

___ 9. A date and time is being set for a weekly meeting. The time is not convenient for you. The times are set when it will be next to impossible for you to make the meeting regularly.

When asked about the time, you look down and almost whisper, "Well, I guess it's okay. I'm not going to be able to come very much, but if it fits everyone else's schedule, it's o.k. with me."

___10. You are the only woman (or man) in a group of men (or women). You are asked to be the secretary of the meetings.

You respond, "I'm willing to do my share and take the notes at this time. In future meetings, I'd like others to take their turn."

ANSWERS TO REVIEW QUESTIONS

1.	P	6.	AG
2.	AS	7.	AS
3.	P	8.	AG
4.	AG	9.	P
5.	AS	10.	AS

Use the spaces below to give assertive responses to the situations which were handled aggressively or passively. These were situations numbered 1, 3, 4, 6, 8, and 9.

1. _____

_____

3. _____

_____

4. _____

_____

6. _____

_____

8. _____

_____

9. _____

_____

SUGGESTED BOOK AND RECORDING

BOOK

Your Perfect Right: A Guide To Assertive Behavior by R.
Alberti: & M. Emmons. San Lois Obispo, California:
Impact, 1970.

RECORDING

Self-Directed Assertiveness Training by R. Rakos & H.
Schroeder. New York: B.M.A., 1976.

Chapter 19

When Do You Turn Aggressive
And When Do You Turn
The Other Cheek?

Now that you understand and can identify behavior that is aggressive, passive and assertive, it is time to put the spotlight on your own life. By now, you probably have discovered that some of your behavior is aggressive or passive. Before you try to change these behaviors, it is best to pinpoint a large number of them so that you can start asserting yourself in those situations that will have the greatest likelihood of success. This chapter should help you "know thyself" a little better and identify some reasonable goals for assertiveness training.

To help you do this, find the chart on page 350. Notice that ten situations are given and seven categories of people are provided. For example, you may not have difficulty refusing requests from subordinates at work, but you may have great difficulty refusing requests from your spouse or from close friends. You may be able to give your opinions easily if they differ with those of friends, but you may have much more difficulty doing so when you are in large groups.

The goal of categorizing your assertiveness in different interactions is to become aware of those situations in which you have the most difficulty. By rating them, you will know where to start practicing new assertive behaviors.

As you fill out this chart, note that the first three types of situations, including refusing requests, handling criticisms, and receiving from others, are situations where others begin the interaction. The list continues with those situations where passivity can result when we simply put off doing anything because we are not forced to act.

Your Inalienable Rights

Notice that each type of situation reflects one of the rights that we have as people. Many people do not realize that they have rights in their relationships with others. Some of us have full knowledge of a long list of obligations, but are only dimly aware of our own rights.

Whether you make up a list of rights from the Declaration of Independence, The Bill of Rights, or the Universal Declaration of Human Rights, your rights are freedoms which people have sought and fought for. Your assertion keeps you free, by upholding these rights.

What are some or your rights? You have the right to refuse a request. In fact, you have the right to say "no" to any request without feeling guilty. Problems people have may well be important and pressing, but you are not required to solve them. You also have the right to change your mind or decide on another course of action.

You have the right to handle criticisms without assuming or acting as if they are always correct. In addition, you have the right to make mistakes.

You have the right to receive things from others and accept them as gifts with no strings attached and, as such, you do not have to reciprocate now or in the future. You have the right to state your needs and to stand up for your rights, even if it sometimes means putting yourself first.

More Rights

You have the right to express your true feelings whether they are positive, warm and pleasurable feelings, or negative, angry and dissatisfied feelings. Part of this right is the right to be the final judge of your feelings. Accepting and expressing your feelings help you to avoid the loneliness that comes from either being unaware of these feelings or being unable to communicate them to others.

If some of your rights are violated, you have the right to give negative feedback so that the other person can choose to respect your rights. You have a right to protest unfair treatment or criticism.

You have the right to your own convictions. If someone is proposing something which you do not like, you have the right to differ with that person and give your opinions.

You also have the right to make requests in the hope that others will help you. Some of us have been taught to deny our own needs and never ask for help or emotional support. Finally, you have the right to make social contacts, to start conversations with others and to build friendships. Without these rights we would live in a dangerous and lonely world. Such a world would be full of distress.

The following chart will help you to assess your own behavior patters. While you fill out the chart, it may be helpful to run through the past week or two and find those situations in your life, where you found yourself acting in an aggressive or a passive manner. The most important problems for stress management are the ones which occur over and over again. Even those to which you give a rating of mildly difficult, are important if they happen often. They are also important because it is usually best to change your behavior on the easier tasks first so as to insure success.

Now, rate your assertiveness in the situations categorized on the next page.

RATING YOUR ASSERTIVENESS IN DIFFERENT SITUATIONS WITH DIFFERENT PEOPLE

Directions: Fill in each of the blocks with a rating of your assertiveness from 0 to 10. A rating of 0 means you have no difficulty at all in asserting yourself. A rating of 10 means you are completely unable to assert yourself.

People: Type of Situation:	Relatives	Friends	Strangers	Authority Figures	Subordi-nates	Service People	Groups
1. Refusing requests							
2. Handling criticisms							
3. Receiving from others							
4. Stating your rights and needs							
5. Expressing negative feelings							
6. Giving negative feedback and confronting others							
7. Differing with others and giving opinions							
8. Making requests							
9. Expressing positive feelings							
10. Making social contacts							

Mildly Difficult Situations Calling For Assertiveness

When you have rated your assertiveness in various types of situations, choose a few real life examples in which you have mild difficulty asserting yourself.   These should be rated around a three on the zero to ten scale.   Write these situations down in the following spaces.   For example, a teacher we worked with wrote down:

Example 1. *Refusing requests from friends: Jane Stoner asked me to help her with the United Fund.*

Example 2 *Stating rights and needs with relatives: John borrows the family car but does not tell us when he will return it.*

Example 3. *Differing with others and giving opinions in groups: Speaking up at the faculty meeting when I disagree with curriculum changes.*

Your Mildly Difficult Assertive Situations:

1. _____

   _____

2. _____

   _____

3. _____

   _____

4. _____

   _____

Moderately Difficult Situations Calling For Assertiveness

Next, make a list of those situations in which you have moderate difficulty asserting yourself. These should be rated around five to seven on the scale. Here is a list that a young lawyer listed.

Example 1. *Making social contacts with strangers:* *Meeting the attractive girl in front of me in line at lunch*

Example 2. *Handling criticisms from authority figures:* *Finding myself tongue tied when the boss points out a mistake.*

Example 3. *Giving negative feedback to subordinants:* *Pointing out a mistake to the older secretary who made it.*

Your Moderately Difficult Assertive Situations:

1. _____

_____

2. _____

_____

3. _____

_____

4. _____

_____

Very Difficult Situations Calling For Assertiveness

Finally, make a list of those situations in which you have a great deal of difficulty asserting yourself. These should have a rating of eight to ten. A homemaker had particular difficulty with situations outside of the home. Her list included the following:

Example 1. *Refusing request from service personnel:*
The waitress asked me to hurry up because there is a large group requiring seating.

Example 2. *Differing with others and giving opinions in groups. Expressing her concern for her childrens safety when the issue of busing came up at a meeting.*

Example 3. *Making requests from authority figures:*
Asking Johnny's pediatrician about the treatment that he is recommending.

Your Very Difficult Assertive Situations:

1. _____

_____

2. _____

_____

3. _____

_____

4. _____

_____

REVIEW QUESTIONS

<u>Directions</u>: Circle the letter in front of the best response to each question. The correct answers are provided on the page following the last question.

1. If we are assertive with relatives, friends and subordinates, we are likely to be

    a. passive with strangers, authority figures and service people.
    b. aggressive with strangers, authority figures and service people.
    c. passive with authority figures, groups and strangers.
    d. None of the above are necessarily true.

2. If we find it easy to refuse requests, make social contacts, and express negative feelings, we are likely to

    a. have difficulty handling criticisms, receiving from others, and stating our rights and needs.
    b. have trouble giving negative feedback, confronting others, and differing with others.
    c. have trouble making requests and expressing positive feelings.
    d. None of the above are necessarily true.

3. In which of the following can we find some of our rights written out:

    a. Declaration of Independence.
    b. The Bill of Rights.
    c. The Universal Declaration of Human Rights.
    d. All the above.

4. Assertiveness

    a. respects the other person's rights.
    b. upholds your rights.
    c. helps to manage stress.
    d. All of the above.

5. Which of the following is <u>not</u> one of our legitmate rights?

    a. We have the right to say "no" to any request without feeling guilty.
    b. We have the right to handle criticisms without assuming they are correct.
    c. We have the right to force others to accept our opinions.
    d. We have the right to express our feelings whether they are positive or negative.

6. Which of the following is not a right?

    a. The right to refuse requests without feeling guilty.
    b. The right to handle criticisms without assuming they are right.
    c. The right to always give more to others than you receive.
    d. The right to state your rights and needs.

7. Which of the following is a right?

    a. The right to differ with others and give your opinions.
    b. The right to do unto others as they do unto you.
    c. The right to embarass others.
    d. The right to bully others.

8. Which of the following is a right?

    a. The right to make requests.
    b. The right to make mistakes.
    c. The right to express positive feelings.
    d. All of the above.

9. Which of the following is <u>not</u> a right?

    a. You should never change your mind.
    b. You should feel free to make known your needs.
    c. You should feel free to make social contacts.
    d. You should never feel you have to agree to a request.

10. The most important problems for assertiveness training in stress management are

    a. those which occur over and over.
    b. those to which you give a high rating.
    c. those which only occur once a month or once a year.
    d. those which you are handling in an assertive manner.

ANSWERS TO REVIEW QUESTIONS

1.	d	6.	c
2.	d	7.	a
3.	d	8.	d
4.	d	9.	a
5.	c	10.	a

SUGGESTED BOOKS AND RECORDING

BOOKS

The Assertive Option: Your Rights And Responsibilities. P. Jakubowski & A. Lange. Champaign, Illinois: Research Press, 1978.

Your Perfect Right: A Guide To Assertive Behavior by R. Alberti & M. Emmons. San Lois Obispo, California: Impact, 1970.

RECORDING

Self-Directed Assertiveness Training by R. Rakos & H. Schroeder. New York: B.M.A., 1976.

Chapter 20

Rolling Up Your Sleeves
And Becoming Assertive

You have taken the first steps toward assertive behavior. You have learned the differences between aggressive, passive and assertive behavior. You have pinpointed the types of situations and the people with whom you have difficulty being assertive. You have rated the difficulty of the situations, and now it is time to begin practicing some assertiveness skills.

The following step-by-step approach to assertiveness training comes from the book, Your Perfect Right, by Robert Alberti, Ph.D. and Michael Emmons, Ph.D. This book started the assertiveness training movement. The steps involve reviewing your behavior, imagining a more assertive approach, role playing the new behaviors, and, finally, trying to be assertive in a situation with a high probability of success.

First, review the lists of mildly, moderately, and very difficult situations which you wrote in Chapter 19. Use the "Personal Assertiveness Practice Guide" on the next page to list and categorize your responses according to whether they were passive, assertive or aggressive. Look at what you say verbally and how you say it nonverbally. Write down your goals by referring to the chart, "Your Apparent Goals and Feelings," in Chapter 18.

Perhaps you are trying to avoid conflict, please, dominate or humiliate, rather than communicate. Consider what you gain by being aggressive or passive and what you might gain by being assertive. You almost always have more to gain by being assertive. If necessary, review the effects on others of your behavioral options and their probable outcomes.

Planning Your Assertiveness

Now that you have reviewed what you are currently doing and chosen to become more assertive, it is time to decide how you might handle the situations better. A good way of finding a

Personal Assertiveness Practice Guide

Directions: Complete the following chart by sequentially listing the mildly, moderately and very difficult situations you listed in Chapter 19. You may want to refer back to Chapter 18 to classify your behavior and the goals of your behavior. Later in this chapter you may learn new ways of asserting yourself. If you do, you can come back to this chart to modify the new behaviors you proposed.

Personally Difficult Assertiveness Situation	Typical Behavior (Verbal and Nonverbal)	Your Behavior (Aggressive, Passive, or Assertive?)	Goal of Behavior	Proposed New Behavior
1. _____	_____	_____	_____	_____
2. _____	_____	_____	_____	_____
3. _____	_____	_____	_____	_____
4. _____	_____	_____	_____	_____

Personally Difficult Assertiveness Situation	Typical Behavior (Verbal and Nonverbal)	Your Behavior (Aggressive, Passive, or Assertive?)	Goal of Behavior	Proposed New Behavior
6.				
7.				
8.				
9.				
10.				
11.				

better way of coping with the situation is to observe someone who is handling it effectively. You may wish to write down a variety of responses that might be more effective than one you are currently using. Later in this chapter, we will suggest many different assertive techniques.

Imagining Your Assertiveness

The next step is to use visual imagery to imagine better ways of handling the problem. Imagine yourself acting in an assertive manner both verbally and nonverbally. Picture how the other person will react and your response. Envision a number of outcomes and how you can handle them.

Role Playing Your Assertiveness

Rather than jumping from imagining your new behavior to trying it out in the "cruel world," it is best to first role play your assertive solutions. Role playing involves taking the role of someone who is acting in an assertive manner. It is often very helpful to use a mirror to check your nonverbal messages. Be sure that you are:

1. Facing the other person from a normal distance.
2. Looking directly at the other person without staring.
3. Keeping your head erect and body relaxed.
4. Leaning toward the other person.
5. Speaking distinctly and firmly, so as to be easily heard.

Try taking the role of yourself and then taking the role of the other person. Finally, try your role once again. Imagine and rehearse all the possible outcomes.

When you role play, be sure to use your relaxation techniques to calm yourself. This will also help you learn a relaxed, calm and firm approach to assertive communication. You may also want to practice your new skills with someone in your family or with a friend. Be sure to switch roles with them and practice both roles several times.

The Real Thing

The next step is to choose a situation which is likely to bring good results and build up your confidence. Talk over your difficulties with members of your family or a close friend. Ask them to help you deal with your problem by encouraging you and by praising you when you report back about your attempts. Then, relax and take the plunge. Afterward, do not be blind to your progress. Reward yourself for acting assertively.

Remember, you do not have to succeed all the time. Just be sure to learn from your mistakes and then practice more effective behaviors in your imagination, your role playing and your daily life. It will take a good deal of practice before you will do these things naturally and automatically.

Taking The Steps To Assertiveness: An Example

A young woman, who was looking forward to graduating from college and getting married, came to one of us for therapy because she was suffering from tension headaches. After finding some relief from relaxation training, it became clear that a major source of stress was her relationship with her fiancee, a senior medical student. Her fiancee often asked her to take care of more errands than she wanted to take on.

Following the steps suggested above, the woman, whom we will call Susan, began by reviewing her behavior. She described the situation that brought the problem to a head in the following way. The weekend before, her fiancee, whom we will call Bill, had spent one of his few days off fishing with his friends. He had been at her apartment a couple of hours before she returned from shopping with her mother. When Bill told her that he was hungry and asked why she was late, she was angry and disappointed that he had not started dinner; but, she apologized and said she would get started right away.

Susan correctly identified her behavior as passive. She had avoided saying what she thought, wanted or felt. Her apology had a hidden meaning of anger and she remembered being tense and hoping that he would see how tired she looked.

Susan realized how much she wanted to please Bill. At the same time, she felt resentful. Thinking back, she remembered how little respect Bill's father had for his wife who never stood up to him or refused his requests before their divorce. She vowed not to fall into the same trap.

Susan started to think of assertive behaviors that she might use. She had a good friend, named Kathy, who was married to a medical student, and seemed to have a very healthy relationship with her husband.

Susan talked with Kathy and then began using visual imagery. She rehearsed new ways of responding to Bill's requests. She also imagined new ways of approaching Bill for a discussion about these issues.

At our next session, Susan reviewed this work, but was advised to slow down. She had picked one of her most difficult situations and one with a lot of personal happiness riding on it. She then used her "Personal Assertiveness Practice Guide" to find an easier situation that was not as critical and had a higher likelihood of immediate success. Susan chose a mildly difficult, but common problem she had with her sister.

After imagining an assertive response to her sister's requests, she role played the behavior. However, with a weak voice and her eyes turned downwards, she did not look like she meant what she was saying. Susan then watched herself in the mirror, started to laugh, and agreed to use a mirror to practice her nonverbal behaviors at home.

After successfully asserting herself with her sister, Susan began role playing some of the new approaches she wanted to use in her relationship with Bill. She practiced with her friend, Kathy, and then tried out her new skills with Bill.

As it turned out, Bill was very concerned that their marriage not end the way his parent's had ended. He was surprised at his actions when Susan expressed her disappointment and described what he was doing. At the next session of therapy, Susan reported that she was proud of her assertiveness and that their communication was steadily improving.

Responding Assertively To The Requests Of Others

The step-by-step approach we just covered is quite effective for those situations in which you need to initiate an assertive behavior. However, there are many situations where you must respond to the actions of other people. We have found it important to practice these situations and role play them repeatedly, because these are the sort of stressful situations where you may respond impulsively.

Let us take the frequent example of a request made by an authority figure at work. Your immediate supervisor asks you to stay a few hours overtime and do some extra work. You have some special plans, and you do not want to give them up. One of the first things to do is to ask for clarification. If you do not understand what is requested of you or its importance, it is difficult to make a decision to either fullfil the request or to refuse it. In this case, it would be important to clarify how pressing the work is and whether it is work which you might be expected to accomplish.

The next step is to know where you stand on the issue. You need to take some time to process the request and make a decision. Even in a situation like the one just given, you may want to say that you need some time to think it over and let your boss know when you will have an answer. Before responding, it is helpful to use a relaxation technique such as scanning or countdown.

Try to use the word "no" when turning down a request. "No" has a great deal of power and clarity. It is a lot better than "Well, I just don't think so...Ah...." Along the same lines, it is important to be as brief as possible. Give your reasons for refusing the request, but avoid long, elaborate justification or explanation. Long excuses can become accusations or reveal your tendency toward over-responsibility. These excuses can be used by the other person to manipulate you.

Try to use "I" messages. In this case, you might say "I won't work overtime tonight." This might be more effective than "I can't work tonight," or "I shouldn't work tonight." Using an "I" message makes it clear that you have made a choice.

The Broken Record Technique

You may find it necessary to refuse the request several times before the person "hears" you. In this case, you can use a technique which has been popularized by Manuel Smith, Ph.D. He called it the broken record. To use the technique you calmly repeat your "no," with or without your original reason for declining. You do so as often as is required. You may find it helpful to practice the broken record technique in your role playing.

One of the best situations to use the broken record is when you are trying to get what you have paid for. It is particularly useful with repairmen, waiters, and waitresses, salespeople, and landlords. In these cases, you continue saying "no" to any compromise which is unsatisfactory. Be sure to do this in a firm, relaxed manner. Role playing these situations can help you to realize how frequently you may have to play your broken record in a situation.

The Power Of Silence

Silence is a very potent form of nonverbal communication. If someone continues to badger you after you have turned on your broken record, use silence. This is particularly useful on the telephone. If you recall the difficulty that one of the authors was having in a loud hotel room, you may be interested to know that silence seemed to be what finally led the manager to make his decision and change the room.

Additional Approaches

You may also want to assert yourself about what is happening when you are being badgered. You may want to say, "I really wish you would stop pressuring me." Or you may want to try saying, "I'm not going to change my mind." If this does not work, you may need to inform the person of what you are going to do next. You may want to say that you are going to change the topic, hang up the phone, or leave. And you may need to do what you say you are going to do.

An additional approach, called the paradoxical statement, has the power of the unexpected. A paradox may lead to exactly the opposite of what you actually say. For example, just before you leave or hang up the phone, you may want to say, "I hope you will write me a letter or call me several more times about this matter. It is really helping me to practice my assertiveness." This often disarms the person badgering you and leaves him offenseless.

The Fogging Technique

Another major technique popularized by Dr. Smith is called fogging. The person trying to be assertive repeats what the other person is saying or asking for. In this way, before he says "no," the person acknowledges the other person's problem and shows that he understands what the other person is communicating.

In relationships with important people, it is also helpful to acknowledge the feelings that the other person may have about your refusal. You may want to reflect his feelings after he has stated them. You may say something like "I know that you've been hoping that I would do it and that this may be a disappointment to you, but I won't be able to."

Try to avoid using the words "I'm sorry." Apologizing is often unnecessary and dishonest. It also tends to compromise your basic right to say "no." You may wish to offer a compromise, but it is important that you realize you have the freedom not to compromise. In the office example we started with, you may want to compromise and work for an hour extra, or come in early the next day. Be sure to refuse the major request clearly and without feeling guilty.

Finally, you have the right to change your mind and refuse a request that you may have originally agreed to. You have to weigh the consequences, but if you find yourself hedging or feeling manipulated, you may want to reconsider your initial decision.

Practice Saying "No"

To practice saying "no" to requests and demands, use the following examples. First, try them in your imagination and then role play them in front of a mirror.

1. A friend asks you for a loan until the next payday.
2. You daughter asks if she may stay out until 3:00 in the morning.
3. You are on a committee and have done your work. Another committee member calls you at the last minute and trys to get you to do some of his work.
4. Your uncle tells you of his plan to visit you for a month. This is the third time this year.
5. A person at work never seems to have a cigarette. He asks you again for one of yours.
6. A salesperson pressures you to buy when you are still undecided.
7. You and your wife are out with friends who want to go for a nightcap. You are tired and want to go home.
8. A friend asks you to make cookies for a bake sale, but you have planned an evening with another friend.
9. Your boss asks you again to postpone your vacation.
10. A friend expects you to help her plan a party.

Taking the Stress Out of Criticism

Criticism you receive from others is another major category of situations for which you may need to practice responding to others in an assertive manner. When someone begins to criticize you, you may find it helpful to use a brief relaxation technique, such as taking a deep breath and saying silently "Relax and let go." This will help you to listen to what the person is saying. If the criticism is vague or ambigiuous, it may be helpful to ask the person to be more specific. The next step may be to state the criticism in your own words. This allows you to check out what you have heard and shows the other person that you understood the criticism.

At this point, it is often helpful to take a moment to relax and decide if the criticism is accurate or useful. You may also want to get in touch with your feelings so you can share them with the person making the criticism. You may feel annoyed, angry or scared. It is often helpful to share these feelings with the other person so that the person will know the effect the criticism is having on you. You may want to express your feelings about the timing, frequency, or accuracy of the criticism.

If the criticism is a fair one, you may find it helpful to ask for specific suggestions and alternatives. It is important to avoid excuses which may turn out to be self-accusations. Try to move toward the future and turn the person criticizing you in the same direction. When sharing your feelings about the criticism, it is important to use "I" statements so as not to put the other person on the defensive. Consider the difference between "You don't understand anything," and "It seems to me that you may not have understood what happened."

By using a relaxation technique, you can avoid an escalating sense of urgency and anger. If you try to match the pace and volume of the person criticizing you, it may lead to an argument. Try speaking slowly, calmly and quietly.

Here are some examples of criticisms to practice with:

1. Your boss says that your work is sloppy.
2. Your supervisor says your work is never on time.
3. You wife says you don't love her.
4. Your child says you don't understand him.
5. Your mother says you don't visit enough.
6. Your girlfriend says you are a cheat.
7. Your teacher says your paper was confusing and meaningless.
8. A new acquaintance says, "Most women don't know what they're talking about."
9. Your students say, that your lectures are boring.
10. A customer says, that what you have done or what you sell is useless.

Common Problems And Their Solutions

Some people can recognize and categorize their behavior, but have difficulty with the next step of imagining vividly better ways of handling the problem. They know what to imagine, but to do so makes them anxious. If you seem to be having trouble visualizing a situation without a great deal of anxiety, you may be conditioned to respond with fear in situations where you might be disliked or rejected. If this is the case, it may be helpful to return to Chapter 13. Practice mental simulation and image rehearsal with relaxation so that you will be less sensitive to what others say and do.

Irrational Beliefs Supporting Passive Behaviors

Another way of handling difficulties with assertiveness is to examine potential irrational beliefs about assertiveness. Lynn Bloom, Karen Coburn and Joan Pearlman in their excellent book, The New Assertive Woman, review irrational beliefs that support passive behaviors. One of their chapters is entitled "What's the Worst that Could Happen--Irrational Beliefs." These irrational beliefs can support passive behaviors whether you are a man or a woman.

You may have unrealistic beliefs about the possible outcomes of a situation involving assertive behavior. Even if the outcome is negative, you may be blowing it out of proportion or assuming that you could not handle it. Some of the irrational beliefs and their rational counterparts include:

Irrational Belief	Rational Counterpart
1. As soon as I am assertive, others will become angry at me.	Others may react positively, neutrally, or negatively. If assertiveness involves legitimate rights, the odds are that you will have a positive response.
2. As soon as I assert myself, people will become angry and I will be devastated.	I will be capable of handling it and I am not responsible for another person's anger. It may well be that person's problem.

3. I want others to be honest and straightforward with me, but if I tell others what I feel or want, I will hurt them.

People may or may not feel hurt, and most people prefer to be dealt with directly.

4. If others are hurt by my assertive behavior, I am responsible for their hurt feelings.

Even if they are hurt, I can let them know I care for them in other ways and they will survive.

5. If I turn down legitimate requests, other people will hate me.

Even legitimate requests can be refused. I can consider my own needs, and I cannot please everyone all the time.

6. I should always avoid making statements or asking questions that might make me look stupid.

I am a valuable human being. The people I want to associate with will accept me as a valuable human being.

Irrational Beliefs Supporting Aggressive Behaviors

Aggression is appropriate for situations in which we are physically attacked. Fearing harm, we strike back to protect ourselves. Unfortunately, we may misperceive a situation as dangerous and become aggressive in unnecessary and ineffective ways. What we think and say to ourselves can determine what we see and do. This is especially true when we jump to conclusions without considering all the evidence.

Just as there are irrational beliefs that support passive behaviors, there are irrational beliefs that support aggressive behaviors. If you are trying to substitute assertive behaviors for aggressive ones, consider some of the false beliefs that often support aggressive behaviors. The irrational beliefs that follow were held by people in a group we led to help them get better control over their tempers and aggressive behaviors. Some of the rational counterparts which the group members found useful are provided next to each irrational belief.

Irrational Belief	Rational Counterpart
1. It's either him or me, and it's not going to be me if I can help it.	We can both win. Let's look for a compromise.
2. If I'm not aggressive, they will be.	Others may respond in many ways--odds are the ways will be neutral or positive.
3. It's a dog-eat-dog world.	What you expect is often what you get.
4. If I don't angrily turn this request down now, I'll have a flood of requests to contend with.	I can be assertive if people later try to take advantage of me.
5. If I don't let them know loud and clear, they won't do what they said they would.	First, I'll see what they say to my firm request. I can always use other assertive techniques if they refuse.
6. You can't teach an old dog new tricks. I always get angry.	Always? Few "always" or "never" statements are true.

Check and dispute your irrational beliefs. Some of them may be interfering with your right to be assertive. Review Chapter 15 about thinking and feeling better if you have trouble recognizing and disputing them.

REVIEW QUESTIONS

<u>Directions</u>: Circle the letter in front of the best response to each question. The correct answers are provided on the page following the last question.

1. All but one of the following steps of becoming assertive are correct. Which one is <u>not</u> correct?

    a. Review and categorize your behaviors as aggressive, passive, or assertive.
    b. Decide how you might handle the situation better, maybe by finding a good role model.
    c. Visualize in your imagination better ways of handling the problem and then role play them.
    d. Choose your most challenging situation and force yourself to do it.

2. Role playing in front of a mirror can help you to

    a. assess your non-verbal signals.
    b. practice your new behaviors.
    c. improve your non-verbal behaviors.
    d. All the above.

3. By maintaining direct eye contact, an erect body posture, and a clear, audible speaking tone, you will be more likely to be perceived and responded to as

    a. passive.
    b. assertive.
    c. non-assertive.
    d. Any of the above.

4. When refusing a request, try to

    a. use the word "no."
    b. give clear justifications and long explanations.
    c. use "you" messages.
    d. apologize in a calm voice.

5. The broken record technique involves

    a. waiting until you can blow off steam by throwing records
        at home.
    b. calmly repeating "no" with or without the original
        reason for declining the request.
    c. apologizing over and over again.
    d. maintaining a passive approach to the situation.

6. Which of the following approaches is not useful in handling
    criticisms?

    a. Use a brief relaxation technique so you can listen to
        what the person is saying.
    b. Take a moment to relax and decide if the criticism is
        accurate or useful.
    c. Avoid muddying the waters with your feelings and provide
        clear excuses.
    d. Use "I" statements so as not to put the other person on
        the defensive.

7. If you feel too anxious to visualize or attempt assertive-
    ness in a situation, you might try

    a. desensitizing yourself to what others say and do.
    b. examining your irrational beliefs that support passive
        behavior.
    c. examining your irrational beliefs that support your
        anxiety.
    d. Any or all of the above.

8. Which of the following irrational beliefs support passive
    behavior?

    a. "Give them an inch and they'll take a mile."
    b. "I have to put others down to protect myself."
    c. "As soon as I am assertive, others will become angry at
        me."
    d. "It's a dog-eat-dog world."

9. Which of the following irrational beliefs support aggressive behavior?

    a. "As soon as I assert myself, people will become angry and I will be devastated."
    b. "I want others to be honest with me, but if I tell others what I feel or want I will hurt them."
    c. "It's either him or me, and it's not going to be me if I can help it."
    d. "If others are hurt by my assertive behavior, I am responsible for their hurt feelings."

10. All but one of the following beliefs support assertive behavior. Which one is <u>not</u> supportive of assertiveness?

    a. "Others may react positively, neutrally, or negatively."
    b. "If I don't let them know loud and clear, they won't do what they said they would."
    c. "People may or may not feel hurt, and most people prefer to be dealt with directly."
    d. "We can both win. Let's look for a compromise."

ANSWERS TO REVIEW QUESTIONS

1.	d	6.	c
2.	d	7.	d
3.	b	8.	c
4.	a	9.	c
5.	b	10.	b

SUGGESTED BOOKS AND RECORDING

BOOKS

Stand Up, Speak Out, Talk Back! by R. Alberti & M. Emmons. New York: Pocket, 1975.

The New Assertive Woman by L. Bloom, K. Coburn & J. Pearlman. New York: Dell, 1976.

When I Say No, I Feel Guilty by M. Smith. New York: Bantam, 1975.

Your Perfect Right: A Guide To Assertive Behavior by R. Alberti & M. Emmons. San Luis Obispo, California: Impact, 1970.

RECORDING

Self-Directed Assertiveness Training by R. Rakos & H. Schroeder. New York: B.M.A., 1976.

Section VI

Planning Your Days
And Your Years

Chapter 21

Managing The Times
Of Your Life

The Faster I Go, The Behinder I Get

How time has fascinated men throughout the ages! "Time, time, oh good, good time, where have you gone?" This has been the lament of the young and the striving. It has also been the lament of the old and the dying. If you have ever wondered where time has gone, you may have been using your time ineffectively. You may know the meaning of the words "The faster I go, the behinder I get."

Not Seeing The Forest For The Trees

One of the best stories we know concerning the ineffective use of time is about a lumberjack, or at least a very powerful young man who wanted to be a lumberjack. This young man wandered through a logging camp on his 18th birthday. He had been raised around the lumbering communities and admired the strong lumberjacks. He told the boss that he wanted a job. Seeing that the boy was large, strong and healthy, the boss quickly agreed. The first day this lad chopped down ten large trees entirely by himself. Now this was quite an accomplishment and the boss was very pleased. He complimented the boy about his energy and strength.

The next day, the boy seemed to work just as hard and just as long, but he only chopped down eight trees. This was still quite respectable. The rest of the week passed and each day the boy worked just as hard and just as long, but each day he produced less and less. On Friday, the boss called the boy into his office after noticing that he had yet to fell one tree. The sun was going down. The boy had worked vigorously all day. He was ashamed because he had produced so little and tears began to roll down his face as he went into the office.

"Sir," he said, "I'm working harder and harder, but I'm afraid I'm a disappointment to you. I have yet to fell one tree today." "Why do you do so little?" the boss said. "I'm really

trying, Sir," the response came. "Have you taken the time to
sharpen your axe, boy?" The boy answered, "No sir, I really
haven't had time because I have been so busy working."

And so the story goes. Today, thousands of people
everywhere in the world tirelessly pursue this fleeting thing
called time. Yet time is the one thing that we are all given in
equal amounts. The rich and the poor all have the same number
of minutes in an hour, hours in a day and days in a year.

What Is Time?

It has been said that your time is your life. If you waste
your time, you waste your life. Saint Augustine said that we
speak of time as if we understand it, but when we are asked to
define it, our mind is blank. Time can be thought of as an
endless series of decisions, small and large, that gradually
shape our lives.

Not only do we have difficulty defining time, but we also
have several misconceptions about time. For example, we often
say "time flies." Of course, time does not fly. Time moves at
a predetermined rate. Another misconception is that we can
"save time." We cannot really save time. We cannot put time in
a bank or collect interest on time that is saved. Can we make
up time? No, once time is spent it is irretrievable. Some say
time is money, but it is only valuable if it is productive or
enjoyable.

We often feel that time and the clock are against us. But
time can be on our side once we have the ability to organize our
lives to use time to our benefit. If the use of time is an
endless series of management decisions, then inappropriate
decisions can produce frustration, lower self-esteem and
increase stress levels.

Danger Signals Of Poor Time Management

There are various danger signals that suggest a person can
benefit from better time management. Read through the following
list and discover if any of these warnings apply to you. Use
the scale under the title to determine your score between 0 and
10 for each item. Record your score in the blank next to each
statement and then add these scores to compute your total time
management score.

TIME MANAGEMENT SCALE

0	1 2 3	4 5 6	7 8 9	10
Never	Sometimes	Frequently	Most of the Time	Always

_____ 1. I am indispensable. I find myself taking on various tasks because I'm the only one that can do them.

_____ 2. Daily crises take up all my time. I have no time to do important things because I'm too busy putting out fires.

_____ 3. I attempt to do too much at one time. I feel I can do it all, and I rarely say "no."

_____ 4. I feel unrelenting pressure, as if I'm always behind and have no way to catch up. I'm always rushing.

_____ 5. I'm working habitually long hours, 10, 12, 14 even 18 hours a day; 5, 6, and 7 days a week.

_____ 6. I constantly feel overwhelmed by demands and details, and feel as if I'm having to do what I don't want to do most of the time.

_____ 7. I feel guilty about leaving work on time. I don't have sufficient time for rest or personal relationships. I take worries and problems home.

_____ 8. I constantly miss deadlines.

_____ 9. I am plagued by fatigue and listlessness with many slack hours of unproductive activity.

_____ 10. I chronically vacillate between unpleasant alternatives.

_____ Total Score

If you scored less than 35 total points, then you may benefit from learning additional time management techniques, but
your stress level is probably not significantly affected by time
pressure. If you scored 36 to 60 you probably could use time
management training to reduce the risk of potential stress
disorders.

If you scored greater than 60, then your life may feel dan-
gerously out of control. People that score over 60 often "don't
have time" for training in stress or time management. They may
put off indefinitely such important decisions as to stop smoking, begin exercising, spend more time with family and friends,
or take vacations. We have a choice whether we wish to allow
time to manage us, or we wish to manage time.

Time, Stress and Productivity

Productivity can increase with the time and energy we ex-
pend, but only up to a critical point. Past this point, additional time and energy become counter-productive. Time management experts use a stress-productivity curve to demonstrate this
finding. If you examine this curve, you will notice that there
is a critical point beyond which increasing time, energy and
stress lead to decreasing productivity. This is the point of
diminishing returns.

STRESS-PRODUCTIVITY CURVE

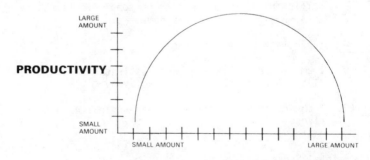

TIME, ENERGY AND STRESS

We mentioned earlier in this book that stress can be a
motivator. Time can also be our friend. However, if you have
too much stress, or too little time, these can become enemies
that lead to many of the problems we listed above. Time can be
your master or your slave. Time management techniques are ways
of gaining control over your life and finding solutions to
various time wasters.

Time Wasters Are Time Robbers

An analysis of time wasters helps to build a firm foundation for good time management. A time waster is anything that
prohibits us from reaching our objectives most effectively.
Time is a perishable asset and, if we are not careful, it can be
taken away without our even noticing it is being stolen. Time
wasters are robbers. They can be divided into two major
categories: Major and minor time wasters.

Major time wasters are the first things that stand between
us and what we want to accomplish. Major time wasters include
problems with our attitudes, goals, objectives, priorities,
plans, and abilities to make basic decisions.

Minor time wasters include those things that distract us
once we are on the way to accomplishing what we want to
accomplish. Minor time wasters can include interruptions that
we face during the day, lengthy meetings of minor importance,
needless reports, extended telephone calls, unexpected visitors,
and many other distractions.

Taking A Time Inventory

Before examining various steps to effective time management
and analyzing time wasters, it is useful to take your own
personal time inventory. To do this, you should use the chart
on page 385, which is broken into 15-minute segments of the
day. Carry this chart with you during a typical day and fill it
in as you go along. It is most helpful to complete this chart
as you go through a normal day. If you try to recall accurately
how you spent your time and how much work you actually
accomplished in a particular day, you might find it difficult or
impossible.

In the categories of the activity column on "Your Personal
Time Inventory," describe activities that suit your particular
business and daily routine. We would like to suggest certain
categories that you may find useful. For example, categories
that are often helpful in taking a time inventory of the working
part of the day include: socializing, routine tasks,
low-priority work, productive work, meetings, and telephone
calls. Helpful categories for when you are not at work include:
telephone calls, television, recreation, errands, commuting,
shopping, household chores, eating, personal hygiene, and
sleeping.

Modify or add any categories that will help you to better understand how you spend your time. Taking a time inventory can help you to separate and examine the various categories of time and how you use them. This allows you to determine if you want to spend more or less time in various activities.

By taking a time inventory, some people learn that they need to limit phone conversations to five minutes, reduce the amount of time spent on preparation for breakfast and eating, shorten the time spent showering and preparing for work in the morning, and restrict the time spent watching television. On the other hand, some people find that their best time for relaxation is in the morning. For this individual, a long casual breakfast may be very effective in helping to management stress.

Although every person is unique, the majority of people find that their most productive work hours and peak-energy periods are in the morning. If there are many interruptions, lengthy meetings, or a lack of priorities and organized objectives in the morning, they may feel that the whole day has been wasted before they reach noon. These people should schedule their most productive work in the mornings.

Now, complete your time inventory and then add up the amount of time spent in each category of activity.

PERSONAL TIME INVENTORY

List the activities you do during the next three days. Use the following <u>Activity Codes</u> and any <u>Personal Codes</u> to describe how your time was spent.

In the <u>Satisfied</u> column place a "+", "0" or "-" to indicate how satisfied you are with how you spent your time. If you are very satisfied or feel the time was spent productively, then place a "+" in column. If you are not satisfied with how you spent the time, but feel it was a necessary part of the day, rate it "0." If you are dissatisfied with how you spent your time or feel it was an unnecessary part of the day, use the "-" for the rating.

Activity Codes:

Socializing - Soc.
Telephone Calls - Tel.
Meetings - Mtgs.
Low Priority Work - L.P.W.
Medium Priority Work - M.P.W.
Productive Work - P.W.
Commutting to Work - Com.

Passive Recreation (reading,
   listening to the radio,
   etc.) - P.R.
Errands - Err.
Shopping - Shop
Household Chores - H.C.
Eating - Eat

Personal Codes:

_____   _____

_____   _____

_____   _____

_____   _____

_____   _____

_____   _____

_____   _____

Date _____

Time	Activity	Satisfaction (+,0,-)	Time	Activity	Satisfaction (+,0,-)
5:00 a.m.			10:00 a.m.		
5:15 a.m.			10:15 a.m.		
5:30 a.m.			10:30 a.m.		
5:45 a.m.			10:45 a.m.		
6:00 a.m.			11:00 a.m.		
6:15 a.m.			11:15 a.m.		
6:30 a.m.			11:30 a.m.		
6:45 a.m.			11:45 a.m.		
7:00 a.m.			Noon		
7:15 a.m.			12:15 p.m.		
7:30 a.m.			12:30 p.m.		
7:45 a.m.			12:45 p.m.		
8:00 a.m.			1:00 p.m.		
8:15 a.m.			1:15 p.m.		
8:30 a.m.			1:30 p.m.		
8:45 a.m.			1:45 p.m.		
9:00 a.m.			2:00 p.m.		
9:15 a.m.			2:15 p.m.		
9:30 a.m.			2:30 p.m.		
9:45 a.m.			2:45 p.m.		

Time	Activity	Satisfaction (+,0,-)	Time	Activitiy	Satisfaction (+,0,-)
(continued)			7:30 p.m.		
3:00 p.m.			7:45 p.m.		
3:15 p.m.			8:00 p.m.		
3:30 p.m.			8:15 p.m.		
3:45 p.m.			8:30 p.m.		
4:00 p.m.			8:45 p.m.		
4:15 p.m.			9:00 p.m.		
4:30 p.m.			9:15 p.m.		
4:45 p.m.			9:30 p.m.		
5:00 p.m.			9:45 p.m.		
5:15 p.m.			10:00 p.m.		
5:30 p.m.			10:15 p.m.		
5:45 p.m.			10:30 p.m.		
6:00 p.m.			10:45 p.m.		
6:15 p.m.			11:00 p.m.		
6:30 p.m.			11:15 p.m.		
6:45 p.m.			11:30 p.m.		
7:00 p.m.			11:45 p.m.		
7:15 p.m.			Midnight		

Time Analysis

Total up the amount of time spent in each category of activity on your time inventory. List below the activity code and the time spent doing the activity. Indicate if you were satisfied (+) with how much time you spent for each activity, or if you were dissatisfied (-). If you were dissatisfied, indicate in the adjustment column how much more or less time you would want to spend on a particular activity.

Activity	Time Spent	Satis- faction (+,-)	Adjustment
Example: *Casual office talk*	*3 hours*	*−*	*2 hours less*
1.			
2.			
3.			
4.			
5.			
6.			
7.			
8.			
9.			
10.			
11.			
12.			
13.			
14.			
15.			

Job Descriptions

Now you have analyzed how you spend your time. We would like to encourage you to decide that it is your choice as to how you use your time. Taking responsibility for the way you use your time is no more, and no less, than taking responsibility for the way you live your life. Doing this allows you to choose to spend your time in ways other than how you spend it now.

We have worked with many people that chronically complain about their job, constant interruptions, and a feeling of always being behind. It is true that some jobs involve coping with many interruptions and "putting out fires." We certainly don't recommend this, but if your job entails dealing with constant interruptions, it is easier to deal with them if you consciously chose this as your job. One clear way to add stress to an already stressful job is to adopt the "I have to" attitude. Do you frequently find yourself saying or thinking, "I have to take care of this because...." or "I have to work late because...."?

Many people find themselves feeling that their jobs are beyond their control. When this happens frequently, it helps to step back and assess the situation in the following way. Sit down and write out a realistic job description. Become aware of your authority and responsibility. Write down all the duties you really take on. Do not be surprised if the job is not what you initially contracted for. Many people find that they are actually doing the wrong tasks--tasks that are unimportant or not even part of their jobs.

Once you have an accurate job description and a list of your duties, then decide if this is really the job you want. If it is not the job you want, you may wish to use assertiveness to renegotiate the job description or duties and take better advantage of the skills and time of others over whom you have authority.

You may also decide that your best choice is to change jobs. It may be wise to check the material about life-change management in Chapter 11 to plan an optimal time period for adding this change stressor. In addition, most people find that the best time to land a new job is when you already have one.

Job searching requires skills many of us never learned or even used. An excellent guide to finding a job is The Trees Jobs Grow On. See the suggested readings and recordings at the end of this chapter.

The Job-Person Fit

Hans Selye points out that among people, "There are race-horses and there are turtles." Most of us fall somewhere between the two extremes. If you are a casual person, you probably do not want to be in a profession where you are always running a race. Your real pleasures may be at home in the evenings watching your children grow up. If you are a real racehorse, then you may find it stressful to sit quietly at home. Different people, have different values and pleasures.

Jimmy Buffet wrote a song called "It's My Job." His words describe an attitude of contentment expressed by a street sweeper as he is sweeping the streets. He sings "It's my job and that's enough reason to go for me." This street sweeper has resolved his values with his job, and he does the best at what he has chosen to do. We all have a choice in life, although sometimes we are put into situations where we can only choose how we will react.

The prisoners of war (P.O.W.'s) in Vietnam responded differently depending on their interpretation of their situation. Some became depressed and only focused on the horror around them. Others used it as a "vacation" for self-improvement and practiced muscial instruments, played golf, wrote books or exercised. Some returned depressed and some returned with new skills.

Many people feel like they, too, are P.O.W.'s, but they mean prisoners of work. You probably have a choice in your vocational endeavors. Write down your job description and decide if this is what you want to be doing. If you choose your present job situation, use the job stress as an opportunity for self-improvement. Follow the guidelines in this chapter to help you better manage your time and job stress. When you fill in your goals and priorities, be sure these are what you truly want. It is easier to reach the goals of your choice, than goals chosen by parents, spouse, colleagues or peers.

The Importance Of Goals

Now we want you to examine what many people discover is their major time waster: a lack of important goals. Goals reflect our purpose in life and have a widespread impact on our life.

Victor Frankl is a Viennese psychiatrist who survived the horror of the Nazi death camps in World War II. In his book Man's Search for Meaning, he describes how those who had a

purpose for living were able to withstand torture and
starvation. The purpose for living could have been revenge,
building a new homeland, or waiting for the allied forces to
arrive. Those without purpose, goals or positive self-direction
died quickly.

Dennis Waitley, in his book The Psychology of Winning,
tells how the Vietnam P.O.W.'s who adjusted most easily upon
returning to freedom were those with goals. The goals could be
as clear and uncomplicated as one P.O.W.'s goal to become the
world's record holder for the number of consecutive sit-ups.

It has been said that two of the greatest tragedies are to
have never had a goal, or to have reached it. Life is a series
of ever growing accomplishments and few people have only one
goal which they reach and then call it quits. Those who do so,
face a major change stressor. Consider the man who "finally"
retires and has no new goals. The emptiness can be devasting.
As you work through this section on goals, we would like you to
consider your future in a number of different ways.

Life-Long Goals

First, imagine that you are very old and you overhear your
grandchildren talking to their friends about you and your life.
What would you want them to say about you and your accomplishments? Use the spaces below to jot down your thoughts about
this.

_____

_____

_____

_____

_____

_____

_____

_____

_____

_____

Next, we would like you to write your own epitaph.   An epitaph is an inscription on a tomb and is written as a tribute to the dead person.   How would you want others to remember you?

_____

_____

_____

_____

_____

As you list your future goals in this chapter, remember that people are goal-seekers by design. We constantly adjust our self-image and subconscious to help us reach goals. Often, our goals are not planned out, or they are dictated by negative self-talk such as "I can't do this very well," or "I just know she's not going to like me."   Many people actually program themselves not to reach goals by using negative self-talk, failing to clearly define goals, or neglecting to make plans for reaching well-chosen goals.

Most people spend more time planning a party or reading the newspaper than they spend planning their lives. Dennis Waitley describes winners as people with a definite purpose in life. He also says, "If you don't stand for something, you'll fall for anything." Keep his words in mind as you explore your goals and the value you place on them.

Goal-Getting

Goals must be obtainable and objectives must be quantifiable. In addition, goals should be flexible in the event that they are blocked by other priorities. For example, if you set a goal to have a luxury automobile, you may find that you spend more per month than you had expected. That may or may not be compatible with the other goals you have.

On a different scale you may have set as a goal to research a new project. If the boss comes in and says the budget has to go to committee tomorrow, then your priorities may shift. Your long-term goal is starting the new project, but without budgeting money for it, you may be doing the research out of your own pocket and on your own time. That is why it is helpful to establish flexible plans for acheiving long-term goals.

We would like you to go through an exercise involving two-minute drills. Use the <u>Goal Cues</u> list below to help you think of categories of goals.

GOAL CUES

New home	Increase earnings	Start exercising
Home improvement	New position	Stop smoking
Lose weight	Family activity	Family communication
Professional skill	Become more patient	New honor
Long vacation	Additional education	Problem solution
Spiritual goals	Short vacation	More spontaneity
New hobby	Increase savings	Play with children
Closer friends	Debts paid off	Community service

Co-worker communi-
  cation
	Manage something
	  better
		More marital satis-
		  faction

First, we ask you to spend two minutes writing down all the things that you would like to accomplish in the next five years. Limber up your imagination and write down anything that comes to mind. Spend only two minutes on this task. Use extra paper if you need to list all of your goals.

FIVE-YEAR GOALS

1. _____

2. _____

3. _____

4. _____

5. _____

6. _____

7. _____

8. _____

Next, list all the goals you hope to accomplish next year. Spend only two minutes and list all your goals for the next year.

ONE-YEAR GOALS

1._____

2._____

3._____

4._____

5._____

6._____

7._____

8._____

Spend only two minutes and write down all the goals you have for the next six months.

SIX-MONTH GOALS

1._____

2._____

3._____

4._____

5._____

6._____

7._____

8._____

Spend another two minutes and this time write down all your goals for the coming month and include any work priorities, self-improvement programs, recreational activities, social functions, family gatherings, etc. Spend only two minutes on this task.

ONE-MONTH GOALS

1. _____

2. _____

3. _____

4. _____

5. _____

6. _____

7. _____

8. _____

Top-Priority Goals

Now that you have created these four lists of goals, we would like you to go back and prioritize each goal. Use an A, B, C format.

A's will include all those items that you rank as being most essential and most desired. These are your "must do's." They are often innovative and require creativity.

B's will include all those items which could be put off for a while, but they are items you feel are still important. These are your "desirable to do" or routine duties.

C's are items that could easily be put off indefinitely with little or no harm. These are your "can waits" and are often just trivia.

After you have prioritized your list, combine the three lists into one by including two A items from each of your long-term, one-year, six-month, and one-month goals. Write these down in the spaces below.

<u>A-PRIORITY GOALS</u>

1._____

2._____

3._____

4._____

5._____

6._____

7._____

8._____

The above list should indicate the most important things you would like to accomplish in the next year. To help ensure that this list really contains your <u>most</u> important goals, we want you to complete another list.

For the next list, imagine you have been told that you have a terminal illness and you will die in one year. During your last year of life you will neither be incapacitated nor experience pain. You will be able to do everything you currently do. In the spaces below, write down your goals for the next year if you knew you would die at the end of the year.

MY GOALS IF NEXT YEAR IS THE LAST YEAR OF MY LIFE

1._____

2._____

3._____

4._____

5._____

6._____

7._____

8._____

Compare the last two lists you have constructed. If these lists are totally different, you may want to consider more seriously some of the GOALS IF NEXT YEAR IS THE LAST YEAR OF MY LIFE list. Below combine the A-PRIORITY GOALS and GOALS IF NEXT YEAR IS THE LAST YEAR OF MY LIFE lists to accurately reflect your most important goals.

CURRENT MAJOR LIFE GOALS   TIMETABLE

1._____   _____

2._____   _____

3._____   _____

4._____   _____

5._____   _____

6._____   _____

7._____   _____

8._____   _____

9._____   _____

10._____   _____

Now that you have selected your current major life goals it is essential to set up a timetable for each goal. Indicate time periods during which the goals can reasonably be attained.

You now have important goals to work toward and a timetable to guide you. These are your top priorities. Translate these goals and projects into monthly, weekly and daily activities. Use these as a guide for your time management for a month.

At the end of the month, review your list to see if you need to make a new list. Sometimes goals are completed and sometimes uncompleted goals remain high in importance. Other goals may drop in importance. Set aside time every day to work on your A-Priority goals. Emphasize the results that you want rather than the activity and try to accomplish at least one step toward each goal every day.

Planning Today Means A More Relaxed Tomorrow

When a sailor is preparing for a voyage, he will chart his course toward his destination and determine what prevailing winds he may expect. Seldom will he be able to predict all the changes of weather, but with the forethought of planning comes the knowledge of which reefs to avoid. He will also plan and rehearse his actions should a sudden squall or a prolonged storm appear. We may take an example from the ocean sailor as we sail on the sea of life.

Anything which arouses a stress response can be called a stressor. How we plan our course with these stressors in mind will have an effect on how well we actually deal with the stress. First, we need to have some sort of a chart for where we are going and what dangers we may expect. Next, we need to know the strengths and weaknesses of the vessel on which we are sailing.

If you know your vocational goal is to become a successful businessman, you should also know your port of destination. To be a successful businessman means many things to many people. Without a specific goal, you may not even know when your ship has come in. A chart does little good without setting a course, estimating a time of arrival and determining a destination.

The vessel needs to be equipped to make the voyage. If the boat has a slow leak or battered sails, you may need to decide to pull into an intermediary port for repairs or continue. If the leak develops a day away from your destination, you may be able to keep it afloat until you return. So it is with living. If we know we have to finish the project by the deadline, we can often keep going. When the deadline is met, we can make our repairs by relaxing and taking time off.

The need may arise to look once again at our chart and see how far we are from our long-term goals. Here is where many people have problems. First, they were not certain how much they have really accomplished. With a sense of time urgency they decide to set off once again without a planned period of time to repair the boat. Something in the back of their minds may be saying "It's better to be doing something without a plan, than doing nothing." What they forget is that making the boat seaworthy and studying the chart to find a plan is far from doing nothing.

By knowing what your goals and plans are, you have a better chance of recognizing the stressors you will encounter and how long you may be exposed to them. Without plans and goals, people never know when they have done enough or where they are on their voyage. It is very hard to relax and take a break, if you don't plan for one or forget when it is breaktime.

An Ounce Of Planning Is Worth A Pound Of Work

The best way to effectively work toward your A-Priority Goals is to plan your day successfully. Here is one of the most powerful rules of time management:

ONE HOUR SPENT IN EFFECTIVE

PLANNING SAVES THREE TO FOUR

HOURS IN EXECUTION.

Crises and mistakes can often be avoided with proper planning. Proper planning will insure that the efforts you make during the day are efforts directed at your main priorities, the major goals that you have set in your life. Without a plan, without a road map, or without a chart for navigation, a person is left adrift on a sea of stress.

The only alternative to charting your own course is reacting to the demands of others. In effect, the decision of how you use your time is made by others who are not likely to have as their goals the same business or personal goals that you have just listed. You can end up on Friday wondering where the week went or on your death bed wondering where your life went.

Work Before Play Or Guilt Without Gain

We often find people with whom we work experience a great deal of guilt about how they spend their day. Many of these people have goals, but get involved in recreational activities before they have advanced toward their goals and earned their recreation. When they do this they feel guilty.

We emphasize play and recreation as part of effective stress management. However, when you feel subconsciously or consciously that you have not earned the right for recreation or play because of wasted time during the day, guilt is the price you pay. This can become a pattern and the feelings of guilt can become attached to play, even after a productive day's work. Recreation and play that become strongly associated with negative emotions such as guilt, no longer provide the intended and needed relief from work.

Scheduling Your Time

Allocate your time according to your priorities. Part of doing this means planning your time every day of your life. Schedule appointments and time to stay abreast of what is new in your field. Schedule time to enjoy recreational activities. You should also schedule time to take care of yourself physically. This is very important and each day we should strive toward taking care of ourselves in the best way we can. The winners in life know that they have only one vehicle and that is their body. Unless they maintain that body, they will grow old much sooner and lose the energy needed to enjoy and accomplish the things they want from life.

You may also want to look back over your important goals and note whether you included a satisfying family life. If you are a workaholic, revise your list of goals and plans on a regular basis to include family and personal goals. There are many very successful people who are also very lonely people.

To-Do Lists

As you work toward the accomplishment of your goals, one technique to help you keep focused on important goals is to keep a daily "To-Do" list. Break your larger goals into very small short-term goals. Meeting some of these attainable short-term goals can be very reinforcing. It gives you an important sense of accomplishment and momentum.

The "To-Do" list includes all the small, short-term goals you would like to accomplish for a particular day. Below is a sample "To-Do" list you can use to plan your day.

TO-DO'S

Item	A, B or C	Plan
1. _____	____	_____
2. _____	____	_____
3. _____	____	_____
4. _____	____	_____
5. _____	____	_____
6. _____	____	_____
7. _____	____	_____
8. _____	____	_____
9. _____	____	_____
10. _____	____	_____
11. _____	____	_____
12. _____	____	_____
13. _____	____	_____
14. _____	____	_____
15. _____	____	_____
16. _____	____	_____
17. _____	____	_____
18. _____	____	_____
19. _____	____	_____
20. _____	____	_____

Notice that each item is rated as A, B or C. If you find yourself doing a C item, such as cleaning out your desk, and your A items aren't finished, then you can be certain that you are probably wasting your time. Work your way down from the A items to the C items.

Many individuals begin with little tasks that are inconsequential or unrelated to the day's goals. These may include filing old memos, checking the sports pages in the newspaper, talking to the secretary about a movie, putting away books, or many other activities. Often we do these little tasks as a way of putting off what really causes us some anxiety, namely our A items.

Find ways of overcoming your anxieties and try to tackle the "tough," important jobs first, not last. The following sections describe additional ways of managing your life to help you manage your time.

Not-To-Do Lists

When you have a particularly tight timetable, you may find it helpful to write down specific things you do not plan to do. Write down the time wasters and time robbers you will avoid. For example, you may write down that you will not answer phone calls unless they are truly urgent, you will not accept visitors, or you will not file anything today. Below is a Not-To-Do list you can use.

NOT TO DO'S

1. _____

2. _____

3. _____

4. _____

5. _____

6. _____

7. _____

8. _____

9. _____

10. _____

Saying "No"

One of the best things we can do for ourselves is learning how to say "no." This is so important that we have devoted a whole section to refusing requests in the chapters about assertiveness training.

Poorly considered commitments may force you to spend time on low priority items. You may also find yourself doing other people's high priority items, which, for you, are not very important. Often people will try to convince you to do their work for them. This requires the ability to say "no" if work is delegated unfairly to you.

The 80/20 Rule

The 80/20 Rule is a very important concept in time management. It is also called the Pareto Principle. The principle will help you to become more comfortable not doing C's. Simply stated, only twenty percent of the tasks that we do, produce 80 percent of the rewards. Another way of putting this is that most people spend 80 percent of their time doing duties which are related to only 20 percent of the total job results.

If you are in sales, this principle can mean that only 20 percent of your customers or calls produce 80 percent of your sales. On the homefront, it is likely that 80 percent of the washing is done on the 20 percent of the wardrobe that is worn most often.

In a list of ten tasks, doing two of them will yield most (80 percent) of the rewards. Find these two tasks because they are prime candidates for your top A-Priorities.

If you are trying to meet a deadline, the 80/20 rule also means that unless you manage your time, you are faced with doing the important 80 percent of the job in 20 percent of the little time left before your deadline!

This is a general rule, but one that has been demonstrated time and time again. Remembering this concept will help you concentrate your efforts on the 20 percent of the tasks that will produce 80 percent of the benefits. The C items and the B items that you have listed will probably not produce what you want to accomplish. Setting your sights on your A items and their related tasks will provide you with the best plan for reaching your true goals. The solution is not in learning how to do everything more efficiently, but in learning to do less more effectively.

Delegation

When you have many B and particularly C items to do, delegate them. Often they can be delegated to a secretary, hired help, spouse, parents, or children.

Diana Silcox, a professional time-management consultant and author of Woman Time, kept a time inventory when she was just beginning to expand her consulting service. She found she was answering every phone call, cleaning her own house, doing her own laundry, and handling her own typing and filing. She reset her priorities so as to establish her right to a rich personal life as well as a challenging professional life. She then hired a maid as well as a secretary, and began sending out her laundry, shopping by phone or mail, and eating out more often.

Before you delegate, determine the time necessary to the task and the time required to explain, instruct and coordinate. Delegate those tasks where the time needed to complete the work is long in relation to the time required to instruct and supervise. Avoid doing things you should delegate, but be sure to avoid delegating those things you should do yourself.

When you delegate work give clear, simple instructions and deadlines. Try to assign activities that will stretch the capabilities of others, share the responsibilities, and make everyone feel like useful members of a team. When these activities have been completed, give feedback to your subordinates. Plan ahead for vacations as well as shorter absences and delegate the work to be done while you are away.

Avoiding Reverse Delegation

Another important part of effective delegation is to follow up periodically on each task that you have delegated. Write down reminders in your appointment book. If a task is given back to you in unfinished or unacceptable form without a reasonable explanation or without sufficient time for redelegation, you are experiencing reverse delegation. Periodic follow-ups can help prevent reverse delegation and procrastination.

Do You Want To Delegate?

Of course, you really have to want to delegate for it to work. You may need to ask yourself some tough questions. Do you see delegation as a loss of power? Can you trust others? Perhaps you need to look at your hiring and firing policies or your management styles.

One Of The Best Places To Delegate

The garbage can is often the best place to delegate something. How many of us can remember poking through routine work, straightening our desks or doing trival tasks, instead of doing our A's? We get a temporary feeling of satisfaction, but even with a neater desk, we still have to face the important items. There are some C's that are better left undone or delegated to the garbage can. Ask yourself "How terrible would it be if I just threw this away?" If your answer is "Not too terrible," then delegate it to your garbage can.

If you find that you just can't discard certain "C" items, then set aside a special drawer or file for them. When the drawer or file gets full, then file everything in an envelop or box and label it "C Items" along with the date. January 2nd every year is a good time to annually go through these C files. Usually it is easy to throw things away when they have aged. If you still cannot throw them away, then transfer them back to your selected drawer or file. Maybe you can delegate them to the wastebasket next year.

The Once Over

It is not always best to file your C's. Something you can practice to help avoid accumulating paperwork is to go through each item only once as you receive it. If at all possible, make a decision at that time.

The best example of this is how to deal with a lot of mail. Throw away any mail you receive and feel you can do without. Once you have scanned a piece of mail or paperwork, you should be able to make a decision about it, write out the decision, immediately turn it back in, mail it out, or throw it away.

Not all mail and paper work lends itself to quick and final action. Some papers and projects need many revisions and polishing. Some decisions really do require a great deal of thought. If you can not take a quick and final action at least do something to advance a project. This may mean nothing more than recording the date and your thoughts after reviewing a project.

Often people become overwhelmed by paperwork simply because they do not make the decisions that need to be made the first time. We are a country of people that tend to collect papers, always thinking that we will need them at some point in the future. Remember to throw away any and all the pieces of mail that you possibly can.

Creative Time Management

One of the most enjoyable ways of managing time is to combine information you have gained from taking a time inventory and from pinpointing your goals. For example, several years ago when one of the authors first read about time management, he took a time inventory and came up with about one and a half hours of daily, work-related commuting. The author drove to and from work and traveled to various places where he consulted. He enjoyed listening to music on the radio while he drove, but sometimes found this boring.

One of the goal cues the author used to establish his long- and short-range goals was additional education. He not only wanted and needed to keep up with new discoveries, but found continuing education to be very exciting. Like many, in response to the "publish or perish" pressures of academia, he had begun to put off this activity and complain that he never had enough time.

The author considered increasing his commuting enjoyment by installing a stereo tape deck so that he could listen to music tapes of his choice. At that point, he remembered how much he had enjoyed listening to some taped lectures from a conference that a colleague had attended. He knew he could not afford to buy enough conference tapes to fill even half of the eight hours of weekly commuting time.

The author went to the library and discovered that the audio-visual department had a large assortment of conference tapes and a series called Audio-Digest Psychiatry. The audio-digest series is available in every medical specialty and has been providing monthly or twice-monthly excerpts of medical conferences for over 27 years!

Advertisements in a weekly magazine introduced him to Books On Tape (P.O. Box 7900, Newport Beach, CA 92660) and some mail order rental libraries. He even learned about a business news magazine on tape, Newstrack, available from the Executive Tape Service (Box 1178, Englewood, CA 80150). A combination of music, lectures and books has not only taken the boredom and frustration out of driving, but has provided a great deal of continuing education and enjoyment.

We have spent some time on this example for several reasons. It reveals an effective planning process that anyone can use to find hundreds of valuable hidden hours. Homemakers who want to have some additional skills or a profession after their children grow up, often make obtaining an education a goal. They can use the same planning process to optimize time spent in repetitive tasks such as ironing, dusting, other housework, and "chauffeuring" the children to and from their activities. These times can be used for home study courses or university home work.

Perhaps one of your goals is to increase your correspondence with friends and family. Make use of odd moments of time spent in beauty shops, waiting rooms and restaurants by keeping post cards and note paper in your purse or briefcase. You may want to conserve time and meet some of your goals by learning how to speed read. You may also decide to carry reading matter with you to make the most of small, here-and-there chunks of time. Combining the results of setting your goals and taking a time inventory can yield exciting possibilities.

The Perfect Person

The perfect person is something that we have yet to find. We have found many people that are perfectionistic; and these are the same people that tend to slow down the works. These people never seem to be able to "see the forest for the trees." WE WILL NEVER BE PERFECT.

The role of man is not consistent with any concept related to the perfectionist. In fact, about 20 percent of everything we do is a mistake. Everyone makes about 2 mistakes for every 10 decisions, and you must realize that you too will bat about 2 for 10. Mistakes are the best tools that we have to help us learn. If you are a perfectionist you should etch in the back of your mind the words "Just get it done." or "Do it!" Too often we tend to want the first draft to be the perfect draft. And that same perfectionism will prevent us from ever getting started on the tasks that will lead to our true goals.

Vary the quality of your efforts. Trying to do your best at everything can actually lead to doing everything adequately, but nothing brilliantly. Said another way, "You cannot be anything if you want to be everything." Allocate your best efforts to your A-priority tasks and strive for acceptable performances in your B- or C- priority tasks.

If you are an executive, match the quality of your efforts to the quality and demands of the project. If you are a homemaker, save some energy from housework, so you can enjoy quality time with your spouse and children. With this in mind, ask yourself "What will happen if I don't do this chore immediately and to perfection?"

Scheduling Interruptions And Quiet Periods

It also helps to build into your daily schedule some time for interruptions, unforeseen problems and the inevitable fires that must be put out. If you schedule times for these, you can avoid rushing and feeling time-pressured.

It is also very important to make reasonable time estimates for the length of various events. If you schedule yourself for 30-minute lunch breaks between important appointments, then in all probability you are going to have difficulties keeping within those time boundaries and enjoying lunch.

You should also be able to set aside periods of time during each day for quiet times when you can focus on relaxing and unwinding. These are times when you should be interrupted only if there is an emergency. Schedule quiet times in your appointment book or you may not take advantage of them.

A Practical Lesson Worth $25,000: Sleep On It!

Dr. George Crane, a business-journalist, recently wrote about a little known incident in which $25,000 was paid for a practical lesson in time management. Charles Schwab, the chairman of the Bethlehem Steel Company once consulted a New York based time management expert named Ivy Lee. He said "My friend, I'll pay you any price if you will just show us how to get more things done." Mr. Lee accepted the challenge and gave Mr. Schwab the following advice.

"At night, spend five minutes analyzing your problems of the following day. Write them down on a sheet of paper, but place them in the order of their importance.

"Then tackle the first item as soon as you reach the office. Stick to it until it is finished; then shift to No. 2.

Test this plan as long as you like; then send me a check for whatever you consider it worth."

Shortly thereafter, Mr. Lee received a check for $25,000 and a brief note from the steel magnate. Mr. Schwab wrote "This is the most practical lesson I have ever learned!" Mr. Schwab added that he had been putting off an important phone call for nine months, but after seeing Mr. Lee he had put it at the top of his first list. The call, he wrote, "netted us $2 million because of a new order of steel beams."

So, to optimize your performance, make a list of the five most important things that you want to accomplish during the next day. Make up this list before you leave work. Schedule quiet time during the last half hour of work. Review what you have accomplished for the day and decide on five important things that you want to do during the next day. Take this list home with you and review it before you go to bed.

The mind, particularly the subconscious mind, has an amazing capacity to work on and plan things at night while we sleep. Often people who are starting a new job will wake in the middle of the night with "a nightmare" of themselves working at the new job and perhaps feeling somewhat overwhelmed. This is simply the unconscious mind working on the new task, and practicing and rehearsing during sleep. You can also mentally prepare yourself on a nightly basis by knowing what your goals are and having a plan for what you want to do the next day.

Remember to plan your playtime and your weekend to make the most of your leisure time. Early in the week, write down your weekend plans and begin the necessary preparations. In this way you won't be left alone or bored when the weekend comes. This is very important for workaholics. On Friday, review your weekend plans just before you go to sleep.

Five Minutes In The Morning

If you have set your priorities for the day, filled out your To-Do List, and slept on the six most important things to do, then you are ready at the beginning of the day to involve other people who will help you in executing your tasks. Spend five minutes in a priority setting conference in the morning. Set aside time to review your plans with the people who are working with you so that they can also plan their days. Often secretaries feel overwhelmed because they see work coming from many different directions and do not know where to start.

The five-minute priority setting conference allows the
secretary as well as the boss to decide which task needs to be
done first. Secretaries should not be put in the position of
guessing what the boss's priorities are. If you are a secretary
be sure to ask your boss the order of things to be done. Use
the techniques from the assertiveness training chapter to help
you establish which items can and cannot be done in a reasonable
day's work.

Always limit the five-minute priority setting conference to
five minutes. Do not allow it to turn into a staff meeting. A
small number of key people should be standing and there should
be no chairs, coffee or danish. It should be very much of a
work-oriented and planning-oriented session with a numbered
agenda to keep the meeting focused.

Planning Other Meetings

The principles of limiting the length and purpose of meetings can make a large cumulative difference over the course of
weeks and months. There is no reason why most meetings have to
take an hour and yet most are scheduled to start and end on the
hour. Generally speaking, work will expand to fill the time
appropriated. Unfortunately, this additional work is not
usually productive work.

Block Interruptions

So often, it is considered proper to have an open door
policy at work. Businesses have also been adopting open space
policies in response to economic and environmental pressures.
Space in businesses costs money and private offices are less and
less the norm. Movable partitions are sometimes being employed
to provide some measure of privacy. However, the overall effect
is that people are now physically working very closely together,
and in open spaces where there are usually more interruptions.
Anytime you are working in an atmosphere where other staff members are permitted to contact you at any time, then your productivity may be threatened.

It has been reported that the typical manager in the United
States is interrupted an average of once every eight minutes.
The interruptions may be from a visitor or from the boss buzzing
on the intercom. Phone calls are common forms of interruptions.
When people take time inventories, they often find that they are
involved in only two hours of essential work in an eight-hour

day. This low productivity can result in working overtime and eliminating needed hours for recreation and family.

Quiet Work Time For Office And Home

There are several different things that you can do to help eliminate the interruptions.   One approach taken by large businesses is to schedule two hours of "quiet" work time into the high productivity period of the day. This period is usually in the morning. Perhaps you can schedule one hour of quiet work time in the early morning when there will be no contact between members of your staff. Workers would not be available to each other at that time. Later in the morning, you could have a coffee break or a period during which staff members would be available to each other. Still later in the morning, you could resume the quiet time for an hour.

Some people find that they can be especially productive in the day if they come in very early when other people are not there. This is not always practical or healthy, and scheduling quiet work time can be an effective way of accomplishing the same thing. This technique also works for the housewife that experiences constant interruptions. Let the friends and relatives know that you are not available at certain times, except for emergencies.

Time Saving Techniques For The Telephone

Another technique that you can use to help block the interruption of phone calls is to make yourself unavailable during part of the day. Phone calls can break up your concentration and often are not important. The critical person in this technique is the person who is answering the phone. If this is a receptionist, the receptionist needs to know the kinds of calls you want to take directly, those you want referred elsewhere, those in which you want the receptionist to provide information, and those from which messages are to be taken. It is also incumbent upon the person that is unavailable to return the calls later in the day so as to maintain credibility.

Check your time inventory to see how much time you spend on the phone when you return, initiate or accept telephone calls. You may find that when you return or initiate a call, it takes more time than when you accept one. Analyze the reasons for this. You may want to set a conscious time limit for each call and use a call timer or pretend you are making a long distance

call at your own expense. When you have used up your allotted
time or you have completed your intended discussion, use your
assertiveness skills to politely close the conversation.

If you are placed on hold frequently you may want to
purchase an inexpensive amplifier to hold the receiver while you
continue working. These devices are very useful for homemakers
who enjoy talking while they work.

Visitors

Another technique is to make yourself available to visitors
only part of the day. Visitors can also be a source of interruption at work and can break up your concentration on an
important task. If a quiet work period is in operation two
hours during the morning then this could also be an ideal time
to have a period without interruptions from visitors.

In order to make this work for you, you would need to
inform key people that you will not be available during particular hours. This may mean that an appointment system becomes
necessary. When you work on an appointment only basis, no one
will have cause to complain when someone "drops in" and you are
unavailable.

Remember that blocking out time for yourself will save
time. THIRTY PERCENT MORE PRODUCTIVITY IS GAINED BY HAVING A
PERIOD WITHOUT INTERRUPTIONS. However, it may also be that your
job is handling interruptions. If that is your situation, you
can practice limiting the length of each interruption.

The First Day Of The Month And Your Daily Calendar

The first day of each month can be a very important time to
take aim toward your goals. Family and social events can be
planned at that time and you can put birthdays or anniversaries
on your calendar. You can also plan time for educational
programs that you may wish to attend during the month. You may
wish to set a goal for yourself to attend at least one
educational program each month. You can schedule this during
the first of the month. You should also take time to put
company activities on your calendar so that you can plan for
these when you make out your schedules.

Your appointment book or daily calendar can be a powerful
tool for time management if you expand its uses. Consolidate
all miscellaneous notes, phone messages and memos in your book

or calendar. This will make the information readily available for use now and retrieval later. As you go through your week, list your activities and quiet periods for the following week.

Part of your appointment book can serve as a place for your To-Do lists, relaxation cues, and meeting agendas. You can also use it to schedule follow-ups on delegated tasks. Car and other maintenance schedules can be written in for the coming year with reminders to make appointments and follow up on work which has been delegated. Anniversaries, birthdays, and other important dates can be entered with notes a week before to purchase gifts or cards.

SUMMING IT ALL UP

The main trust of this chapter is how to manage your time more effectively. Time is a major asset and it should be managed just as we manage any other valuable asset. Perhaps one of the most important things that we covered was setting up your goals so that you know where you are going. Having a plan and working toward it is an important part of life. It is also an integral part of learning how to manage time.

Before you go on to the next chapter, we would like to review what we think are the major points about setting goals. These are the steps that we feel you have to read and reread, practice and practice again. Remember that rehearsal and practice is the way to accomplish your goals. The following list is a summary of what you need to do to insure that you are spending most of your time getting where you want to go in life and enjoying what you want to experience in life.

1. Put your goals in writing. If you did not complete that section as you went through this chapter, then you probably do not have any goals. You have only wishes. If you have not put a goal into writing, then it is not a goal--it is just a wish.

2. Goals must be better than your very best, but believable. If I did not jog and set a goal to run a marathon in two weeks, I would not believe I could do it and I would probably become frustrated and stop trying. If I were to set a goal that I would run one mile in two weeks, it would be a goal that I could believe and work toward everyday. Your goals must be better than where you are now, but they must be believable.

3. Set up short-term goals. It is very rewarding to have reached a goal. If you make all of your goals long-term, then you will become discouraged because you are less likely to receive short-term rewards and reinforcements.

4. Goals should be set for all areas of your life. Set up business and professional goals, but also set up goals related to family, physical health and spiritual growth. If you only set up work goals, you are sitting on a stool that is balanced on one leg; and, if anything should happen to that leg, you will end up sitting on your tailbone.

5. Set up long-term goals and personal accomplishments as well as short-term goals. You should know who you want to be and what you want. If you read magazines about cars because your goal is to have a faster car, then you will be pulled toward that goal subconsciously. If you set up goals to have a nice house and you read related magazines such as Architectural Digest, then you will be drawn toward that goal. If you read travel brochures about distant parts of the world, you will probably travel more than if you had only read magazines about gardening.

6. Vividly imagine the accomplishment of your goals. See yourself accomplishing what you set out to accomplish. The winners in life rehearse time and time again, seeing themselves being successful and attaining their goals.

When the astronauts first landed on the moon, they described it as being just as they imagined and rehearsed. One astronaut, as he stepped onto the moon, described it as "old home week," because he had simulated being there so many times before.

When they launched the recent space shuttle, the physiological stress response of the astronauts was minimal. They had practiced time and time again doing just what they were doing. Any of us who had not practiced being in the space shuttle would have had such great increases in blood pressures and pulse rates that we would have been able to literally feel our heart pounding. But the astronauts had rehearsed time and time again and vividly imagined the accomplishment of their goal. This is what the winners do in life. They not only set their sights on their goal, but they imagine themselves acquiring that goal.

7. Goals must be ardently desired. If you just want something a little bit, then you may not work and strive toward it; and, in all probability, you will not accomplish it. You need to really want the goals that you are working toward. This

is why we have emphasized the importance of establishing
personal long-term and short-term goals.

You have to make a commitment like, "I want to be the best
salesman in the company in eighteen months," or "I want to have
my house decorated beautifully in one year." If you really want
to be a world traveler, you have to commit yourself to seeing at
least one foreign country a year.

A perfect example of a commitment to a goal is reflected in
what Jack LaLanne does on each birthday. Jack LaLanne is a
world famous physical fitness expert. Each birthday he
establishes a different goal. Recently, he swam in icy waters
pulling a rope that was attached to several boats full of
people, one person for each year of his life. He is committed
to the goal of physical fitness and he shows it in everything he
does.

Time management is not a skill that you will acquire from
reading this chapter or from reviewing the suggested materials
listed at the end of this chapter. You must practice and live
some of these techniques of time mamangement. This may take you
two months, maybe six months. Remember, as long as you are
striving toward a goal, and as long as you are practicing the
necessary techniques, then you will accomplish what you are
working toward.

REVIEW QUESTIONS

Directions: Circle the letter in front of the best response to
each question. The correct answers are provided on the page
following the last question.

1. Which of the following is a signal of poor time management?

    A. Feeling guilty about leaving work on time.
    B. Habitually working long hours.
    C. Always feeling behind.
    D. All of the above.

2. Time wasters include

    A. people who walk instead of run to catch a bus.
    B. anything that prohibits us from reaching our objectives
        most effectively.
    C. lack of goals.
    D. B and C.

3. The time and stress-productivity curve demonstrates

    A. that increasing stress increases productivity, but only
        up to a point.
    B. that increasing stress always increases productivity.
    C. that increasing time spent on a project will always
        increase productivity.
    D. A and C.

4. The majority of people find that the most productive time
    is in the

    A. morning.
    B. afternoon.
    C. evening.
    D. between midnight and six a.m.

5. "There are racehorses and there are turtles." This means

    A. we can become anything we want.
    B. we need to evaluate who we are and what our goals and
        values are.
    C. some people have a natural ability to keep slower or
        faster paces.
    D. B and C.

6. In the book Man's Search For Meaning, Victor Frankl described how people with a purpose in life could

   A. withstand torture.
   B. withstand starvations.
   C. always win at what they attempted.
   D. A and B.

7. Your current major life goals should include

   A. five-year and one-year goals.
   B. six-month and one-month goals.
   C. goals you would establish if you knew you would die in one year.
   D. All of the above.

8. One hour spent in effective planning saves _____ hour(s) in execution.

   A. up to one.
   B. one to two.
   C. three to four.
   D. zero.

9. "To-Do" lists help us focus on important goals by listing tasks or projects and rating them as

   A. A's.
   B. B's.
   C. C's.
   D. All of the above.

10. An important rule in time management is that

   A. 20 percent of the tasks we do, produce 80 percent of the value.
   B. 30 percent of the tasks we do, produce 70 percent of the value.
   C. 40 percent of the tasks we do, produce 60 percent of the value.
   D. all tasks are of equal value.

ANSWERS TO REVIEW QUESTIONS

1.	d	6.	d
2.	d	7.	d
3.	a	8.	c
4.	a	9.	d
5.	d	10.	a

SUGGESTED BOOKS AND RECORDINGS

BOOKS

Getting Organized by S. Winston. New York: Warner, 1978.

Getting Things Done by E. Bliss. New York: Bantam, 1978.

How To Get Control Of Your Time And Your Life by A. Lakein.
    New York: Signet, 1973.

Sidetracked Home Executives by P. Young & P. Jones. New
    York: Warner, 1981.

RECORDINGS

How To Get Control Of Your Time And Your Life by A.
    Lakein. Waco, Texas: S.M.I., 1980.

The Trees Jobs Grow On And How To Find The One For You by J.
    Gallagher & K. Nathan. Houston: Biobehavioral, 1980.

Section VII

**Enhancing Health
And Preventing Disease:
When Your Body Wears
Out, Where Are You
Going To Live?**

Chapter 22

Keeping Your Body
"Tuned Up"

In Collaboration With
Nema Frye, M.S., R.D.

The benefits of regular exercise and good nutrition are popluar topics of conversation today, and science is providing a growing body of knowledge to make possible a separation of fact and fancy. Exercise and nutrition can be of importance in the prevention of illness and in the enhancement of health. The next two chapters will offer some reasonable guidelines to help you incorporate proper nutrition and regular exercise into your life. These are essential ingredients in combating the "wear and tear" of stress.

Regular exercise not only has physiological benefits, but psychological benefits as well. Advantages that have been associated with regular exercise include: a greater ability to concentrate, a reduced risk of heart attack, more energy, a firmer appearance, reduced anxiety and depression, better sleep and better control of body weight.

The Stress Response

In the first chapter of this book, we reviewed the sympathetic nervous system's response to stress. If you recall, the body responds with preparation for fighting or fleeing. Our heart beats faster, our blood pressure soars, our breathing quickens, our perspiration increases, our muscles tense, and our body pours stored sugars and fats into the blood stream. In addition, a signal originating from the hypothalamus contributes to the secretion of adrenalin.

Exercise provides a way of releasing a great deal of the muscle tension and general physical arousal accumulated in our responses to stress. Rather than fighting a tiger or fleeing from a bear, we can hit a punching bag or jog around the track.

Exercise As Relaxation

One very important benefit of exercise is muscle relaxation. In response to stress, our bodies often become tense. This tension can accumulate, especially after a long day. One way to relax after a tense day is to engage in some type of exercise. You will find that, after exercising, your muscles are relaxed and calm.

Using exercise to relax, is far better than another common release used at the end of a day's work -- alcohol. Drinking alcohol adds another stressor, and can ultimately lower your ability to manage stress.

The Role Of Exercise Today

As man became industrialized, he developed more and more labor-saving devises. Physical activity was no longer necessary for survival and became a form of recreation. When we rediscover play and enjoy body movement, we restore a sense of control and wholeness to our lives. Since you are the sum of physical and mental activities, exercise can be self-enhancing and improve your responses to not only physical stressors, but social and mental stressors as well.

Exercise As A Mental Release

Exercise can be used to clear your mind. One frustration which you may face during the workday, is reaching the point where your mind is so cluttered that it is impossible to concentrate. You might reach a point where problems seem impossible to solve. This is an excellent time to go for a walk, jog or swim. People who exercise, report that time away from working diligently on a problem actually gives them a chance to sort everything out in a more relaxed way.

To give you an example, a colleague of ours reached an impasse while working on the development of a new health program. After working on crucial scheduling problems for several hours, she seemed no closer than when she started. In a continual effort to solve these problems, she went to a co-worker to discuss the schedule. Still, no solution was reached.

At this point, the workday was over, and the two workers decided to exercise together. During their 20 minutes of jogging, the scheduling problem was discussed. By the end of the run, the problem had been solved. It is not clear if this happened because the pressure was off, or simply because their minds were more creative in another environment. But it worked! This is common among people who exercise regularly.

Exercise And Self-Image

For many people, their body image is a stressor. Whether they are overweight, too "flabby" or not as muscular as they would like to be, the end result is that they are unhappy with themselves. People who begin an exercise program, find that their self-image improves and they feel better emotionally.

How Does Exercise Physically Help Us To Manage Stress?

When we are in good physical condition, we have a greater capacity to resist stress and strain. We react more slowly and less drastically to environmental, physical and psychological stimuli. Physiologists have repeatedly shown that a regular exercise program will improve endurance, reduce total peripheral resistance in blood circulation, lower systolic and diastolic blood pressure, increase the inner size of arteries, increase the number of capillaries, lower blood lipids and improve lung capacity and muscular strength. This all adds up to an increase in endurance and a greater resistance to fatigue.

The heart becomes more powerful and more efficient with appropriate exercise. A conditioned heart beats more slowly at rest and during work. It also acquires a greater pumping capacity.

A simple way to express this is summed up in the old phrase, "Use it, or loose it!" Approximately 80% of the adult population today is not active enough to properly arrest physiological dacay. Such an inactive life style is said to be a slow form of suicide. It actually requires very little time to obtain and maintain an adequate level of fitness. This is often misunderstood, because when one thinks of a physically fit person, too often the athlete comes to mind. It is not necessary to spend the number of hours and endure the strenuous training of a professional athlete to be considered physically fit. If this is true, how does one define physical fitness?

Components Of Physical Fitness

A person is considered physically fit if he or she is engaged in activities that bring about three fitness components: cardiorespiratory endurance, flexibility and muscular function. These can be remembered as the three S's: Stamina, Suppleness, and Strength.

Cardiorespiratory endurance is the ability to perform moderately strenuous, large muscle exercises for relatively long periods of time. Large muscle exercises include walking, cycling, swimming or jogging. A relatively long period of time is defined as 20 to 30 minutes. The word, "cardiorespiratory," represents the knowledge that these activities depend a great deal on the capacity of the heart and the lungs.

Flexibility is defined as the range of motion about a joint, or simply the ability to move a body part from one extreme position to another. Touching your toes is an example of the range of motion about the hip joint.

Muscular function includes muscular strength, muscular endurance and muscular power. Muscular strength is the force that a muscle can exert against a resistance, while muscular endurance is the ability of that muscle to resist fatigue. Muscular power is the result of strength and the speed at which the force can be applied.

If you perform the same exercise everyday, you will not increase your strength or endurance. This goal is reached only by stretching your abilities a small increment each day. The isometric exercises that Charles Atlas made famous, increased strength, but only in the skeletal muscles. The heart and the lungs were left out of many of these fitness programs.

All three fitness components are important. However, for the adult, cardiorespiratory endurance is considered the most important fitness component. The work of Dr. Kenneth Cooper in the area of aerobics is an example of an approach to exercise which emphasizes cardiorespiratory fitness. Because of the importance of cardiorespiratory fitness, the remaining discussion will deal largely with exercises and activities that bring about improvement in this area. These are also the types of activities which are most helpful in reducing stress.

Cardiorespiratory Endurance

There are several activities which improve cardiorespiratory endurance. Examples include: basketball, cycling, jogging, racquetball, rope jumping, ice and roller skating, snow and water skiing, swimming, tennis, and vigorous walking and dancing. All of these activities have something in common that causes an increase in cardiorespiratory endurance -- they are "aerobic."

An "aerobic" activity is one which utilizes oxygen in producing energy. An "anaerobic" activity takes place in the absence of oxygen. An example of an anaerobic activity is running at top speed, but only for a short period of time. In reality these two systems work simultaneously. Any activity that is continued for several minutes will be using oxygen and is, therefore, considered "aerobic."

A pioneer in the area of exercise, Dr. Kenneth Cooper, used this knowledge in writing a number of books, and a tape program. These are highly recommended for anyone interested in beginning an exercise program. All the information you need for a variety of activities is included in the material, as well as a system to help the beginner measure his or her improvement.

How Much Exercise Do I Need?

What about the "how hard," "how often" and "for how long" of exercise? Exercise specialists refer to these as the frequency, duration and intensity of exercise. It may surprise you to learn just how little time and effort is needed to obtain an adequate amount of exercise to develop cardiorespiratory endurance.

The recommended frequency of exercise is a minimum of three times per week. These three days should not be three continuous days, but scheduled so that there is a day of rest between the days of exercise. However, once you have increased your cardiovascular endurance, you may want to exercise five or six days a week to enjoy the recreation and help relieve stress.

The duration of exercise or the number of minutes one should exercise each time is 20 to 30 minutes. This should be continuous exercise rather than 10 minutes in the morning, 10 minutes at noon and 10 minutes in the evening.

The intensity of the exercise session is not as easy to convey as the frequency and duration. A simple test of intensity is how a person feels. If it is not possible to talk while exercising because you are breathing too hard (known as the "talk test"), then you are exercising too vigorously. A more scientific and individualized indicator is a person's heart rate or pulse.

The heart rate is an excellent measure of how much stress a person is undergoing. With exercise, the heart rate will increase in direct proportion to the intensity of the exercise. First, you must learn how to take your pulse. This requires practice. To learn, please follow the directions below.

FOUR PLACES TO TAKE YOUR PULSE

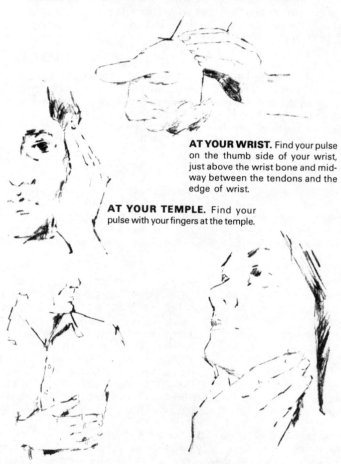

AT YOUR WRIST. Find your pulse on the thumb side of your wrist, just above the wrist bone and midway between the tendons and the edge of wrist.

AT YOUR TEMPLE. Find your pulse with your fingers at the temple.

OVER YOUR HEART. Find your pulse with your hand over the left side of your body, just below the breast.

AT YOUR CAROTID ARTERY. Find your pulse with your fingers between the adams apple and the large muscles on the side of your neck.

The average heart rate of an individual is aproximately 72 beats per minute. This varies a great deal from one individual to another, and it depends on many things, such as age, sex, level of fitness and medications. How high should your heart rate be during exercise?

To achieve cardiorespiratory benefits, a person should work at 70% to 85% of his or her MAXIMUM HEART RATE. The MAXIMUM HEART RATE can be estimated (as shown below) and then used to calculate the TARGET HEART RATE for exercise (which is 70% to 85% of the MAXIMUM HEART RATE).

To calculate Maximum Heart Rate:

220 minus your age in years equals MAXIMUM HEART RATE.

Example: If you are 50 years of age:

220 - 50 = 170 beats per minute, you MAXIMUM HEART RATE is 170 beats per minute.

Now fill in the blanks and calculate your MAXIMUM HEART RATE

220 - _____ = _____ beats per minute

To calculate Target Heart Rate Range:

The TARGET HEART RATE RANGE is 70% to 85% of the MAXIMUM HEART RATE, so compute 70% and 85% of the MAXIMUM HEART RATE. Using the example above:

.70% of MAXIMUM HEART RATE equals_____ beats per minute

.70 x 170 = 119 beats per minute

85% of MAXIMUM HEART RATE equals _____ beats per minute

.85 x 170 = 140 beats per minute

The example's TARGET HEART RATE RANGE is between 119 and 144 beats per minute.

Now fill in the blanks and calculate your TARGET HEART RATE RANGE:

.70 x ___ = ____ beats per minute

.85 x ___ = ____ beats per minute

During exercise, your heart rate should remain in your TARGET HEART RATE RANGE.

To make it easier to take your heart rate during exercise, you can take your pulse for 10 seconds. You will need to convert your one-minute (60 second) TARGET HEART RATE RANGE into 10-second rates. This is done by dividing the lower and upper number of your TARGET HEART RATE RANGE by 6 and remembering that this is the range of numbers for a 10-second interval. If your TARGET HEART RATE RANGE is 120-144, then the number of beats in a 10-second count should be roughly between 20 and 24. This is shown in the example below.

To calculate TARGET HEART RATE RANGE for 10-second intervals:

Divide Lower Range of TARGET HEART RANGE by 6 to get the 10-second rate.

Example: $\dfrac{\text{Lower Range}}{6} = \dfrac{119}{6} = 20$ is the 10-second rate

Divide Higher Range of TARGET HEART RANGE by 6 to get the 10-second rate.

Example: $\dfrac{\text{Higher Range}}{6} = \dfrac{144}{6} = 24$ is the 10-second rate.

TARGET HEART RATE RANGE is between 20 and 24 beats per 10 seconds.

Now fill in the blanks and calculate your 10-second TARGET HEART RATE RANGE:

$\dfrac{\text{lower range}}{6} = \dfrac{\rule{2em}{0.4pt}}{6} = \rule{2em}{0.4pt}$ is the 10-second rate.

$\dfrac{\text{higher range}}{6} = \dfrac{\rule{2em}{0.4pt}}{6} = \rule{2em}{0.4pt}$ is the 10-second rate.

My TARGET HEART RATE RANGE is between _____ and _____ beats per 10-seconds.

If you are just beginning an exercise program, it is a good idea to exercise in the lower part of the target heart rate range so that you will be able to exercise the recommended duration of 20 to 30 minutes. You may be surprised at how little it takes to elevate your heart rate to the target range if your life has been sedentary.

A few words of caution are warranted. Too much exercise, too soon, will not only discourage you but will be adding another stressor to your life. If you are over 35 years of age, it is advisable to have a physical examination and a Treadmill Stress Test before beginning an exercise program. This test of physical working capacity is performed while walking on a tread- mill. During this test, the physician administering the test is able to observe how your heart responds to various exercise loads. Remember, if you are over the age of 35 years or in poor physical condition, do not begin an exercise program without first consulting your physician.

Earlier, we pointed out that it is often good to exercise soon after you experience a stress response. However, this advice does not apply to severe emotional stress. When you have experienced a major stressor, you may not be able to benefit or survive the added physical stressor of exercise. If you get angry at your boss and go out jogging, you may tend to overdo it. Do not let this happen. Have an exercise specialist give you an exercise prescription, and be sure to use moderation!

Becoming More Fit: Getting Started

If you have not yet begun a formal fitness program, then increasing your general activity level is an excellent place to begin. Small changes are significant. Just as the goal of fitness training is not to make you a star athlete, the goal of getting started is not to make you a fitness fanatic. Our goal is to help you take the first step toward becoming fit, avoid tripping over common problems and help you continue your efforts.

There are probably as many reasons as there are people to explain why so many of the well-informed procrastinate starting an exercise program. Research from the Surgeon General's 1979 report, entitled Healthy People, showed that although individ- uals knew that regular exercise was an important health habit, few people were practicing regular exercise. If you feel you are too busy to exercise, then refer to Chapter 21 and apply the time management techniques to help you get started.

Let's discuss some of the reasons frequently given for not exercising. For some people, memories of pain after exercise is what keeps them from beginning to exercise again. Pain from exercise is unnecessary, and is usually brought about by exercising incorrectly. If one properly warms up and cools down after exercise, and does not do too much too soon, then there will be little or no pain. You can improve your body's strength and endurance without causing pain. Use pain as a signal that you are doing too much. Stiffness and muscle pain should not be used as signs that you are getting stronger.

Another reason which is often used for not starting an exercise program involves the expense. Although some sports and activities do require an investment or a fee, not all exercise programs are expensive. In fact, many of the best exercises are free. It is important to remember when you are selecting an activity, that the lower the costs in terms of time, money, or inconvenience, the more likely it is that you will continue the program.

Lack of knowledge on how to exercise properly is another concern of people who do not exercise. The information in this chapter is sufficient to help you start exercising. The books in the Recommended Reading List will provide you with additional information from many experts. Another suggestion is to enroll in an exercise class. This has the advantage of providing you with information, as well as involving you in a support group of individuals who are also beginning an exercise program.

The more fun the exercise is to you, the more likely it is that you will continue it. Fitness does not have to be a lonely, torturous activity. In fact, finding another person with whom you can enjoy exercising helps tremendously. So, find a "buddy" and arrange to meet this person on a regular basis. Not only will this person be a support for you, but you will provide that same support for him or her.

Some people feel embarrassed when starting an exercise program. Find others at your same level of fitness with whom to exercise. Avoid being competitive and afraid of not "winning." If you tend to be competitive, avoid competitive events at the beginning of a fitness program. Competition often brings out a blind determination that is not always safe.

It is important to remember that, if weather or scheduling problems force you to miss a day of exercise, DO NOT GIVE UP ALTOGETHER! Instead, just return to the regular schedule as soon as possible. Exaggerating your "failure" and criticizing yourself will only add another emotional stressor.

A common misconception about exercise is that it will bring about fatigue. If approached sensibly, this is not true. As a matter of fact, people report that incorporating regular exercise has increased their level of energy, increased their alertness, and made them more relaxed.

Incorporating Exercise Into Your Regular Activities

Listed below are several ways with which you can begin to increase your activity level even if you are not ready to begin a formal exercise program. These suggestions will help you manage stress by giving you healthy breaks.

1. Become a "stair person" by taking the stairs for at least a few flights instead of relying entirely on the elevator. Try going down stairs first, and then up stairs.

2. Stand instead of sitting.

3. Walk the longer distance, rather than taking a short cut.

4. Park the car farther away from your work place or the shopping center, and walk the distance.

5. If you use public transportation, get off a stop earlier and walk the extra distance.

6. Walk to a nearby restaurant instead of driving or having them deliver.

7. If you have a pet, walk the pet farther, faster, or more often.

8. Walk or cycle to a nearby store instead of driving.

9. When playing golf, do not use a golf cart for all the holes.

10. In department stores, take the stairs instead of an escalator.

11. Take a walk, rather than sitting down for a coffee break.

12. Use a distant restroom, rather than the one closest to your desk.

One of the authors remembers getting a call from the telephone company encouraging him to buy still another telephone extension so he "wouldn't run the little woman ragged." He was told that this could save as much as seventy miles of walking each year. After discussing this with his wife, they decided they could save the money for sporting equipment and use the walking to burn off as much as three pounds every other year!

This concept can apply not only to telephone extensions, but also to many of the labor-saving devices we are offered. In fact, the exercise machines that can be purchased are simply labor-making contraptions that compensate for the reduction in physical activity caused by labor-saving machines. Home robots are around the corner and will place even more importance on the sort of recreational exercise and energy-increasing ingenuity we have been talking about.

To make any of these suggestions a permanent part of your life, you will need to make exercise a real priority. Make it as convenient as possible. Remember, if you are too busy to exercise, you are too busy.

How To Stick To Your Exercise Plans

In choosing an exercise plan or a sports activity, consider some of the obstacles to getting started and some of the ways you can help yourself stick with it. For example, you may not have the money to buy some expensive sports equipment that you want. Maybe it is a tennis racket, a bicycle, a swimming membership, or a pair of hiking boots. This is an obstacle, but it can also be an aid to fitness.

You may find it helpful to make the equipment into a reward to be earned by increasing everyday activities that you are capable of doing without a financial expense. This is a far better alternative than waiting until you can afford the expensive sports equipment. For example, it is usually better to begin brisk walking before jogging or skiing, so walk everywhere you can and make a chart to show your progress in scheduled walking. Then, reward yourself after a certain number of days of such activity.

One author's wife joined a health spa and chose to pay for it in monthly installments. In this way, she knew she would be reminded every month to make full use or even increase her use of the membership.

Try to find some companionship for your chosen activity. As we suggested earlier, try to find someone at your own level of ability. Agree together to meet on a regular basis and make a commitment to keep these dates. If this is not possible, try to make your walking or jogging more fun. Bring along a pocket radio or cassette tape recorder and find a place with pleasant scenery. Be sure to pat yourself on the back for every move in the direction of better health.

The time you spend thinking of the right activity with the right company will pay off in the long run. Beware of the "four day phenomenon". The researcher that coined this term found that most dieters and exercisers take on too much too soon and give up after roughly four days. Try to find activities that you can imagine doing regularly.

An Example Of A Formal Exercise Program

Included below is a sample exercise plan. Because walking is convenient, inexpensive and a good starting point, it is used as an example. When beginning an exercise program, be sure to keep detailed records. For each time that you walk, you should note the time, distance and heart rate achieved during exercise. It is also important to record any feelings that are associated with the exercise. For example, leg pains, stomach cramps, and the more pleasant feelings such as "felt great today."

There are several calendars available that provide a record-keeping form which details the information just mentioned. It is also easy to construct your own form of record keeping.

Remembering that is is important to take it leisurely at first, a good objective for the first week of exercise is to walk three times for 30 minutes each time. After each walk, return home and record the time, the distance, how you felt and the heart rate that you achieved during exercise. If you consistently fall below your TARGET HEART RATE RANGE this first week, do not be too concerned. It is more important to establish the habit of being outdoors or on a track, three times a week for 30 minutes each time. As you become more comfortable in spending that time walking, then you can walk at a faster pace or you can jog a little to get the heart pumping within the TARGET HEART RATE RANGE. An example of some record keeping for the first few weeks of exercise is shown below:

Week 1

       Sunday   Walked: 30 minutes
                     Heart Rate: 110
                     Distance: 1-1/2 mile
                     Felt a little tired

Tuesday   Raining--did not walk

Thursday   Walked: 30 minutes
Heart Rate: 110
Distance: 1-1/2 mile
Not tired at all today

Week 2

Sunday   Walked, Jogged: 30 minutes
Heart Rate: 130
Distance: 2 miles
Breathing a little harder today, but felt good

Tuesday   Walked, Jogged: 30 minutes
Heart Rate: 130
Distance: 2 miles
Feeling great!

Thursday   Walked, Jogged: 30 minutes
Heart Rate: 130
Distance: 1-3/4 miles
Tired today, was walking slower. A little
disappointed that I didn't go the full 2 miles--
but on second thought - I'm doing great!

Week 3

Sunday   Jogged: 30 minutes
Heart Rate: 135
Distance: 2-1/2 miles
Felt stronger today than ever!

Tuesday   Party after work, so I wasn't able to jog. Will
try to jog tomorrow.

Wednesday   Jogged: 30 minutes
Heart Rate: 135
Distance: 2-1/2 miles
Felt OK while jogging - but really pleased,
since I missed yesturday, that I was flexible
enough to exercise today.

Thursday   Jogged: 20 minutes
Heart Rate: 135
Distance: 1-1/2 miles
Feeling tight today, so I didn't go as far.

Week 4

Sunday   Jogged: 30 minutes
                Heart Rate: 140
                Distance: 3 miles
                Feeling great!

Tuesday   Jogged: 30 minutes
                Heart Rate: 140
                Distance: 3 miles
                Feeling great!

Thursday   Jogged: 30 minutes
                Heart Rate: 140
                Distance: 3 miles
                Feeling great!

If this person totalled the distance covered each week, it would be obvious that the distance increased from Week 1 to Week 4. The total distance for Week 1 was 3.0 miles; for Week 2, the total distance covered was 5-3/4 miles; for Week 3, the total distance covered was 6-1/2 miles; and for Week 4, a total of 9 miles was covered. If you were to graph this, you would see a gradual increase in the amount of distance that could be covered in the same amount of time. Also, if you had been noting how you felt each time you returned from walking, you would probably begin to notice that the walking became easier with less pain and with more enjoyment as time went on. Dr. Kenneth Cooper, in his books and tape program on aerobics, has devised an excellent point system which is based on heart rate and distance covered. We recommend it for anyone who is beginning an exercise program.

REVIEW QUESTIONS

<u>Directions:</u> Circle the letter in front of the best response to each question. The correct answers are provided on the page following the last question.

1. Exercise can

    a. relax tense muscles, while avoiding the stress of drugs.
    b. improve our self-image.
    c. promote clear thinking and creativity.
    d. All the above for most people.

2. A regular exercise program will

    a. raise blood pressure.
    b. decrease lung capacity.
    c. decrease the size of the inside of arteries.
    d. improve endurance.

3. An inactive life style is a slow form of suicide. To obtain and maintain an adequate level of fitness, a person has to

    a. become an athlete.
    b. spend the number of hours athletes spend.
    c. devote surprisingly little time and almost
        no pain.
    d. exercise five minutes twice a week.

4. Fitness is made up of all, but one of the following components

    a. cardiorespiratory endurance.
    b. sweat-gland activity.
    c. flexibility.
    d. muscular function.

5. For the adult, _____ is considered the most important fitness component.

    a. cardiorespiratory endurance
    b. flexibility
    c. sweat-gland activity
    d. muscular strength

6. For the average American adult, exercise specialists recommend exercising

   a. three times per week.
   b. twenty to thirty minutes per session.
   c. within your target heart rate.
   d. All of the above ways.

7. To determine your target Heart Rate Range

   a. subtract your age in years from 220 and add your age to 220 for both ends of the range.
   b. subtract your age in years from 220 and multiply it by .70.
   c. subtract your age in years from 220 and multiply it by .85.
   d. calculate the lower range in b and the higher range in c.

8. To get started exercising

   a. have a physical examination and a Treadmill Stress Test first, if you are over 35 years of age.
   b. examine some of the reasons you do not now exercise.
   c. try incorporating exercise into your regular activity by taking the stairs instead of the elevator, and by walking instead of driving.
   d. All of the above are useful.

9. Cardiorespiratory exercise includes all of the following except:

   a. weight lifting.
   b. bicycling.
   c. running.
   d. swimming.

10. To increase the likelihood of continuing your exercise plans

   a. reward yourself for each small step.
   b. try to find some companionship for your chosen activity.
   c. avoid the "four day phenomenon" by doing a little bit more each day.
   d. Try to do all of the above.

ANSWERS TO REVIEW QUESTIONS

1. d	6. d
2. d	7. d
3. c	8. d
4. b	9. a
5. a	10. d

SUGGESTED BOOKS AND RECORDINGS

BOOKS

Aerobics For Women by M. Cooper & K. Cooper. New York: Bantam, 1973.

The Complete Book of Running by J. Fixx. New York: Random House, 1977.

The Magic Of Walking by A. Sussman & R. Goode. New York: Simon and Schuster, 1967.

The New Aerobics by K. Cooper. New York: Bantam, 1970.

Stretching by R. Anderson. New York: Random House, 1980.

RECORDINGS

Comprehensive Exercise Guide by M. Mahony. New York: B.M.A., 1982.

The Joy Of Fitness by S. Main & B. Sample. Victoria, British Columbia: Joy Of Fitness Production, 1981.

Run For Your Life by K. Cooper. Waco, Texas: S.M.I., 1975.

Chapter 23

Stress Management Through Nutrition And Weight Control

In Collaboration With
Nema Frye, M.S., R.D.

The relationship between exercise and stress has been studied for years, but the relationship between nutrition and stress has only recently received the attention it deserves. Much of the interest in this area has come from the knowledge that stress imposes additional demands on the body. First, let us review how our eating habits are related to stress.

The Relationship Between Stress And Eating Habits

People respond to stress in different ways: some smoke, some drink alcohol, and some increase or decrease their food consumption.

How do these behaviors relate to our stress cycle? Consider the example of overeating. The net effect of overeating is a weight gain. In our society, this weight gain can become still another source of stress to the person. Thus, we begin to see a vicious cycle:

stressful situation -- overeating -- weight gain -- more
    stress -- more overeating -- more weight gain --

The most important thing to realize in this cycle is that the episode of overeating did not solve the problem, unless the stressor was hunger. In most cases, the stressor that may have triggered the person to eat is probably still there. We recommend all of the coping techniques discussed in this book for helping individuals through stressful situations. As you will learn, maintaining a proper diet is also an important technique for managing stress.

Another response to stress is consumption of alcoholic beverages. Using alcohol to manage or avoid managing stress is similar to overeating. Alcohol just adds another stressor. Not only does it fail to solve the original problem, but it brings other problems with it!

Stress is often used as an excuse for not eating properly. A common example is the person who complains that there is not enough time to take a lunch break. Instead of taking a break, he consumes candy bars from the vending machines or skips the meal altogether. If you find yourself saying "I don't have time to eat," we recommend you study the chapter on time management. Make good eating habits and regular meals a priority.

Can improper eating habits actually cause stress? Yes. If, over a period of time, one does not consume adequate amounts of nutrients, then the stores of these nutrients become depleted. The person is then more susceptible to disease and less able to adapt to other stressors.

For example, pregnancy is considered a positive change in a woman's life, but it is also a stress on the body. If the woman has not adequately prepared for the pregnancy by eating properly during the months before conception, then there is a greater risk associated with the pregnancy. Therefore, by maintaining good eating habits, our body is prepared for any additional demands made upon it.

Proper nutrition can be used to help to cope with stress. Exercise has often been used this way, but only recently have scientists begun considering proper eating as a coping strategy. We feel strongly that it is. All too frequently, we see people who are "stressed" or feel depressed and have a low self-esteem because of their body image. In this situation, the individual's concern over his or her body weight is a stressor; and proper eating habits can be a coping strategy.

There is another advantage to eating properly. People that exercise regularly and eat properly "feel good" about themselves. These positive feelings are an important part of other coping strategies, especially those we presented in the chapter on thinking and feeling better. When your self-esteem is high, other parts of your life seem less stressful, because you view the world through the eyes of a winner.

What Makes Up A Healthy Diet?

In the pages that follow, you will find guidelines for healthy eating. These are from the 1980 <u>Dietary Guidelines for Americans</u> by the U. S. Department of Agriculture and by the U. S. Department of Health and Human Services. There is a great deal of controversy in the area of nutrition today; but, all agree that these guidelines are sound and safe.

These guidelines are intended for the general population, specifically those who are free from disease. They may not be specific enough for those people on a special diet for aa diagnosed condition. Remember, no guidelines can guarantee health or well being, because in addition to diet, health depends on many things. Food alone will not make a person healthy -- but good eating habits, combined with regular exercise and stress management, can improve your health.

Dietary Guidelines For Americans

The seven dietary guidelines are:

1. Eat a variety of foods.

2. Maintain your ideal weight.

3. Avoid too much fat, saturated fat and cholesterol.

4. Eat foods with adequate starch and fiber.

5. Avoid too much sugar.

6. Avoid too much sodium.

7. If you drink alcohol, do so in moderation.

Eat A Variety Of Foods

You need about 40 different nutrients to stay healthy. These include vitamins and minerals, as well as amino acids (from proteins), essential fatty acids (from vegetable oils and animal fats), and sources of energy (calories from carbohydrates, proteins and fats). These nutrients are in the foods you normally eat. Water is also an essential nutrient.

Research has shown that the body uses nutritional re- serves when a person is under stress. The reserves most clearly depleted are protein, B-Vitamins, Vitamin C and Vitamin A. But it is important to realize that these reserves can be replaced and maintained by consuming balanced meals. Supplements are usually unnecessary.

Most foods contain more than one nutrient, but no single food item supplies all the essential nutrients in the amounts that you need. Therefore, you should eat a variety of foods to insure an adequate diet and one that will replace nutrients lost while under stress.

The greater the variety of foods you consume, the less likely you are to develop either a deficiency or an excess of single nutrients. Variety also reduces your likelihood of being exposed to excessive amounts of contaminants in any single food item.

One way to assure variety and a well-balanced diet is to select foods each day from each of several major groups. For example, eat fruits and vegetables; cereals, breads, and grains; poultry, fish and lean meats; dried peas and beans; and cheese, yogurt, skimmed or low-fat milk.

Fruits and vegetables are excellent sources of vitamins, especially Vitamin A (dark-green vegetables and yellow vegetables such as carrots, squash and sweet potatoes) and Vitamin C (citrus fruits, peppers, baked potatoes, and strawberries). Whole grain and enriched breads, cereals and grain products provide B-vitamins and iron. Meats supply protein, fat, iron and other minerals, as well as several vitamins, including thiamine and Vitamin B_{12}. Dairy products are major sources of calcium and other nutrients. A regular intake of balanced meals based on the above foods is a preventive measure in avoiding the effects of stress.

Caffeine, on the other hand, has been shown to affect the central nervous system, often making people nervous and putting them on edge. Some nutritionists have called coffee a stress-packed beverage. It is the worst offender with up to 155 mg. of caffeine in each cup; instant coffee is next with about 70 mg.; and, tea or cola soft drinks are runner ups, with 30 to 65 mg. per 12-ounce can. So, limit or avoid caffeine, especially when you are under stress. If you want to drink something warm, try a grain-based beverage, such as Postum.

Maintain Your Ideal Weight

If you are overweight, your chances of developing some chronic disorders are increased. Obesity is associated with high blood pressure, increased levels of blood fats (triglycerides and cholesterol), and diabetes. All of these

are associated with increased risk of heart attacks and
strokes. Thus, you should try to maintain an "ideal" weight.
But, how do you determine what the ideal weight is for you?

There is no absolute answer. The table below shows
"acceptable" ranges for most adults. For most people, their
weight should not be more than it was when they were young
adults (20 or 25 years old). Later in this chapter, we will
discuss techniques for weight control.

SUGGESTED BODY WEIGHTS

Range of Acceptable Weight

Height (Feet-Inches)	Men (Pounds)	Women (Pounds)
4'5"		92-119
5'0"		94-122
5'1"		99-128
5'2"	112-141	102-131
5'3"	115-144	105-134
5'4"	118-148	108-138
5'5"	121-152	111-142
5'6"	124-156	114-146
5'7"	128-161	118-150
5'8"	132-166	122-154
5'9"	136-170	126-158
5'10"	140-174	130-163
5'11"	144-179	134-168
6'0"	148-184	138-173
6'1"	152-189	
6'2"	156-194	
6'3"	160-199	
6'4"	164-204	

For those of you who are now at your suggested body weight, it is important to know that the average American gains one-half to one full pound per year between the ages of 20 and 50. Keep an eye on these creeping pounds resulting from what some have called our country's "thorn of plenty"! It may be helpful to adopt some of the suggestions on weight control as a preventive measure.

Do not attempt to reduce your weight too far below the acceptable range. Severe weight loss may be associated with nutritional deficiencies, menstrual irregularities, infertility, hair loss, skin changes, cold intolerance, severe constipation, psychiatric disturbances and other complications.

If you lose weight suddenly or for unknown reasons, see a physician. Unexplained weight loss may be an early sign of an underlying disorder.

Avoid Too Much Fat, Saturated Fat And Cholesterol

Americans, with diets high in saturated fats and cholesterol, tend to have high blood cholesterol levels. These individuals usually have greater risks of having heart attacks than people eating low-fat, low-cholesterol diets. It is believed that this occurs because eating extra saturated fat and cholesterol will increase blood cholesterol levels in most people.

However, there are wide variations among people. These variations are related to heredity and the way a person's body uses cholesterol. Some people can consume diets high in saturated fats and cholesterol and still maintain a normal blood cholesterol level. Other people, unfortunately, have high levels of blood cholesterol even if they eat low-fat, low-cholesterol diets.

There is controversy about the best recommendations for healthy Americans. But for the U.S. population as a whole, a reduction in our current intake of total fat, saturated fat and cholesterol is sensible. This suggestion is especially appropriate for people who have high blood pressure, smoke, or have a family history of heart disease.

To avoid too much fat, saturated fat and cholesterol:

1. Choose lean meat, fish, poultry, dried beans and peas as your protein sources.

2. Limit your use of eggs and organ meats (such as liver).

3. Limit your intake of butter, cream, hydrogenated margarines, shortenings, palm oil, coconut oil and foods made from such products.

4. Trim excess fat off meats, remove skin from chicken.

5. Broil, bake or boil rather than fry.

6. Read labels carefully to determine both amount and types of fat contained in foods.

Eat Foods With Adequate Starch And Fiber

The major sources of energy in the average American diet are carbohydrates and fats. To a lesser extent, proteins and alcohol also supply energy. While decreasing your fat intake, you should increase your calories from carbohydrates so as to supply your body's energy needs.

A common misconception about carbohydrates is that they are high in calories. This is not true. In trying to reduce your weight to an "ideal" level, carbohydrates have an advantage over fats: carbohydrates contain less than half the number of calories per ounce of fats!

Complex carbohydrates are better than simple carbohydrates. Simple carbohydrates, such as sugars, provide energy, but little else in the way of nutrients. Complex carbohydrate foods, such as beans, vegetables, whole grain breads, cereals and grain products, contain many essential nutrients.

Increasing your consumption of certain complex carbohydrates can help increase dietary fiber, which is advantageous because the average American diet is relatively low in fiber. Eating more foods high in fiber tends to reduce the symptoms of chronic constipation and other gastrointestinal disorders. There is also concern that low-fiber diets might increase the risk of developing cancer of the colon, but evidence is inconclusive at this time.

To be sure that you eat enough fiber, you should consume fruits, vegetables, and whole grain breads and cereals. There is no reason to add fiber to foods that do not already contain it.

To eat more complex carbohydrates daily:

1. Substitute starches for fats and sugars. For example, eat whole grain crackers for a snack instead of candy.

2. Select foods which are good sources of fiber and starch, such as whole-grain breads and cereals, fruits, vegetables, beans and peas.

Avoid Too Much Sugar

The major health hazard from eating too much sugar is tooth decay. The risk of tooth decay is not simply a matter of how much sugar you eat. The risk increases the more frequently you eat sugar and sweets. This is especially true if you eat between meals, and if you eat foods that stick to the teeth. For example, small, but frequent snacks of sticky candy or day-long use of soft drinks, may be more harmful to your teeth than a large amount of sugar consumed at one time.

Contrary to widespread opinion, sugar alone in your diet has not been proven to cause diabetes. The most common type of diabetes is seen in obese adults. For these people, avoiding sugar, without losing weight, will not solve the problem. There is also no convincing evidence that sugar causes heart attacks or blood vessel diseases.

Estimates indicate that, on the average, Americans use more than 130 pounds of sugar a year. This includes, not only sugar in the sugar bowl, but the sugars and syrups in jams, jellies, candies, cookies, soft drinks, cakes and pies. Sugars are also found in products such as breakfast cereals, catsup, flavored milks and ice cream. Frequently, the ingredient label will provide a clue to the amount of sugars in a product. Ingredients are listed in descending order from the greatest quantity to the smallest quantity. So, if a product lists sugar as the third of 15 ingredients, you can be sure it is high in sugar.

To avoid excessive sugars:

1. Use less of all sugars, including white sugar, brown sugar, raw sugar, honey and syrups.

2. Eat less of foods containing sugar, such as candy, soft drinks, ice cream, cakes and cookies.

3. Select fresh fruits or fruits canned without sugar rather than fruits canned in syrup.

4. Read food labels for clues on sugar content--if the names sucrose, glucose, maltose, dextrose, lactose, fructose or syrups appear first, then there is a large amount of sugar.

5. Remember, how often you eat sugar, is as important as how much sugar you eat.

Avoid Too Much Sodium

Table salt contains sodium and chloride. Both are essential elements and should not be avoided altogether. Sodium is present in many beverages and foods that we eat, especially in processed foods, condiments, sauces, pickled foods, salty snacks and sandwich meats. Baking soda, baking powder, monosodium glutamate (MSG), soft drinks and even many medications (many antacids, for instance) contain sodium.

The major hazard of excessive sodium is for persons who have high blood pressure. Not everyone is equally susceptible. It is true that sodium intake is but one of the factors known to affect blood pressure, but it is one that we can control.

At present, there is no good way to predict who will develop high blood pressure, though certain groups, such as blacks, have a higher incidence. Individuals with a family history of high blood pressure are also more susceptible. Low-sodium diets may help to prevent high blood pressure.

Most Americans want more sodium than is needed. Consider reducing your sodium intake, and use less table salt. Eat sparingly those foods which are high in sodium. Remember that up to half of sodium intake may be "hidden," either as part of naturally occurring food or, more often, as part of a preservative or flavoring agent that has been added.

To avoid too much sodium:

1. Learn to enjoy the unsalted flavors of foods.

2. Cook with only small amounts of added salt.

3. Add little or no salt to food at the table.

4. Limit your intake of salty foods, such as potato chips, pretzels, salted nuts and popcorn, condiments (soy sauce, steak sauce, garlic salt), cheese, pickled foods and cured meats.

5. Read food labels carefully to determine the amounts of sodium in processed foods and snack items.

If You Drink Alcohol, Do So In Moderation

Alcoholic beverages tend to be high in calories and low in other nutrients. Even moderate drinkers may need to drink less if they wish to achieve ideal weight.

Heavy drinkers face additional problems. They often lose their appetites for food, so that the essential nutrients are not obtained. Vitamin and mineral deficiencies occur commonly in heavy drinkers. This is, in part, because of poor intake, but also because alcohol alters the absorption and use of some essential nutrients.

Heavy drinking may also cause a variety of serious conditions, such as cirrhosis of the liver and some neurological disorders. Cancer of the throat and neck is much more common in people who drink and smoke than in people who do not. Impotence is common in men that have a history of consuming large quantities of alcohol.

Sustained or excessive alcohol consumption by pregnant women has been associated with birth defects. Pregnant women should avoid alcohol or limit their intake to the amount their physician recommends.

One or two drinks daily appear to cause no harm in adults. If you drink, you should do so in moderation.

WEIGHT CONTROL

Is there a proven method to help one obtain and maintain one's ideal body weight? Yes!!! It is a three step formula and it is really quite simple.

1. If caloric use is greater than caloric intake then weight loss occurs.

2. If caloric use equals caloric intake then weight is maintained.

3. If calorie use is less than caloric intake then weight is increased.

Do not let anyone try to fool you--calories do count! All diets that cause a loss of weight do so because the caloric intake is less than the person's caloric expenditure. Some diets cause a faster weight loss than others, but this is often because of a loss in body water, not body fat.

Although the formula above is simple, it would be misleading to assume the problem is a simple one. Losing weight and maintaining that weight loss is a major problem with American people today. Why?

1. Eating habits are learned. To maintain a weight loss permanently, poor eating habits must be changed to new and good ones. Only those diets which bring about a change in eating habits will be successful on a long-term basis.

2. To lose one pound of body fat, one must take in 3500 calories less than is expended. A reasonable goal is to reduce caloric intake by 500 calories per day. This will produce a loss of one pound each week (7 x 500 calories = 3500 calories or one pound). Avoid the harmful effects of near starvation and its companion of stressful malnutrition.

3. Because Americans are so sedentary, it is difficult for the caloric expenditure to exceed the caloric intake (thereby bringing about a weight loss) without restricting calories and increasing activity. Both of these require a change in behavior.

4. People are often unrealistic in their expectations about how many pounds can be lost and in what period of time. Be patient!

Example:

A 30-year-old woman consuming 1400 calories was maintaining her weight. She had tried a 1000-calorie diet, given to her by her doctor, and became frustrated after one week because she had not lost any weight. Why?

If 1400 calories is required to maintain weight, and you begin a 1000-calorie diet, then you have a 400 calorie deficit per day.

$$3500 \div 400 = 8.75 \text{ days}$$

With a 1000-calorie-a-day diet, it would take her 8-9 days to lose one pound. Because she was sedentary, her weight loss occurred very slowly. By following the recommendations in the chapter on exercise (exercise 30 minutes three times per week), she could lose one pound in approximately 6 days.

It is helpful to remember that weight gain does not occur overnight, so it is unrealistic to expect it to disappear overnight. It is helpful to keep in mind that a weight lose of any amount is better than a weight gain. Remember, the average American gains 15 to 30 pounds between the ages of 20 and 50 years.

5. Most people underestimate the number of calories in food and overestimate the calories they burn off during exercise. For example, if you drink one eight ounce glass of your favorite soft drink, you probably have consumed about 100 calories. If you wanted to burn off your soda, you would have to run about a mile, bicycle for two miles, play tennis for a quarter of an hour, or garden for about a third of an hour. If you eat six potatoe chips, plan on swimming for about ten minutes, playing golf for about twenty, or running for about seven minutes.

The best exercise for loosing weight is one described by one of our high-school coaches and health teachers: Push yourself away from the table!

Behavior Modification And Weight Control

This highly successful approach to weight loss concentrates on changing eating behaviors. New eating behaviors are the keys to the maintenance of any weight loss. These techniques must be practiced just like any of the techniques for stress management. There are four categories of techniques that are included in most behavior modification programs.

1. Self monitoring--Record keeping is an essential part of becoming aware of your eating habits. Where? With whom? Doing what? At what time? Under what conditions? These are all questions that will familiarize you with the "why" of your eating patterns.

2. Stimulus control--After keeping records, it usually becomes apparent that there are various stimuli other than true hunger which trigger or bring about your desire to eat. Control of these stimuli will help you to reduce the intake of food. Some of the most powerful stimuli for eating are actually food cues. So, avoid leaving food in sight and avoid stocking your pantry with attractive snacks that are not nutritious.

3. Goal setting--Short-term and long-term goals are important in helping you to approach weight loss realistically. It is important to reward yourself for achieving goals, because this positive reinforcement is motivating in itself. Some of the best rewards are clothing in your new size and equipment for hobbies other than cooking and eating.

4. Relaxation--Just as relaxation techniques helped in managing stressful situations, they can also help to "get through" those times where you are tempted to eat in response to anger, frustration, boredom, depression, etc. Try to eat slowly, chew your food thoroughly, and relax between bites. Breathing from your stomach area will not only relax you, but also help you to become aware of cues that you are full.

Caloric Restriction And Weight Control

As a country, we are actually eating slightly less (3%) than during the early 1900's, yet there are an estimated 80 million Americans who are overweight. Why? Because we are more sedentary.

Another reason is the kind of food we eat. Compared to the early 1900's we now consume less calories, but more fat, less complex carbohydrates and more simple carbohydrates. Why is this important? A diet higher in fat and lower in carbohydrates is a diet containing a smaller quantity of food. In other words, we are consuming a smaller amount of food and, yet, it has a higher concentration of calories.

Recommendations for controlling weight:

1. Learn new eating behaviors through self-monitoring, stimulus control, and reward. Avoid the "rhythm method of girth control" by making changes you can live with the rest of your life. Remember, small caloric changes can have a major impact over a year or a lifetime.

2. Reduce caloric intake. It is possible that, if you reduce the fat intake, you could successfully reduce total caloric intake without reducing total quantity of food eaten. A study comparing obese and non-obese doctors showed the major difference between the two groups was their fat intake.

3. Increase physical activity. Muscle is heavier than fat. So, if you reduce the calories you are eating and increase your exercise, your weight may be an underestimate of your health. New findings in obesity research, suggests that a man's waistline or the amount of fat in skin-fold measurements for women, may be the best measures of obesity.

4. Practice stress management to help decrease eating in response to stressful situations.

5. When you have trouble sticking to the above guidelines, do not give up and tell yourself you are a failure. Tell yourself you are human and start following your plan again, right away.

REVIEW QUESTIONS

<u>Directions</u>:   Circle the letter in front of the best response.
The correct answers are provided on the page following the last
question.

1. Overeating and overdrinking can

    a. be a response to stress.
    b. become additional sources of stress.
    c. still leave one with malnutrition.
    d. All of the above are true.

2. The U.S. Departments of Agriculture and of Health and
    Human Services list seven dietary guidelines for
    Americans. Which of the following was not one of the
    guidelines?

    a. eat a variety of foods.
    b. maintain ideal weight.
    c. eat foods with greater amounts of sodium.
    d. avoid too much fat, saturated fat and cholesterol.

3. Research has shown that the body loses nutritional reser-
    ves when a person is under stress. These reserves
    include

    a. protein.
    b. B-Vitamins.
    c. Vitamins C and A.
    d. All of the above.

4. It is important to eat a variety of foods because

    a. no single food item supplies all the essential
        nutrients in the amount you need.
    b. variety increases the likelihood of exposure to
        excessive amounts of contaminants.
    c. you are more likely to develop an excess of a single
        nutrient.
    d. you are more likely to develop a deficiency of a
        single nutrient.

5. Pick out the so called "stress-packed" ingredient.

   a. dark-green vegetables
   b. caffeine
   c. yellow vegetables
   d. citrus fruits

6. To avoid too much fat, saturated fat and cholesterol, it
   is important to do all of the following except:

   a. choose lean meat, fish, poultry, dried beans, and peas,
      as your protein sources.
   b. limit your use of eggs and organ meat (such as liver).
   c. eat plenty of hydrogenated margarines, shortenings,
      palm oil, and coconut oil.
   d. limit your intake of butter and cream.

7. Eating food high in carbohydrates means

   a. increasing the amount of fat in your diet.
   b. increasing the number of calories in your diet.
   c. decreasing your dietary fiber.
   d. eating beans, vegetables, whole grain bread, cereal
      and grain products.·

8. Which of the following should be reduced to lower the risk
   of heart disease?

   a. sodium
   b. fruit
   c. adequate starch and fiber
   d. moderate amounts of alcohol

9. To lose weight, it is recommended that one

   a. decrease caloric intake from overeating.
   b. increase caloric consumption by exercise.
   c. lose about one pound per week by changing eating
      habits.
   d. All of the above.

10. Self-monitoring, stimulus control, goal setting and relaxa-
    tion are all parts of a recent advance in weight control
    called

    a. behavior modification.
    b. exercise physiology.
    c. zero-based nutrition.
    d. None of the above.

ANSWERS TO REVIEW QUESTIONS

1. d	6. c
2. c	7. d
3. d	8. a
4. a	9. d
5. b	10. a

RECOMMENDED READINGS AND RECORDINGS

BOOKS

Food for Sport by N. Smith. Palo Alto, California: Bull, 1976.

Habits Not Diets by J. Ferguson. Palo Alto, California: Bull, 1976.

The Help Your Heart Eating Plan by Methodist Hospital Diet Modification Clinic, Houston: Methodist Hospital, 1979.

Permanent Weight Control: A Total Solution To The Dieter's Dilemna by M. Mahoney & K. Mahoney. New York: W. W. Norton, 1980.

The Pritikin Program For Diet And Exercise by N. Pritikin & P. McGrady. New York: Grosset & Dunlap, 1979.

Realities Of Nutrition by R. Deutsch. Palo Alto, California: Bull, 1976.

Rating The Diets by J. Berland & The Editors of Consumer Guide. New York: Signet, 1980.

Slim Chance In A Fat World: Behavioral Control Of Obesity by R. Stuart & B. Davis. Champaign, Illinois: Research, 1978.

COOKBOOKS

Fat-Free Recipes by N. Lampen. London, England: Faber &
Faber, 1977.

The Live Longer Now Cookbook by J. Leonard & E. Taylor. New
York: Grosset & Dunlap, 1977.

RECORDINGS

Comprehensive Smoking Cessation Program by B. Danaher & E.
Lichtenstein. New York: B.M.A., 1980.

Comprehensive Weight Control Program by A. Marston & M.
Marston. New York: B.M.A., 1980.

Section VIII

Putting It All Together

Chapter 24

Putting It All Together
And Making It Work For You

Falling Down And Picking Yourself Up Again

The habits of a lifetime cannot be changed overnight. Change takes time. Sometimes a year or two of dedicated practice. But if you do not change sometime during that same year or two, your blood pressure elevations could become chronic, your stomach lining could open in a painful ulcer, you could be plagued with headaches or you could suffer any number of other stress-related disorders.

There is no magic to transform you instantly into a successful stress manager. However, we have seen hundreds of people make tremendous progress when they apply and practice the techniques presented in this book.

What will happen if you stop practicing your stress management techniques? Will you immediately return to the chronic stress responses of your old lifestyle? First, even if you have totally dedicated yourself to practicing these techniques, there will probably be times when you forget to "Relax and let go." We all get overconfident at times.

Both authors have been practicing, teaching and researching various stress management techniques for over a decade. They still find themselves tense and rushing at times. They recognize their stress faster now, more than ever before, by listening to their bodies and then they return to regularly scheduled stress management practice. The stress spiral can be broken!

Do not get discouraged if you find that you occasionally fail to handle certain stressors in the best way. If life is to be judged, it should be judged on a "best efforts" basis. You may wish you had done something better. You can imagine, plan and practice toward doing better. But, to look back with discouragement, is not a realistic way to approach life. Don't let initial failures or temporary set-backs stop you from trying!

Is Failure A Part Of Success?

All of science is based on failures. Thousands of unsuccessful experiments were necessary for such discoveries as the light bulb and pasteurized milk. Behind most successful people are numerous failures. These winners in life try to learn something from every experience.

The following is the history of one of life's winners who overcame many failures and personal hardships: He lost his job; suffered defeat in a campaign for legislature; faced failure in business; won an election for the legislature; lost his sweetheart to a fatal disease; experienced a nervous breakdown; lost an election for Speaker in the legislature; lost in a race for Congressional nomination; won an election to Congress; lost renomination; rejected for land officer; lost an election for the Senate; lost in a race for the Vice-Presidential nomination; and, suffered a second defeat in a Senate election. Two years after his last defeat, Abraham Lincoln was elected President of the United States.

We can all benefit from adopting the "stick-to-it" attitude of Lincoln. Accept any initial failures or set-backs as part of the trial and error that will bring you a little closer to eventually being a successful stress manager. Most people don't fail, they just give up trying.

Positive Self-Control

Dennis Waitley, the psychologist who wrote the Psychology of Winning, lists the ten characteristics of successful people. By being successful, he means much more than financial success. He studies people that succeed in managing stress and living satisfying lifes. Dennis Waitley's emphasis is on mental health and not mental illness. His ten qualities of a winner include:

1. Positive Self-Awareness - understanding where you are coming from
2. Positive Self-Esteem - liking yourself
3. Positive Self-Control - making it happen for yourself
4. Positive Self-Motivation - wanting to and deciding you can
5. Positive Self-Expectancy - deciding next time that you will do even better
6. Positive Self-Image - seeing yourself changing and growing
7. Positive Self-Direction - having a game plan

8. Positive Self-Discipline - practicing mentally
9. Positive Self-Dimension - valuing yourself as a person
10. Positive Self-Projection - reflecting yourself in how you walk, talk and listen

All of these characteristics are important for successful living; and, we highly recommend Dr. Waitley's books and tapes. His characteristic of positive self-control means that winners say, "I make it happen for me." Losers say "It always happens to me." Dr. Waitley's proverb for living is "Life is a do-it-to-myself project. I take the credit or the blame for my performance."

The Freedom To Choose

Self-control means you have the freedom to choose alternatives. If you believe your life is dictated by luck, fate or circumstances, then you are open to doubts and fears. You don't have to do anything in life. Take the hunger strikers, for example. They decided they did not even have to eat. You decide to do things because they are the best choices among the available alternatives to help you reach your goals.

We hope you decide to break out of the habit of stressful living and into the skills of stress management. We know that you can! Positive self-control is a stress-management skill and habit which puts you in control of your life. Not managing stress is also a habit. Habits take years to form, and habits die hard, or they die with the person. Everything you do is a habit.

One of the best ways to break a habit, is to replace it with a good one. Rather than concentrating on which stressful habits you are not going to do, begin to concentrate on which stress management habits you will practice and develop.

Making Excuses Versus Taking Responsibility

If you are like most people, there will come times when you encounter difficulty in exchanging familiar habits for new ones. If you slack off practicing your new stress management skills, then examine your excuses. We ofter hear excuses such as "I'm too busy today," "I'm too tired," or "This isn't working."

Do not be lured by these excuses. Of course, they are partially true. You may be busy, tired or progressing slowly. These excuses are also partially false. It is not because you are busy, tired or progressing slowly that you cannot practice the exercises. Take responsibility for your decision to choose one activity over another by saying "I am busy closing out the books for the end of the month. I could do the exercises, but I choose not to." Remember, you are in the driver's seat in your life.

The excuses you give for not rehearsing stress management are probably the same excuses you have used for years to keep yourself locked into a stress cycle. Sometimes these excuses are based on faulty premises and misunderstood need systems.

Understanding Your Needs: Survival And Safety

In order to feel comfortable, most people have certain needs that must be met. If your car started to leak gasoline and caught fire, then your strong need for safety would supersede any need to get to the destination toward which you were driving.

Psychologists, particularly Dr. Abraham Maslow, have helped us to understand that our needs are often hierarchical. Food an shelter are usually considered to be at the top of our need hierarchy. Next come needs for physical safety. Most people in today's world can fulfill these basic needs. It may be helpful to acknowledge the role other needs may play and how we try to fulfill them.

When we fail to recognize our other needs, we begin to feed into our stress spiral. Recognizing your other needs, will also help you to attack any excuses for not practicing your stress management skills.

The Needs For Security And Belonging

The need for security and stability motivates people toward stable relations, insurance policies and dependable jobs. A strong need for affiliation and belonging, means we would value family, avoid disagreements and attempt to have everyone like us.

Could strong needs for security and affiliation interfere with stress management? Yes. A middle-aged woman we worked with believed her family would reject her if she did not have all of her housework done before she practiced relaxation. Since the work of the housewife is never done, she found little time to relax. She had the strong universal need to be appreciated. She wanted to be secure, not "rock the boat," and have everyone like her.

Taking positive self-control of her life, she was able to examine her needs and discussed these with her family. She reread the chapters on assertiveness training. She discovered her family did not reject her if she took time for herself, but instead they wanted her to do this. In fact, her family had felt guilty because she was always doing for others, instead of herself. She met her needs for relaxing and replenishing her store of energy, and she sacrificed none of her needs for a secure family relationship.

Believe it or not, a strong need for the respect of others can also interfere with stress management. We worked with a lovely woman in her middle thirties who was in an important management posistion. Her need for the respect and admiration of others nearly prevented her from learning more about managing stress. She was not able to join the stress management class until she explored this need and brought it into balance with her other needs for a healthy body. Why? She was afraid someone would find out she was in the class, think she could not manage stress, and lose respect for her.

The Esteem Needs

If you are an energetic person who likes to succeed, you may have a strong need for achievement and accomplishment. Enthusiasm may push you to take on too many stress management exercises at once. You may overdo your practice at first, as you strive toward a goal of perfect stress management in 10 days. You may find you have set unrealistic goals and your program is too rigorous. Often, the over-achiever feels guilty about not reaching goals, begins to lose interest and makes excuses about already being overextended. Soon, practicing the techniques is put off indefinitely and the person has burned out, before even getting a good start.

If you have a strong need for achievement, then be sure to go slowly with the stress management practice. Don't expect too much, too soon. You will begin to feel more energy as a result of the relaxation training. Consider your long- and short-term goals. You may wish to use this energy for recreation and hobbies, rather than funneling it back into still more work.

Another strong need that may interfere with stress management is the need for power and control. If you find that you cannot delegate enough responsibilities to give you time to practice relaxation, then review the time management and assertiveness chapters.

Rate the strength of your various needs. Use a number from zero (no need) to ten (extremely strong need) and put your rating next to each need listed below.

_____ Power and control

_____ Achievement and accomplishment

_____ Esteem and respect

_____ Affiliation and belonging

_____ Security and stability

_____ Health and physical well-being

Now, ask yourself if, and how, your strongest needs may help or interfere with practicing what you have learned in this book. How strong is your need for a healthy body? For some people, their need for a healthy body is not stronger than their need for the things they gain by having a stress symptom!

In some cases, a spouse has to do the cooking, take out the garbage, or keep the house quiet, if the person with the symptom is tired, suffers from a headache, or has an elevated blood pressure reading. For others, a backache or an ulcer can offer power and control. How would your life be different if you did not have your stress-related problems? Is there anything you might have to give up?

The Highest Need On The Hierarchy

If one has fulfilled the needs we have reviewed, then what is left to strive for? The highest need on Dr. Maslow's hierarchy is the need for self-actualization. This is the need for self-fulfillment, for realizing ones potentials, and for becoming what one is capable of becoming. As you learn to meet your other needs, strive to find the joy of self-fulfillment.

Reviewing Your Progress

Have you already gained a great deal from practicing the techniques in this book? Could you gain more? Review this book and underline the particular techniques that worked for you. Review your scores on the different self-assessment scales that helped you analyze the specific areas of stress in your life.

Do you need more work on relaxing your muscles? Could you benefit from biofeedback for headaches? Do you want to break a habit such as smoking? Is now the time to begin exercising? Should you select books from the reading list to gain further knowledge of time management? What about the Psychology of Winning books and tapes?

You may find it helpful to set aside a few hours at the first of every month to review your stress management progress. Spend some time identifying the frequency and intensity of your stress responses. Look for the sources of your stress. These may be changes in your life such as new situations you are facing, new feelings you are experiencing, or new foods or drinks you have added to your diet.

Once you have reviewed your progress, develop a plan to cope with the stressors or to avoid them. Consider using some or all of the techniques you have learned in this program. Finally, put your stress management plan into action.

This book, and other books or recordings, may not be sufficient to help you with all situations. You may want to become involved in an ongoing support group or obtain some professional counseling to help you with becoming a successful stress manager.

Support Groups To Help You Through Crises In Living

In the past few years, many support networks have broken down. This is probably one of the reasons why we are experiencing such increases in stress today. For example, years ago people could count on a consistent and faithful family network that would help in times of crises. In addition, we were much less mobile, and people tended to become very friendly with neighbors. The neighborhood was once a support network within itself.

Because support groups are often very important in helping people manage their stress, we have included in Appendix II a list of support groups. You may wish to refer to it during particular life crises and for stress-related disorders you face. We have categorized these according to the type of crisis during which the group could offer the most support.

Religion - A Source Of Strength

Religious fellowship, spiritual principles, and faith in something greater than man, can be major sources of strength for daily living and times of crisis. A sign we saw in front of a church reads, "If God seems far away, who do you think moved?" Once again; the choice is ours.

Perhaps you could benefit from getting more involved in the church or synagogue you belong to. If you have moved recently and need to find one in your new community, call the leader of the one you left and ask for a referral--most have national directories, if they don't know of one in your area. You can also look in the yellow pages of the telephone book under churches or synagogues. If you are traveling, most hotels have a directory of nearby places of worship and the hours of their services.

Most churches and synagogues have groups for single people, teenagers, and other members of the congregation. These can provide new social contacts and sources of lasting friendships. Service groups affiliated with various religious denominations are listed in the Encyclopedia of Associations which can be found in most libraries.

Professional Counseling

If you find yourself continuing to struggle with serious conflicts and problems, we strongly recommend you seek professional counseling or therapy. There are a number of mental health professions whose members offer the sort of help you may need.

Not all psychologists provide clinical services. The authors are clinical psychologists. After completing a liberal arts college education, clinical and counseling psychologists are trained in a psychology graduate program for a minimum of four years before interning for a year and receiving the Ph.D. Following this work, clinical psychologists must be supervised in most states for at least one and sometimes two years in a health care facility before taking an examination to become certified by the state board of examiners. Clinical psychologists offer personality, intellectual and vocational testing, as well as psychotherapy.

Psychiatrists complete a general curriculum in a medical school and then do a specialized psychiatric residency for about four years. Psychiatrists conduct psychotherapy, but they do not provide psychological testing. They prescribe medications and psychologists do not.

Other mental health professionals include social workers, nurses, ministers and counselors. Not all the members of these professions are trained to provide direct clinical services. It is best to inquire if a social worker or a nurse is specifically a psychiatric social worker or a psychiatric nurse. Many counselors are primarily involved with vocational or spiritual work and are not trained in psychotherapy.

Mental health professionals may be listed under their specialty in the yellow pages. Some work in mental health clinics or other institutions which are also listed in the telephone book.

To find the Community Mental Health Center in your area, you may need to look in the white pages of your telephone book under State Department of Human Resources, Division of Mental Health. Alternatively, the department may be listed under the name of your state. These centers are federally funded and are required to provide you with mental health services at a cost based on your ability to pay.

Most communities are also served by an institution which is a member of the Family Service Association of America. These institutions also provide professional mental health services and can be found by looking in the white pages under Family and Children's Services or Family Counseling and Children's Services. To find still other sources of both professional and paraprofessional help, consult your yellow pages under the listing Social Service Organizations.

Recommendations of friends or other professionals who have knowledge of the therapist or institution are more informative and helpful than telephone listings. Most psychotherapists are also listed in national registries. In addition, local county or state associations list names of their members in specific geographic areas with their specific specialties. Local universities may also be a source of information.

It is wise to ask what training the counselor or psychotherapist has had and what sort of work he or she specializes in. Never hesitate to explore the credentials of the professional you are interviewing to work with. If your counselor wants to learn more about relaxation training you might suggest a book we have written for fellow clinicians, entitled, <u>Stress Management: A Conceptual and Procedural Guide.</u>

An Invitation

We would very much appreciate hearing from you. One of the ways you can do this, is to write us about this book. If there are parts that were difficult, let us know. If there are parts that were particularly helpful, let us know this as well. We would also very much like to learn about any additional ways you have found to manage stress and enhance your wellness.

This is not the end, but the beginning. The winners in the game of life have a game plan. We hope your plan includes finding the excitement of managing stress every day of your life.

Good luck; and, may your stressors always be manageable!

SUGGESTED BOOKS AND RECORDINGS

BOOKS
<u></u>

I Can If I Want To by A. Lazarus & A. Fay. New York:
    Warner, 1978.

RECORDINGS
<u></u>

Psychology Of Winning by Denis Waitly. Chicago:
    Nightengale-Coenant, 1978.

Appendixes

Appendix I

Music For Stress Management

The power of music to promote change is not a new concept. The Bible, Greek as well as Roman literature, and Egyptian records discuss music as a therapeutic device. Wild beasts and trees were charmed by Orpheus. Ulysses had his crew put wax in their ears to avoid hearing the song of the Sirens which could lead them to destruction. The poets have written about the "power" of music to calm or stir the emotions, and to inspire or suppress "desire." Men march off to war with a song on their lips. We respond affectively to music.

The ways in which music affects us are varied. There are many studies demonstrating the relaxing physiological responses to music such as: changes in breathing, cardiac blood pressure, blood supply, and galvanic skin responses. The first observations on the physiological effects of music are attributed to a French musician, Gretry (1741-1813). Gretry took his pulse by placing the fingers of one hand on the artery in the wrist of his other hand and noted accompanying changes as he sang at different tempos. In 1880, Dogiel tested the influence of music on the circulation of blood in humans by means of a special device called a plethysmograph. In 1927, Schoen and Gatewood reported data from 20,000 persons that demonstrated changes in mood which were produced by music.

According to Diserens, the following effects of music are generally accepted: Music (1) increases bodily metabolism; (2) changes muscular activity; (3) affects respiration; (4) produces marked effects on pulse and blood pressure; and (5) affords the physiological basis for the creation of different emotions.

Possibly the greatest importance of music, as it relates to the study of stress management, is the range and intensity of its associational value. It can serve as a stimulus for a wide variety of reactions, both pleasant and unpleasant. Music and the images it evokes are far more specific to the unique experiences of the listener than is true of languages. Farnsworth claims that, for most people, the real essence of music lies in the fact that it gives each person an opportunity to project his private experience through his own personal images. Therefore, appropriately selected music can enhance the relaxation experience through calming images, as well as promote physical relaxation.

We suggest trying some of the selections listed below because research has shown they can help most people to enhance their relaxation experiences. Since everyone responds differently, you should make your own evaluation of each recommendation. We have also included natural environmental sounds which many people find calming.

CLASSICAL-INSTRUMENTAL MUSIC BY J. S. BACH

Concerto for Two Violins, "Largo" (Columbia).

Harpsichord Concerto in F Minor, "Largo" (Columbia).

English Suite #3, "Sarabande" from Masters of the Guitar, Vol. 1 (Victor).

Solo Harpsichord Concerto in G Minor, "Largo" (Vox).

Concerto in G Minor for Flute and Strings, "Largo" (Columbia).

Solo Harpsichord Concerto in F Major, "Largo" (Vox).

Solo Harpsicord Concerto in C Major, "Largo" (Vox).

MEDITATIVE LISTENING EXPERIENCES

Paul Horn, Inside (The TajMahal) (Epic).

Paul Horn, Inside 2 (Epic).

Tony Scott, Music for Zen Meditation (Verve).

Tony Scott, Tibetan Bells (Verve).

Walter Carlos, The Four Seasons (Verve).

ENVIRONMENTAL SOUNDS

Environments "The Psychologically Ultimate Seashore" (Atlantic).

Environments #2 "Down At New Hope, Pennsylvania" (Atlantic).

Environments #8 "A Country Stream" and "Wood-Masted Sailboat" (Atlantic).

Appendix II

A Guide To Self-Help Groups

What is a Self-Help Group?

A self-help group can provide valuable assistance and support to its members in dealing with their mutual problems and in improving their psychological well-being. Most self-help organizations were started by members who shared common life experiences and problems. Groups are usually controlled by their members and rely on the efforts, skills, knowledge and concern of their members as their primary source of help.

How Effective Are Self-Help Groups?

A recent survey of 1,800 outpatient psychiatric facilities in the United States found that about half (48%) make either frequent or occasional referrals to self-help groups. In evaluating the usefulness of self-help groups, about 85% of the professionals rated the effectiveness of the groups as very high, high or average. This suggests that the general attitudes of professionals toward self-help groups are quite favorable.

Self-help groups contribute in many ways. They provide a social treatment which can not only improve the quality of life for their members, but also help prevent further difficulties. The groups offer their members information, comfort, emotional support, and a sense of belonging. The public commitments to change, made by members, often serve as sources of motivation to succeed. The desire to avoid letting one's friends down and the hope of gaining the group's approval for success can be very positive and very powerful forces for many people.

Self-help groups also sponsor public information programs designed to remove commonly-held prejudices and prevent discrimination against their members. In addition, they often support legislation and research of benefit to their members.

How Can I Find A Self-Help Group?

There are several ways of finding a self-help group in your area to meet your needs. If you know the name of the group, the telephone book can be an excellent place to start. Many of the groups are also listed in the yellow pages under the section "Social Service Organizations." Some newspapers have a "Calendar of Events" section and announce the times and places of the local weekly meetings. Other sources of referral are friends or local professionals, who are usually familiar with area resources. In addition, a local social service directory may be available from your chamber of commerce or your public library.

If you are unable to find your local group or chapter, contact the national headquarters listed below. Ask for the name, phone number, and address of the chapter nearest you.

Does A Group Exist For My Problems?

If you do not find a group that meets your needs in the list below, you may find one in the Encyclopedia of Associations edited by Nancy Yakes and Dennis Akey which is available in most libraries. The Encyclopedia of Associations lists current addresses and telephone numbers for all of the associations. Much of the information provided below was obtained from the encyclopedia.

If you still are unable to find a group, consider forming one. Find other people with the same problem and/or local mental health professionals who can help you start a group.

NAMES AND ADDRESSES FOR SOME OF THE
LARGE, NATION-WIDE SELF-HELP GROUPS

Alcoholics Anonymous
General Service Board
468 Park Avenue, South
New York, NY 10016

Alcoholics Anonymous (AA) was founded in 1935. Today, there are over a million members in over 30,000 local groups. Alcoholics Anonymous is an international fellowship of men and women who share the common problem of alcoholism. Members share their recovery with others seeking sobriety. The groups follow the twelve suggested steps of Alcoholics Anonymous. As with a number of other self-help groups, Alcoholics Anonymous has a strong belief-system which appeals to its members. In this case, the belief-system is that of the Christian religion. Family members of alcoholics can receive help through groups associated with Alcoholics Anonymous, mainly Al-Anon and Al-Ateen.

Checks Anonymous
c/o Bob Houston
P.O. Box 81548
Lincoln, NE 68501

Over thirteen hundred persons convicted of passing bad checks have joined this self-help group since 1963. Although it began in the Nebraska Penial and Correction System, similar organizations are located in eleven other prisons and reformatories in the United States. The activities include vocational assistance, as well as educational programs of speakers, films and group discussions. The group also provides information to bankers and business men in the hope of lowering the incidence of bad checks. In addition, it conducts an active program of restitution for the victims of checks offenders.

Divorce Anonymous
P.O. Box 5313
Chicago, Il 60680

> Divorce Anonymous was founded in 1949 as a fellowship of men and women who help one another with marriage and divorce conflicts. The meetings involve group therapy, discussions and lectures.

Gamblers Anonymous
2705-1/4 West Eighth Street
Los Angeles, CA 90005

> This group was founded in 1957 and now has over 6,500 members in over 278 local groups. Gamblers Anonymous is a "fellowship of men and women who have joined together in order that they may stop gambling and help other compulsive gamblers to do the same."

Golden Ring Council Of Senior
    Citizens Club
c/o ILGWU
1710 Broadway
New York, NY 10019

> This council involves over 50 clubs across the United States and is dedicated to promoting better living conditions for elderly people, social activities in clubs, and social action to improve legislation.

Gray Panthers
3700 Chestnut Street
Philadelphia, PA 19104

> This consciousness-raising group of both younger and older adults was founded in 1971 to combat discrimination against people on the basis of their age. The group has an information and referral service. It conducts seminars and research, as well as advising and acting as a catalyst for organizing local groups which now number over 80.

La Leche League International
9616 Minneapolis
Franklin Park, IL 60131

This international organization was founded in 1956 and now involves over a hundred thousand members in approximately 4,000 groups in 42 countries. The organization certifies leaders who arrange a series of four monthly meetings of women who are interested in breast feeding their infants. The goals are "to foster good mothering through breast-feeding and thus to encourage closer and happier family relationships."

Make Today Count
514 Tama Building
Box 303
Burlington, IA 52601

Make Today Count with over 9,000 members in 115 state groups was founded in 1974. It brings together cancer victims, their families and the public to discuss the misconceptions and realities of the disease. Make Today Count offers help not only to cancer patients, but to all victims of incurable and fatal diseases. Meetings consist of educational programs, films, tapes and discussions.

Mended Hearts
721 Huntington Avenue
Boston, MA 02115

Founded in 1951, the organization's 8,000 members are persons who have successfully undergone heart surgery or have supported a family member or friend through such an operation. In 85 local groups, members join to provide advice, encouragement and services to others facing or undergoing heart surgery. The group also conducts research and assists the medical profession.

Optomist International
4494 Lindell Boulevard
St. Louis, MO 63108

> This international federation of business, industrial, and professional men's service clubs was founded in 1919. It now involves over 120,000 members in 39 districts and 3,500 local groups. The clubs are dedicated to inspiring respect for law, promoting interest in good government, and aiding and encouraging the development of young people.

Overeators Anonymous
2190 190th Street
Torrance, CA 90504

> This group was founded in 1960 and now has over 4,000 local groups. Overeators Anonymous uses many of the same principles and traditions of the Alcoholics Anonymous program. The goal is for men and women to meet and share their experiences so as to offer one another strength and hope in recovering from what they call compulsive overeating.

Parents Anonymous
2810 Artesia Boulevard, Suite F
Redondo Beach, CA 90278

> This group was founded in 1970 and now involves over 8,000 adults who have abused their children or who have become interested in child abuse problems. The 880 local groups strive to rehabilitate child abusers and insure the physical and emotional well-being of their children. The members meet in voluntary groups and try to keep contact between meetings on the telephone or in person.

Parents Without Partners
7910 Woodmont Avenue, Suite 1000
Washington, DC 20014

This organization was founded in 1957 and now serves 160,000 members in 1,000 local groups. Parents who have become single by widowhood, divorce, separation or otherwise, join together to alleviate their problems with respect to the welfare and upbringing of their children, and the attitudes of the society toward single parents.

Recovery, Inc.
The Association of Nervous
    and Former Mental Patients
116 South Michigan Avenue
Chicago, IL 60603

This organization was founded in 1937 as an independent self-help group to prevent relapses in former mental health patients and chronicity in nervous patients. Its members now number over 7,000 in over 1,000 groups. The approach is based on a method developed by Dr. Abraham A. Low, a neuropsychiatrist.

Stroke Club International
805 Twelfth Street
Galveston, TX 77550

The Stroke Club International, with over 5,000 members was founded in 1968. Stroke victims become active members, and individuals interested in the problems of stroke victims become associate members. The Stroke Clubs provide instructions for stroke victims and their families, aid them in finding employment, and provide mutual aid, hope and encouragement. The meetings are held monthly and qualified speakers discuss medical aspects of stroke, and members share their progress and problems.

Wives-Self Help Foundation
8001 Roosevelt Blvd.
Smylie Time Building, Suite 408
Philadelphia, PA 19153

> This self-help group was founded in 1974 for those people interested in improving their marital, family or personal lives through self-help counseling. The group provides immediate emotional support, strives to develop the client's potential for self-help, operates a hot line, and a guidance program through the mail. It also conducts seminars on particular issues of women and helps to train mental health professionals for work with abused family members.

Women For Sobriety
P.O. Box 618
Quakertown, PA 18951

> This organization was founded in 1975 and involves over 3,000 female alcoholics in 200 local groups. The groups use a program of thirteen statements that are designed to help women find a new way of life through a new way of thinking.

TO GIVE IS ALSO TO RECEIVE

The following group is not a self-help group. Information about the Volunteers of America is provided here because there are times when helping others is the best way of helping oneself.

Volunteers Of America
340 West 85th Street
New York, NY   10024

This group was founded in 1896 and involves over 44 state groups and 750 service centers throughout the country. Founded as a religious social welfare organization, the group provides spiritual and material aid to those in need. If you feel you can benefit from the experience of becoming a volunteer, this organization can help you to become involved with the handicapped, prisoners, families in need, the aging, unwed mothers, and hundreds of other groups of the needy.

Home
Practice
Charts

HOME PRACTICE CHART

DIRECTIONS: For each week of your stress management program, record the date in the blank next to the week number. Space is provided to record your practice twice a day. The codes for what you practiced are defined below. Write the code of the technique you practiced in the appropriate blank next to session (1) and session (2) for each day. Next to the code, write in the number of minutes you practiced. In the last two columns, write in your relaxation ratings. Remember, 0 means total relaxation and 100 means total tension.

CODES FOR WHAT YOU PRACTICED:

Name of Technique	Code
Progressive Relaxation	PR
Scanning Relaxation	SR
Deep Muscle Relaxation	DM
Countdown Relaxation	CD
Autogenic Training	AT
Imagery Training	IT
Mental Simulation	MS
Other Training	OT

WEEK 1   DATE _____

Day/Session		What You Practiced	Minutes Practiced	Relaxation Ratings (0-100) Before	After
1	(1)				
	(2)				
2	(1)				
	(2)				
3	(1)				
	(2)				
4	(1)				
	(2)				
5	(1)				
	(2)				
6	(1)				
	(2)				
7	(1)				
	(2)				

WEEK 2   DATE _____

Day/Session		What You Practiced	Minutes Practiced	Relaxation Ratings (0-100) Before	After
1	(1)				
	(2)				
2	(1)				
	(2)				
3	(1)				
	(2)				
4	(1)				
	(2)				
5	(1)				
	(2)				
6	(1)				
	(2)				
7	(1)				
	(2)				

HOME PRACTICE CHART

DIRECTIONS: For each week of your stress management program, record the date in the blank next to the week number. Space is provided to record your practice twice a day. The codes for what you practiced are defined below. Write the code of the technique you practiced in the appropriate blank next to session(1) and session(2) for each day. Next to the code, write in the number of minutes you practiced. In the last two columns, write in your relaxation ratings. Remember, 0 means total relaxation and 100 means total tension.

CODES FOR WHAT YOU PRACTICED:

Name of Technique	Code
Progressive Relaxation	PR
Scanning Relaxation	SR
Deep Muscle Relaxation	DM
Countdown Relaxation	CD
Autogenic Training	AT
Imagery Training	IT
Mental Simulation	MS
Other Training	OT

WEEK 3   DATE _____

Day/Session		What You Practiced	Minutes Practiced	Relaxation Ratings (0-100)	
				Before	After
1	(1)				
	(2)				
2	(1)				
	(2)				
3	(1)				
	(2)				
4	(1)				
	(2)				
5	(1)				
	(2)				
6	(1)				
	(2)				
7	(1)				
	(2)				

WEEK 4   DATE _____

Day/Session		What You Practiced	Minutes Practiced	Relaxation Ratings (0-100)	
				Before	After
1	(1)				
	(2)				
2	(1)				
	(2)				
3	(1)				
	(2)				
4	(1)				
	(2)				
5	(1)				
	(2)				
6	(1)				
	(2)				
7	(1)				
	(2)				

HOME PRACTICE CHART

CODES FOR WHAT YOU PRACTICED:

Name of Technique	Code
Progressive Relaxation	PR
Scanning Relaxation	SR
Deep Muscle Relaxation	DM
Countdown Relaxation	CD
Autogenic Training	AT
Imagery Training	IT
Mental Simulation	MS
Other Training	OT

WEEK 5   DATE _____

Day/Session	What You Practiced	Minutes Practiced	Relaxation Ratings (0-100) Before	After
1 (1)				
(2)				
2 (1)				
(2)				
3 (1)				
(2)				
4 (1)				
(2)				
5 (1)				
(2)				
6 (1)				
(2)				
7 (1)				
(2)				

WEEK 6   DATE _____

Day/Session	What You Practiced	Minutes Practiced	Relaxation Ratings (0-100) Before	After
1 (1)				
(2)				
2 (1)				
(2)				
3 (1)				
(2)				
4 (1)				
(2)				
5 (1)				
(2)				
6 (1)				
(2)				
7 (1)				
(2)				

HOME PRACTICE CHART

DIRECTIONS: For each week of your stress management program, record the date in the blank next to the week number. Space is provided to record your practice twice a day. The codes for what you practiced are defined below. Write the code of the technique you practiced in the appropriate blank next to session (1) and session (2) for each day. Next to the code, write in the number of minutes you practiced. In the last two columns, write in your relaxation ratings. Remember, 0 means total relaxation and 100 means total tension.

CODES FOR WHAT YOU PRACTICED:

Name of Technique	Code
Progressive Relaxation	PR
Scanning Relaxation	SR
Deep Muscle Relaxation	DM
Countdown Relaxation	CD
Autogenic Training	AT
Imagery Training	IT
Mental Simulation	MS
Other Training	OT

WEEK 7   DATE _____

Day/Session		What You Practiced	Minutes Practiced	Relaxation Ratings (0-100)	
				Before	After
1	(1)				
	(2)				
2	(1)				
	(2)				
3	(1)				
	(2)				
4	(1)				
	(2)				
5	(1)				
	(2)				
6	(1)				
	(2)				
7	(1)				
	(2)				

WEEK 8   DATE _____

Day/Session		What You Practiced	Minutes Practiced	Relaxation Ratings (0-100)	
				Before	After
1	(1)				
	(2)				
2	(1)				
	(2)				
3	(1)				
	(2)				
4	(1)				
	(2)				
5	(1)				
	(2)				
6	(1)				
	(2)				
7	(1)				
	(2)				

HOME PRACTICE CHART

DIRECTIONS: For each week of your stress management program, record the date in the blank next to the week number. Space is provided to record your practice twice a day. The codes for what you practiced are defined below. Write the code of the technique you practiced in the appropriate blank next to session (1) and session (2) for each day. Next to the code, write in the number of minutes you practiced. In the last two columns, write in your relaxation ratings. Remember, 0 means total relaxation and 100 means total tension.

CODES FOR WHAT YOU PRACTICED:

Name of Technique	Code
Progressive Relaxation	PR
Scanning Relaxation	SR
Deep Muscle Relaxation	DM
Countdown Relaxation	CD
Autogenic Training	AT
Imagery Training	IT
Mental Simulation	MS
Other Training	OT

WEEK 9 DATE _____

Day/Session	What You Practiced	Minutes Practiced	Relaxation Ratings (0-100) Before	After
1 (1)				
(2)				
2 (1)				
(2)				
3 (1)				
(2)				
4 (1)				
(2)				
5 (1)				
(2)				
6 (1)				
(2)				
7 (1)				
(2)				

WEEK 10 DATE _____

Day/Session	What You Practiced	Minutes Practiced	Relaxation Ratings (0-100) Before	After
1 (1)				
(2)				
2 (1)				
(2)				
3 (1)				
(2)				
4 (1)				
(2)				
5 (1)				
(2)				
6 (1)				
(2)				
7 (1)				
(2)				

FREE OFFER*

BUY THIS BOOK and send for your **FREE** relaxation and stress management recording. Edward A. Charlesworth, Ph.D., one of the authors of this book, developed this recording to teach you relaxation skills you can use anywhere. Discover how to control your stress response with cue-controlled relaxation. Many patients use this recording to help them fall asleep at night without sleeping pills. Produced in a sound studio by a professional narrator, the recording is complete with music and natural environmental backgrounds.

If you prefer, use the coupon below to receive a **SPECIAL 20% DISCOUNT** off the price of the complete, three cassette *Relaxation and Stress Management Program* by Edward A. Charlesworth, Ph.D.

This **NATIONALLY ACCLAIMED PROGRAM** includes six highly effective techniques. The techniques are presented on three studio-recorded cassettes complete with music and natural environmental backgrounds and a 52-page guide. The program is stored in a handsome binder with built-in pockets for each cassette and the guidebook. Regularly $29.95. With the coupon below and your sales receipt, your cost is only $23.97 plus $1.50 postage and handling.

★Simply fill in the coupon below and send it with your sales receipt and $1.50 to cover postage and handling to:

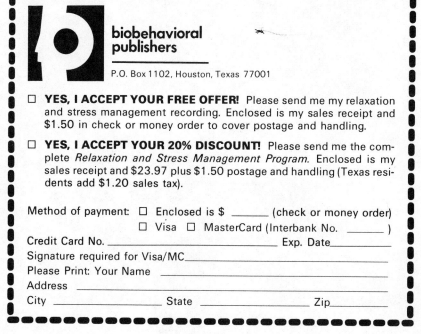